ic Service Employ
cations in Europe

This book provides an up-to-date analysis of the restructuring of public service employment relations in six European countries: Germany, France, Italy, Spain, Denmark and the UK. Each chapter on national systems is written by international experts in the field and is organized around a set of themes and policy issues, including:

* the impact of fiscal crises, and of increasing macro-economic integration within the European Union, on the scope and organization of public services
* changes in the patterns and status of public service employment
* the shift from centralized administration to new models of devolved management
* changes in the organization and policies of public service trade unions
* reforms in the structure, process and outcome of collective bargaining
* patterns of conflict and co-operation between unions, managers and the state.

The book begins with an introductory analytical framework for assessing changes in public service employment relations and explore the variation in national experience. Evidence for a partial convergence in the patterns of public service employment relations between countries, and between public and private sector employment relations within each country is examined.

Comprehensive and controversial, *Public Service Employment Relations in Europe* is essential reading for any one interested in industrial relations, HRM, public administration or comparative social policy.

Stephen Bach is Lecturer in Industrial Relations at Warwick Business School, University of Warwick. He has published widely on public sector industrial relations and health service employment relations. **Lorenzo Bordogna** is Associate Professor at the Department of Social Studies, University of Brescia, Italy. He has published widely on trade union organization. **Giuseppe Della Rocca** is Partner, Management e Innovazione, Milan and teaches industrial sociology at the University of Calabria, Italy. He has published widely on union organization, workplace industrial relations and the management of change in the public services. **David Winchester** is Senior Lecturer at Warwick Business School, University of Warwick. He has researched and published on public service employment relations for more than twenty years and, more recently, has specialized in teaching comparative industrial relations courses, especially on West European countries.

Routledge studies in employment relations
Series editors: Rick Delbridge and Edmund Heery
Cardiff Business School

Aspects of the employment relationship are central to numerous courses at both undergraduate and postgraduate level.

Drawing on insights from industrial relations, human resource management and industrial sociology, this series provides an alternative source of research-based materials and texts, reviewing key developments in employment research.

Books published in this series are works of high academic merit, drawn from a wide range of academic studies in the social sciences.

Rethinking Industrial Relations
Mobilisation, collectivism and long waves
John Kelly

Social Partnership at Work
Workplace relations in post-unification Germany
Carola M. Frege

Employee Relations in the Public Services
Themes and issues
Edited by Susan Corby and Geoff White

The Insecure Workforce
Edited by Edmund Heery and John Salmon

Public Service Employment Relations in Europe
Transformation, modernization or inertia?
Edited by Stephen Bach, Lorenzo Bordogna, Giuseppe Della Rocca and David Winchester

Public Service Employment Relations in Europe

Transformation, modernization or inertia?

Edited by

Stephen Bach, Lorenzo Bordogna, Giuseppe Della Rocca and David Winchester

London and New York

First published 1999 by Routledge
11 New Fetter Lane, London EC4P 4EE

Simultaneously published in the USA and Canada
by Routledge
29 West 35th Street, New York, NY 10001

Routledge is an imprint of the Taylor & Francis Group

In editorial matter and selection ©1999 Stephen Bach,
Lorenzo Bordogna, Giuseppe Della Rocca and David Winchester;
in individual contributions, © 1999 the contributors

Typeset in Baskerville by Graphicraft Limited, Hong Kong
Printed and bound in Great Britain by TJ International Ltd, Padstow, Cornwall

British Library Cataloguing in Publication Data
A catalogue record for this book is available from the British Library

Library of Congress Cataloging in Publication Data
Public service employment relations in Europe: transformation,
    modernization or inertia? / Stephen Bach, Lorenzo Bordogna,
    Giuseppe Della Rocca and David Winchester.
        p.   cm. – (Routledge studies in employment relations)
    Includes bibliographical references and index.
    1. Employee-management relations in government – European
Union countries – Case studies.   2. Collective bargaining –
Government employees – European Union countries – Case studies.
3. Trade-unions – Government employees – European Union
countries – Case studies.   4. Civil service – European Union
countries – Case studies.   5. Government efficiency – European
Union countries – Case studies.   6. Decentralization in government
– European Union countries – Case studies.   7. Industrial relations
– European Union countries – Case studies.   I. Bach, Stephen,
1963–   . II. Series.
HD8013.E854P83   1999
331′.0413514–dc21   99-10532
                            CIP

ISBN 0–415–20342–2 (hbk)
ISBN 0–415–20343–0 (pbk)

Contents

Tables

Contributors

Ramón Alós Department of Sociology, University of Barcelona.

Søren Kaj Andersen Industrial Relations Research Group (FAOS), Department of Sociology, University of Copenhagen.

Stephen Bach Industrial Relations Research Unit, Warwick Business School, University of Warwick.

Lorenzo Bordogna Department of Social Studies, University of Brescia.

Carlo Dell'Aringa Department of Economics, Catholic University of Milan.

Giuseppe Della Rocca Management e Innovazione, Milan.

Jesper Due Industrial Relations Research Group (FAOS), Department of Sociology, University of Copenhagen.

Pere Jódar Department of Political Science, University of Barcelona.

Jacint Jordana Department of Political Science, University of Barcelona.

Berndt K. Keller Department of Political Science, University of Konstanz.

Jørgen Steen Madsen Industrial Relations Research Group (FAOS), Department of Sociology, University of Copenhagen.

Phillippe Mossé Laboratoire d'Economie et de Sociologie du Travail (LEST), Aix-en-Provence.

Robert Tchobanian Laboratoire d'Economie et de Sociologie du Travail (LEST), Aix-en-Provence.

David Winchester Industrial Relations Research Unit, Warwick Business School, University of Warwick.

Preface

This book arose out of the meetings of a research network which linked scholars with an established interest in public sector employment relations in Europe. The impetus for the research was the belief that public service employment relations were an under-researched area of industrial relations, despite the immense challenges that faced national governments in their attempts to modernize the public services. The aims of this book are twofold. The primary aim has been to develop systematic and authoritative national case studies of public service employment relations based on a common framework of analysis. This proved to be a formidable challenge, given the diversity of national systems. Second, the national studies and the introduction provide the starting point for a systematic and thematized comparative analysis of public service employment relations. In our view informed comparative analysis hitherto has been hindered by the absence of detailed and up-to-date national studies.

The book's origins derive from a research workshop in Rome during January 1996, organized by ARAN, the Italian public sector bargaining agency. Fourteen papers were presented which provided an initial analysis of the restructuring of public sector employment relations in nine countries within the European Union. Many of the participants expressed a willingness to undertake further research and to produce a more systematic analysis of current trends in each country. Members of the research network continued to meet on a regular basis and presented some comparative papers at the International Industrial Relations Association Eleventh World Congress in Bologna during September 1998.

The overall framework for each country's study, and the drafts of these chapters, were discussed in a series of workshops held at the Universities of Brescia, Milan and Warwick during 1996–98. All the national case studies were informed by the authors' primary research interests in the area, but focused also on secondary sources of data and analysis. The selection of countries was based on several criteria. First, in economic terms we have included the four European members of the G7 group of leading world powers – Britain, France, Germany and Italy. Second, recognizing the diversity of practice between Northern and Southern Europe, we have included countries from both the 'North' (Britain and Denmark) and the 'South' (Italy and Spain). Third, we wished to address explicitly variations in the extent and scope of change, and, from our early discussions, identified countries that might illuminate the range of possibilities from transformation to modernization to inertia. Also we did not want to replicate existing publications that collected brief or selective accounts from numerous countries, so we chose fewer, more comprehensive and detailed national studies. We have not therefore attempted to include all European countries or extended our remit to include Central and Eastern Europe.

The book and the continuing research contacts sustained by the network would not have been possible without the administrative and financial support of a number of organizations. We would like to thank ARAN, CREAP, the ETUI (particularly Reiner Hoffman and Giuseppe Fajertag) and the Universities of Brescia and Warwick for their financial support. We have benefited immeasurably from the discussions that we were able to have with contributors on these occasions, and we are grateful to the authors for their patience in responding to our numerous requests and queries whilst editing this book.

Stephen Bach
Lorenzo Bordogna
Giuseppe Della Rocca
David Winchester

1 Europe

Changing public service employment relations

Stephen Bach

Since the 1980s there has been sustained interest in reforming public service employment relations across Europe. The pressure for reform has arisen from concerns about high levels of public expenditure and their potentially detrimental effects on national competitiveness in a more global economy. These macro-economic constraints were reinforced by the Maastricht convergence criteria for membership of Economic and Monetary Union (EMU) and the provisions of the 1997 growth and stability pact, maintaining the pressure on national governments' fiscal policies. To these macro-economic pressures can be added the micro-economic scepticism that traditional patterns of public service employment relations can ensure the recruitment, retention and satisfactory performance of public service workers in responding to increased citizen expectations about service quality and efficiency. In most countries the characteristic features of public service employment relations, including intricate systems of administrative and legal regulation, centralized systems of pay determination, rudimentary forms of human resource management, and entrenched union influence, have all been subject to increasing critical scrutiny.

There is much at stake for governments, employers and trade unions. Governments remain directly or indirectly the employers of public service workers (accounting for 20–30 per cent of the work force) and control of the public sector paybill is central to effective economic policy. Moreover, the political sensitivity of many public services ensures that all governments continue to monitor closely the behaviour of producers and consumers. For public service employers, many of the proposed structural and employment reforms bolster their authority, but also hold them more to account for organizational performance. Whilst for trade unions, faced with the prospect of membership decline and continuing pressures to accept employers' demands for flexibility, the public services remain a crucial arena of economic and political influence.

This introduction addresses several issues. It first considers whether the comparative analysis of public service employment relations is distinctive. It goes on to explore the challenges facing the public sector and whether macro-economic integration within the European Union, and other pressures for reform, are producing greater similarity in the structure and outcome of public employment regulation. It next outlines the analytical framework of the national chapters and

explores the main developments in terms of state, employer and trade union policy and of collective bargaining practice which inform each contribution. The scope and direction of reform in each country are then assessed and variations in terms of transformation, modernization or inertia are explored. Different outcomes reflect variation in the objectives and extent of reform and the obstacles to these policy initiatives. It concludes by assessing how far macro-economic constraints and the process of restructuring have led to convergence between countries. In addition, the degree to which there has been erosion of the separation between public and private sector employment relations within each country is considered.

The characteristics of public service employment relations

There has been detailed consideration of changing industrial relations in Europe based mainly on experience in the private sector (Bamber and Lansbury, 1998; Ferner and Hyman, 1998; Van Ruysseveldt and Visser, 1996). These and other studies examine whether distinctive national systems of employment regulation can survive the pressures arising from globalization and European integration. They invariably emphasize the persistence of national diversity and reject the strong version of the 'convergence' thesis. In contrast, the question of convergence has traditionally been less relevant to public services because they have been shaped so strongly by distinctive national state traditions. Whilst this has discouraged interest in systematic comparison, it might be expected that the common pressures to reform the public services would have spawned an interest in cross-national comparative research.

Public sector comparative research has emerged strongly at the sub-sectoral level. Differences between countries in structure, financing and proposals for welfare reform have stimulated interest in international experience, with some consideration of employment practices in health services (Altenstetter and Björkman, 1997; Bach, 1998) local government (Naschold, 1996) and the civil service (Bekke *et al.*, 1996; Hood and Guy Peters, 1994). Does the increased attention to sub-sectoral developments, alongside increased European integration, imply that national comparisons of public services are no longer of academic or policy interest?

The nation state, with unique legal and administrative characteristics, remains pivotal in explaining trends in the public sector. A blend of the specific features of individual state traditions with their unique administrative cultures; the historical development of the welfare state, incorporating a particular post-war settlement between capital and labour; and the economic and political characteristics of each country have borne strongly on the evolution of public sector employment relations. In the language of political scientists there is strong evidence of path dependence. These influences can be contrasted with comparative studies of private sector industrial relations. They are increasingly alert to the influence of product market competition in diluting specific patterns of national industrial relations, hence the vigorous debate about the implications of 'globalization' (see Ferner and Hyman, 1998: xix). In particular the actions of transnational companies and their interest in 'regime shopping' has been highlighted (Streeck, 1992).

Until recently there was scarcely any equivalent pressure in the public services, with the important exception of the impact on public utilities and public enterprises of the twin processes of deregulation and privatization (see Lane, 1997). Transnational companies operate in the public sector, but public services remain firmly in the control of national governments and have been protected from the chill winds of international competition, being a core component of each country's social protection system. Self-evidently, public services cannot be relocated from one country to another, preventing the type of concession bargaining engaged in by transnational companies in their negotiations with the work force and trade unions.

Trends in national patterns of public sector employment relations none the less are of interest to policy makers and the social partners (Hegewisch *et al.*, 1998; OECD, 1995; Olsen, 1996; Treu, 1987). The OECD Public Management Service has been the primary source of information about employment relations trends. Focusing on management practice, it has developed a strong critique of the current public sector employment model. Its publications advocate a model of human resource management which borrows heavily from existing private sector 'best practice'. How far these prescriptions are appropriate, and the extent to which national practice follows this policy agenda, are not fully addressed in the OECD studies. There is little other information available, especially in comparison with studies covering the private sector. This may arise, in part, from difficulties in gaining funding for public sector research, but what is clear is that public sector employment relations are ripe for reappraisal.

Challenges to the public sector

A major challenge to existing patterns of public service employment relations arises from the belief that the growth of public expenditure is unsustainable, and that the size and scope of the public sector require reappraisal. Public expenditure trends have been viewed as providing important pointers to illuminate national experience, although comparisons are not straightforward (see Adema, 1998; Foster and Plowden, 1996).

Table 1.1 reports public expenditure trends/GDP ratios on a standardized basis for OECD countries, and shows that there are considerable variations in the experience of countries. Britain has historically had relatively low levels of E/GDP, as has Spain, although Spain's has accelerated sharply since 1980. France, Italy, Germany and Denmark have much higher levels of E/GDP growth, but it is only in Denmark that expenditure growth seems to have slowed significantly. These figures indicate that, despite the long-standing debate about fiscal crisis, few countries appear to have had much success in reining in public expenditure.

This limited success reflects primarily the growth in transfer payments (social security benefits and pensions) rather than expenditure on services, such as education

Table 1.1 Public expenditure/GDP ratios on a standardized basis for selected OECD member countries 1950–95 (%)

Country	1960	1970	1980	1985	1990	1994
UK	32.6	38.8	42.9	44.0	39.9	43.2
West Germany	32.0	38.6	47.9	47.0	45.1	49.1
Italy	30.1	34.2	41.9	50.9	53.2	54.1
France	34.6	38.5	46.1	52.1	49.8	54.8
Spain	13.7	22.2	32.0	41.1	42.0	56.1
Denmark	24.8	40.2	56.2	59.3	58.6	48.0
United States	27.8	31.7	31.8	33.2	33.3	33.5
Japan	20.7	19.4	32.0	31.6	31.7	35.8
Total OECD	28.5	32.3	37.3	39.7	39.2	41.4

Sources: OECD (1992); OECD (1995), table 28.

Note
The data are measured according to the standard definitions of the OECD-UN systems of accounts. The definition of public expenditure used is 'total outlays of government'. The entry for 'Total OECD' is weighted average for those countries for which information is available. 1985 and 1990 data refer to General Government Outlays.

and health care. These trends reflect political difficulties in reducing social security benefits; a combination of sluggish growth and record levels of unemployment across the European Union and, throughout most of the 1990s, unfavourable demographic trends. Whether these trends amount to a fiscal crisis remains an open question, but the important point is that policy makers have acted as if a fiscal crisis existed. The difficulties in stemming transfer payments have led national governments to place some of the burden of adjustment on public services and their work force. This has extended beyond attempts to control the public sector paybill and the reform of collective bargaining institutions to a more concerted attempt to raise efficiency within public services, without necessarily addressing fundamental problems of reforming the welfare state (Ferner, 1994).

In addition to concerns about the cost of public services, there has been more persistent criticism of the quality of public service provision and the failure to meet citizens' expectations in terms of access, equity, speed of service and effectiveness. In education, anxieties about the extent to which the education system contributes to economic performance, limiting social exclusion and producing responsible citizens is widespread. A variety of shortcomings in terms of access, equity, professional accountability and effectiveness bedevil systems of health care (Bach, 1998), whilst central government civil servants have been characterized as remote élites ill-adapted to respond to citizens' concerns. Overall increasing levels of prosperity, and improvements in customer service and convenience in private sector services, have encouraged citizens to make unfavourable comparisons with patterns of service delivery in the public service sector (Flynn and Strehl, 1996). The widespread introduction of public service charters is testament to the pressure to improve the reliability of public services and to make them more sensitive to the needs of their users.

Public services have been criticized for their relatively low levels of productivity. There has traditionally been recognition that the scope for productivity improvements in the public sector is lower than the private sector because of the labour-intensive character of public services, the so-called relative price effect, which has limited the scope for dramatic increases in productivity associated with technological innovation. None the less this recognition has not blunted the desire for reform and it is widely believed that inflexible employment practices and limited opportunities for career progression have contributed to poor performance and staff demotivation (OECD, 1995). Many of the chapters echo these concerns in their assessment of national experience.

A final stimulus to the reform of public service employment practices may have arisen from the process of economic and political integration in Europe. The convergence criteria for participation in membership of EMU specified that each member state's deficit should not exceed 3 per cent of GDP and that total government debt should not exceed 60 per cent of GDP. These were viewed as blunt, but highly visible, policy goals which forced many governments to contain public expenditure and put public sector jobs in jeopardy.

The Maastricht convergence criteria have undoubtedly been an important influence on recent changes in public service expenditure in many countries, but its significance should not be accepted uncritically. As noted above, it has been rising levels of unemployment in particular and the associated transfer payments which have driven pressure to curb public expenditure – although it has clearly been convenient for politicians to blame sensitive tax increases, or plans to restrict public expenditure, on the EMU process. With the political complexion of European governments shifting towards the centre-left in recent years, the appetite for further politically contentious austerity measures may have been blunted. Finally, as the capacity of national governments to shape economic policy has been reduced, their reliance on public sector pay and employment policies becomes a more significant component of macro-economic policy. The combined influence of more global and integrated financial markets and the monetary constraints associated with the single currency regime has eroded many of the economic policy instruments traditionally available to member states. Consequently governments are clinging more tenaciously to those aspects of economic policy which remain in their grasp, not least the cost and efficiency of public services.

The framework

Comparative analysis between countries requires that similar phenomena should be examined in each country. There are significant differences in the size, scope and role of the public services between European countries. None the less each chapter follows broadly the same lines and is organized around a core set of themes and issues. This study defines the public services as employment in public administration and publicly funded and managed services. A defining feature of these services is that in most countries, they have been subject to specific forms of employment regulation, frequently distinguished from the private sector by a separate employment statute. Each country study focuses on the core public services; central and local government, health and education, although the degree to which sub-sectoral variations are central to the analysis differs between countries. In some countries railway or postal workers retain their public employment status and these instances are noted, but not explored in detail. Public enterprises and public utilities fall outside this categorization and are excluded, although as public service reforms are often linked with broader processes of privatization, where relevant these developments are noted.

State policies

Many of the characteristics of public service employment which traditionally differentiated it from the private sector derived from the unique role of the state as employer. The 'political contingency' (Ferner, 1988) – the need for governments to be sensitive to their electoral constituency – are to the fore in the government's role, directly or indirectly, as public service employer. These considerations encourage governments to promote stability and order in the conduct of public service industrial relations through elaborate systems of administrative and legal rules. In many instances, especially in Southern Europe, the state has been a source of patronage and acted as 'employer of last resort', cushioning many citizens from unemployment, but with detrimental consequences for managerial accountability and efficiency. Public services have developed along centralized, hierarchical and technocratic lines with a framework of administrative rules, often determined unilaterally by government on the basis of administrative law, rather than industrial relations considerations of joint regulation.

By the 1990s the economic and political context had altered, placing strains on the prevailing pattern of public service employment. A key question is whether these macro-economic constraints are leading to a greater similarity of public sector restructuring within Europe as Massey (1997), among others, suggests. A first consideration is the variability in state structures. In some countries there is a legacy of a strong state with a formidable capacity to initiate far-reaching reforms which permeate the whole public sector. In other countries, power is dispersed, reflecting the devolution of power from the central state, or an historical orientation to a federal system of governance. Overlying these differences are distinct public service traditions which impact on the influence wielded by élite civil servants and the degree to which they have discretion or are tightly constrained by elaborate administrative or legal regulation.

A second consideration is the link between state structures and political power. The political complexion of a government may have a bearing on public service reform, but it is a rather crude indicator of state policies. Related considerations include the need to be sensitive to the stability or fragility of governments and the links with broader coalition politics, as well as the phase of the electoral cycle. These features illuminate the political culture – whether authoritarian and adversarial, or inclusive and consensual – which may impinge on the capacity, direction and pace of reform.

These differences can be illustrated by consideration of a dominant aspect of debate about recent state policy, namely privatization. From its original association with the sale of public enterprises the term often has been broadened to include all initiatives to encourage private sector participation in the provision of public services (Rondinelli and Iacono, 1996). In the public services the best known form of privatization has been associated with the private provision of public services, but contracting-out appears to have been less widespread than is often suggested. Governments may have been reluctant to adopt a policy which has ideological connotations associated with the 'new right' and which could jeopardize specific national forms of social partnership.

The absence of fully fledged forms of privatization has not dampened the enthusiasm for related policy initiatives which have tried to increase efficiency and alter the incentive structures within the public services. Decentralization of budgetary and personnel decision making to lower tiers within organizations, often associated with the breaking up of public services into more independent units, has been a widespread policy objective. In some countries, such as France and Spain, these developments represent an attempt to break with traditionally highly centralized state structures, although the extent to which this type of legacy can be easily transformed is a theme taken up by the country chapters.

Within an overall approach which favours decentralizing public services and devolving decisions to managers, the emphasis can differ. Some governments view devolution as a means to unblock the hierarchy, fostering better personnel practice and improved service standards – an emphasis which resonates with some aspects of reform in France, Denmark and Spain. For others, of which Britain is a prime example, devolution, tight budgetary constraints and some degree of competition have been used to squeeze efficiency gains out of public services, but at the risk of jeopardizing service standards. The key point to emphasize is that the primary purpose of state intervention has been to restructure public services in the expectation that this would be a catalyst for change which would alter employment practices over time.

The focus on restructuring the state apparatus can be contrasted with state initiatives directed towards the reform of terms and conditions of employment. These have focused on reforming specific public service employment regulations and pay determination mechanisms to make them more akin to practice in the private sector, as has occurred, for example, in Italy. An important question is whether the reform of employment practices without accompanying changes in the organization and incentive structure of the public services will fulfil the expectations of reformers. This in part depends on the actions of employers.

Employers' policies

In recent years there has been a shift from equating public sector employment relations almost exclusively with the institutions of collective bargaining and legal enactment, towards a consideration of the policies and practices of employers (Bach and Della Rocca, 1998). Does this increased interest in employers' policy suggest that they have become the dominant actor in the reform of public services? To address this question requires an understanding of who the employers are within the public services and what authority they have to shape employment practices. The characteristics of public service employers are often viewed as distinctive, with management authority divided between a number of parties, at different levels within the state, with potentially conflicting interests. These characteristics often spawn formal or informal processes of multilateral bargaining which inform considerations of employer policy within the public services (Kochan, 1974; Treu, 1987).

These characteristics also impinge on the role of employers' associations, which is viewed as more complex and less well defined than in the private sector (Keller *et al.*, 1998). These difficulties arise from the diffusion of managerial authority, the co-ordination of employer interests, which may straddle different levels of government and distinct sub-sectors, and the extent to which employer authority is dependent on the regulatory framework devised by the state. The discretion of employers' associations has been severely limited by the policies of the state in areas such as pay determination. State promotion of policies of organizational restructuring, decentralized collective bargaining and managerial devolution has shifted attention from the formal policies of employers' associations to the practices of managers within the public services. These reforms have led some commentators, especially Anglo-Saxon writers, to detect that there has been a shift from public administration to public management, labelled the New Public Management (NPM) in which public sector managers mimic private sector best practice (Hood, 1991; Pollitt and Summa, 1997; Ridley, 1996). In these frequently prescriptive accounts, it is suggested that the New Public Management refers to a bundle of measures, not all of which emerged for the first time in the 1980s, but underlying an apparently disparate set of management practices are three key dimensions.

The first concerns the extent to which a stronger management function, held accountable for performance, has emerged. It requires the development of professional managerial roles and the use of a range of corporate management techniques, the adoption of which is aimed at improving efficiency and effectiveness. A second issue concerns the degree of change in organizational structures; the extent to which monolithic public service organizations are broken into separate units with more devolved management practice. A third element is market-orientated, and explores whether the public sector can shift from management by hierarchy to management by contract. Competition may be encouraged by competitive tendering and internal markets. These reforms fragment previously integrated organizations and replace them with competing units linked by a series of contracts.

Does the evidence support the strong version of the NPM model? Is it mainly an Anglo-Saxon phenomenon or does it have relevance to the experience of continental Europe? In many countries there have been sustained attempts to develop more sophisticated managerial systems, and authority has been ceded to lower levels within the nation state, albeit often within strict central government regulations. In Britain, and to some degree in France and Italy, there have been initiatives to strengthen the role of managers, especially in sectors such as health which face severe financial pressures. To what extent does the modest increase in the use of managers with experience outside the public sector and the employment of managers on fixed-term contracts endorse the NPM model? Even in countries where the signs of the new public management are less apparent, such as Germany, there has been vigorous debate about managerial reform, particularly within the municipalities.

These changes in employer practice are open to another interpretation; namely that, although in most countries there is general acceptance that a more efficient public service requires more effective management, this is not necessarily equated with developing a managerial role modelled on the precepts of NPM. This arises from the distinctive characteristics of management in the public domain. In comparison with the private sector, trade union membership remains high and managers are more likely to be trade union members than their private sector counterparts. This raises the question of whether managers share some or most of the values of their work force and, if so, whether they may be unwilling to alter fundamentally management practices. These reservations are reinforced by the presence of distinct professional and occupational identities among public service staff, often shared by their managers, which may instil opposition to the widespread implementation of managerial values. In addition, within formalized and legalistic systems of public administration there may be limited scope for the exercise of management prerogatives, a point highlighted by the German case. Finally, the capacity to implement public management reforms, which requires more sophisticated systems of human resource management, may be constrained by the underdevelopment or absence of a specialist personnel function in many parts of the public sector.

Trade unions

Public service trade unions, like their private sector counterparts, face perennial challenges: their effectiveness in organizing and mobilizing their members' interests; their capacity to aggregate these interests in a manner which maintains solidarity (or at least prevents fragmentation and division) and their ability to maintain the authority and cohesion of their organizations. These long-standing questions of trade union purpose, organization and strategy take particular forms in the public services, reflecting the distinctive characteristics of public service employment.

The composition of the work force, with its relatively high proportion of women, employed in white-collar and professional occupations has been an important influence on the character of public service unions. Many grew out of professional associations with privileged professional concerns about status, service quality and influencing state policy rather than a narrower focus on terms and conditions of employment backed up, if necessary, by the threat of industrial action. Although this tradition has been eroded as their members' concern to maintain their terms and conditions of employment has come to the fore, the legacy continues to impact on public service trade unionism, especially in sectors such as health and education in which professional concerns remain especially prominent.

In marked contrast to the private sector, some public service trade unions remain detached from the dominant peak-level confederation(s) or are affiliated to wholly public sector confederations. Public service trade unionism has not been immune from the influence of distinct national patterns of unionism, and the impact of union mergers is becoming more significant, as the creation of Unison in Britain and the merger plans of the ÖTV in Germany illustrate. None the less organization on the basis of occupation has remained a more enduring characteristic than in the private sector. This structural characteristic reflects and reinforces more general trade union divisions based on ideological and other differences and, more recently, increasing competition for members to safeguard against loss of membership.

Trade unions as secondary organizations attempt to organize and represent workers whose aspirations and employment conditions have been influenced strongly by the state in its differing roles as employer, economic regulator and legislator. These roles blend economic and political concerns and ensure that the 'political contingency' impacts on union practice. Trade union policy has been primarily focused on the national level and the capacity to influence governments to maximum effect. This approach has been shaped by highly centralized systems of pay determination and the prominent role of trade unions in welfare state policy debates and administration in some countries. It is only recently that the limitations of this form of trade union practice have emerged. In particular, highly centralized and bureaucratic forms of trade unionism may not have the capacity to adapt to the challenge of more decentralized forms of management. Moreover, traditional trade union practice has been implicated in the criticism of the quality of public services which is a ubiquitous feature of current debates.

These issues should not conceal the fact that public service trade unions retain many advantages over their private sector counterparts, not least their high levels of membership and density. They face little or no hostility from employers in recruiting members; few organizational constraints because their potential membership is often concentrated in large employment units and has greater job security; and their potential members appear to be favourably disposed to union membership (see, for example, Jorgeson and Lind, 1992, cited in Lind, 1995). Various attempts to 'deprivilege' the status of public sector employment, however, pose some of the greatest challenges for trade unions. Although state policies have varied, there have been widespread attempts to erode the advantages traditionally associated with public service employment. The spread of various forms of 'precarious employment', a stronger emphasis on performance and accountability and alterations in employment status have undermined the differences with conditions in the private sector.

Differences remain, however, between and within countries, in the nature of trade union responses to restructuring proposals. In Britain trade unions were not only excluded from planning and implementing reforms but were explicitly targeted as an impediment to change and a concerted attempt was made to reduce their influence. It is scarcely surprising that in these circumstances trade unions opposed the Conservative government's agenda, albeit with limited success, and remain highly ambivalent about the public sector policies of the Labour government. In France the aims and outcomes of reform have been more modest, but some of the same adversarial dynamics as seen in Britain are evident. French governments have oscillated in their commitment to involving the trade unions in their reform plans, although the conflicts of December 1995, and the subsequent electoral demise of the Juppé government, testify to the risks of such a course of action. A second approach to reform has been more consensual, and the trade unions have been more willing to engage with government measures, as in Denmark and Italy. For example, in Italy the contractualization of public service employment so that employment status is more similar to the private sector was broadly welcomed by the trade unions. Finally, in Germany where the modernization process has been limited, public sector trade unions, whilst opposed to neo-liberal plans for privatization have been open to the types of reform which have been implemented in some of the municipalities and the ÖTV has been integrally involved in debates about modernization.

This schematic presentation illustrates the variability of trade union responses at national level but conceals important differences between trade unions within individual countries which arise from the divisions noted earlier. These differences have been brought into sharp relief by reform plans which force trade unions to confront issues which lay dormant when public service expenditure and employment were expanding during the first three decades of the post-war period. Unions have been forced to decide whether they endorse or oppose modernization strategies, and a myriad of other consequences for union purpose and organization flow from their decisions. Many of the dilemmas are illustrated by the changes in the level and scope of collective bargaining.

Collective bargaining

It is usual within the comparative literature on collective bargaining, based mainly on private sector experience, to differentiate between the coverage, level, scope and forms of bargaining (Windmuller, 1987). Within the public services the prevailing pattern of private sector collective bargaining in each country has been an important influence, but the analysis is complicated by the distinct and variable role of the state. This has resulted in the slow and uneven growth of collective bargaining in many countries.

There are several distinctive features of public service collective bargaining practice. A primary consideration for governments has been whether joint regulation of terms and conditions of employment is the most appropriate mechanism for public sector pay determination. The implied uncertainty arises from the essential or statutory nature of public services, which often precludes the use of industrial action, an integral component of the exercise of power within the collective bargaining process. In addition, governments have been uncertain whether collective bargaining has been the most appropriate mechanism to reconcile tight control of the public sector paybill with broader macro-economic constraints. For these reasons, the division between unilateral regulation and collective bargaining has been contested, but to what extent has this boundary shifted in recent years in favour of collective bargaining?

As the following chapters show, there seems to have been a general move towards the recognition of collective bargaining rights for larger groups of public employees. The increased coverage of collective bargaining is in marked contrast to the experience of the private sector, in which some weaknesses in the coverage of collective bargaining have emerged, albeit with wide variations between countries. The shift towards decentralization of bargaining has exacerbated these difficulties under certain conditions (Katz, 1993). The evidence from the national chapters suggests that the extension of collective bargaining has not been universal or unqualified. Strong elements of unilateral regulation may continue alongside formal systems of collective bargaining – because of its uncertain status, as in France, or because some groups remain outside the collective bargaining machinery, as in Britain and Germany. Even when there is no formal system of collective bargaining the formal institutional arrangements for pay determination often disguise the complex forms of 'arm's-length' bargaining and lobbying undertaken by the social partners, as the British and German cases illustrate.

A second distinctive feature of the public services bargaining process is its multilateral character (Kochan, 1974), with the employers' side exhibiting a considerable dispersion of power between government ministers, state officials, politicians and the managers of public services. The resolution of internal conflict within the employers' side complicates negotiations; and a similar process arises among trade union participants. A key problem for employers and trade unions has been their capacity to minimise internal divisions to ensure that the differences do not jeopardize their bargaining goals. One of the most elaborate illustrations of the complex coalitions that shape the bargaining process can be found in the Danish experience, but whichever methods are favoured to maintain unity, they are influenced strongly by the level at which collective bargaining occurs.

The question of bargaining level has been considered the most important dimension, which influences many aspects of labour relations behaviour and trade union practice (Clegg, 1976). Katz (1993), referring to private sector practice, suggests that the shift towards decentralized bargaining poses challenges for trade unions because it prevents wages being taken out of competition and fosters concession bargaining at workplace level. Have the same trends been evident in the public services or have the traditionally more centralized systems of public sector pay determination remained intact?

As Bordogna and Winchester (1998) suggest, the implications of decentralized collective bargaining are quite different in the public and private sector. First, in the private sector, individual firms having previously ceded responsibility for collective bargaining from firm level to an employers' association have subsequently chosen to decentralize bargaining, abandoning multi-employer bargaining, and focusing on setting their own terms and conditions of employment at enterprise level. In the public sector the starting point of the process is usually reversed; the state has the responsibility for pay determination and, in some cases, has decided to delegate responsibility for some terms and conditions of employment to individual employers or single units of the administration (Dell'Aringa, 1997).

Second, governments have been reluctant therefore to risk losing control of the public sector paybill by encouraging decentralized collective bargaining. But this type of analysis does not necessarily preclude all types of decentralization because forms of 'organized decentralization' (Traxler, 1996) may be possible which combine tight overall expenditure control with scope for employers to negotiate forms of flexibility agreement at more local level. The changing structure of collective bargaining has implications also for the patterns of conflict and co-operation within the public sector.

Traditionally the public services have been much less strike-prone than the private sector and this has derived, in part, from the restrictions on industrial action placed on employees providing essential services. This pattern has altered markedly and the public sector has become far more important as an arena of conflict. As the national chapters show, the patterns of conflict and accommodation take a variety of forms, from defensive struggles against privatization and work intensification to more offensive action by occupational groups, critical of official trade unions for failing to safeguard their interests. The emergence of the *cobas* in Italy and the *co-ordinations* in France are illustrative of such conflicts. The implications of decentralized bargaining practice and devolved management responsibility have shifted attention away from the traditional focus on national patterns of mobilization, but the implications are not straightforward. Whilst individual country experience points to the emergence of more fragmented micro-level conflicts which extend beyond industrial action to problems of staff morale and absenteeism, at the same time, enhanced managerial discretion at local level can also allow more co-operative patterns of employment relations to be established between the social partners at local level.

Transformation, modernization or inertia?

Taken together, these developments in state, employer and trade union policies indicate that the last decade has been a momentous one for public services in Europe. Alongside perennial macro-economic concerns about 'fiscal crisis', a more sustained attempt to reform the governance and employment structures of the public services was made in the 1990s. For national governments, containing public expenditure has been a necessary but not a sufficient condition of economic competitiveness, and the emerging orthodoxy has been that more fundamental forms of structural adjustment are necessary. Against this backdrop there has been a shift in the manner in which the public services are conceptualized.

Analysis of employment practices is no longer confined to assessing long-standing features of administrative regulation with policy makers concerned to explore the dynamics of change and reform. The prism through which public service developments are viewed has a harder, more utilitarian edge with the language of modernization, decentralization, performance and privatization featuring more prominently in discussions of public service employment relations.

The task of comparing reform trajectories in countries with widely different political systems, economic policies and constitutional structures is a complex process which can be captured only imperfectly by the subtitle of this book: *transformation, modernization* or *inertia*. None the less what do we signify by these terms? *Transformation* implies a purposeful, intensive and sustained attempt to alter the basic organizational principles of the public sector. Specific outcomes might include the establishment of novel organizational forms, the reconfiguration of power relations and alterations in the governance structure of the public services, for example a shift from hierarchical to market relations (see Ferlie *et al.*, 1996). *Modernization* has become a ubiquitous term of discussion about public services reform and has been used loosely to signify a wide range of reforms in the public services. In contrast to transformation, modernization is an intermediate category which embodies more gradual and less intensive attempts at reform, and the persistence of strong elements of continuity. *Inertia* signifies much more limited change and although it may signify resistance on the part of interest groups, or inactivity on behalf of governments, it may also reflect a conscious decision to retain the core values and forms of administrative regulation prevalent in the public services in some cases. What has been the experience of the six countries explored in the following chapters?

The public service reforms in Britain have the greatest claim to the epithet 'transformation'. A distinctive feature of the British experience is that there have been both substantial reforms of the administrative structures of the state and concerted attempts to reform employment relations. Public services have been reorganized and responsibility for aspects of employment relations has been devolved to managers. This has been accompanied by a marked accretion of managerial power to the detriment of trade unions, often reinforced by forms of market competition. There has been a strong emphasis in government policy that public sector management practice should mimic private sector best practice. Measures to decentralize collective bargaining and introduce human resource management techniques, such as individual performance-related pay, forms of direct participation and the use of numerical flexibility have been designed to produce a convergence of public and private sector practice. What were the preconditions for this sustained attempt to transform employment relations?

The most familiar explanation is a political one, with the assumption that the Conservative government's ideological hostility to the public sector and its trade unions unleashed radical reforms. This forms part of the explanation, but although eighteen years of continuous Conservative government may have been a necessary condition for radical reform, it was not sufficient; particular characteristics of the political system and British state sustained radical reform. With no system of proportional representation or tradition of coalition government, Conservative governments were relatively free to pursue a radical agenda of reform, secure in the knowledge that the opposition was weak and divided. The determination of the Conservative government to pursue this agenda was aided by the absence of a written constitution and the tradition of parliamentary sovereignty, which places few constraints on the government of the day. Moreover, there is a relatively weak tradition of administrative law which civil servants apply in their dealings with organizations and individuals (Ridley, 1996).

Although trade union density is relatively high compared with the private sector in Britain, there is no legally codified system of co-determination in the public sector and only a weak tradition of social partnership. The influence that trade unions have exerted through voluntary forms of joint consultation has depended on their bargaining strength and the willingness of managers to acknowledge the value of consultation. In a harsher economic and ideological climate, and with managers taking their cue from developments in direct participation in the private sector, trade unions were vulnerable to a sharp diminution in their influence. All these characteristics allowed much greater scope to reform the public sector than in any other European country. The capacity of the central state to intervene directly has led to radical reforms in organizational structures, management roles and the spread of marketization, but also, paradoxically, elements of continuity. The centripetal forces associated with central decision making and tight expenditure control in the British public sector have prevented the same degree of change in employment practices.

The experience of Germany is almost diametrically opposed to that of Britain and there are fewer signs of modernization. Until recently there has been much less anguished debate about public expenditure and public sector efficiency, reflecting, in part, the more modest and more diffuse role of the state than in many other countries. In addition, the immense challenges posed by reunification required the transplantation of the system of public administration and employment rules to the new *Länder*, which diverted attention away from the challenges faced by the public sector in the former West Germany, at least in the short term. In contrast to many countries the debate about modernization has been less concerned with central government initiatives and more orientated to the policies of individual states and municipalities.

There have been few initiatives to alter the administrative structures of the state or the system of labour relations. Collective bargaining (which formally excludes *Beamte*) is highly centralized and there are few pressures towards decentralization. The most contentious issue has concerned the special status of the *Beamte*, but any reform requires the explicit consent of the trade unions and a broad political consensus among the different political parties which at present is a distant possibility, not least because *Beamte* are well represented in parliament and can exert informal influence through a number of channels.

Employer policy has evolved in an incremental manner, with some adoption of management techniques derived from the private sector. These techniques have been grafted on to an existing dense network of administrative and legal regulations.

The existence of fairly elaborate rights of co-determination has diluted moves to develop a managerial culture, and is reflected also in a fundamental ambivalence about the utility of adopting wholesale the tenets of the new managerialism. It is among the trade unions that alternative modernization strategies are being debated.

The experience of Germany reveals therefore a continuing commitment to a traditional system of administrative regulation, with some scope for employers at local level to pursue incremental changes in working practices. There has been limited pressure for reform and because of the federal structure of the German state the capacity of central government to initiate fundamental reforms of labour relations is heavily constrained. Although there are signs that a note of greater urgency has been injected into the debate about the reform of the public sector this requires the mobilization of a high degree of support from a variety of constituencies which skews debate towards an acceleration of incremental change rather than a radical break from past practice.

The Italian case can be interpreted as an attempt to modernize the public services in an environment which has been conducive to some reforms of employment practices and collective bargaining, but where the weakness of the central state has prevented the formation of a coalition of interests to enable more far-reaching reforms of administrative structures. The most far-reaching changes have been in the sphere of collective bargaining with the 'privatization' of the employment relationship after 1993 which placed employment contracts in the public sector on the same basis as those in the private sector. Trade unions, which were closely involved in discussions about the reforms, remain well organized at workplace level and were not opposed to adopting the two-tier system of collective bargaining which prevails in the private sector. Attempts to implement policies associated with the New Public Management have been more difficult to achieve, despite strong desire to develop more professional managers and grant autonomy to civil servants to protect them from political influence. The attempts to 'empower' management have been constrained by the continuation of an all-encompassing framework of administrative and legal regulations, and the blend of political and administrative authority with strong elements of clientelism. Organizational structures have been slow to change and devolution of managerial responsibilities has been limited.

The defining feature of Spain's process of modernization has been the rapid expansion of the public services, which were underdeveloped during the Franco period. It was important for all governments to maintain the momentum of public service expansion as a tangible expression of the transition to democracy. This process of expansion has been accompanied by radical reforms of the central structure of the state. Authority has been decentralized with the establishment of a new administrative tier (*autonomous communities*), with wide powers, which has altered the responsibilities of civil servants and incorporated elements of budgetary devolution. The motivation behind these reforms was not only to modernize the state, but also to defuse the tension between centralism and separatism within it, although the extent to which the tensions have been overcome rather than recast in a different guise is open to question.

Alongside this dispersion of political authority, there have been some attempts to establish institutional industrial relations practices, with the role of the trade unions consolidated and the emergence of collective bargaining, albeit in a highly ambiguous form. These developments have been uneven, with few substantial reforms of management practice, which remains highly circumscribed by the weight of the strong legal tradition. The legacy of the Franco era has been significant, not least rudimentary personnel practice, reliance on legal regulation and a culture of political patronage. In addition the ban on civil servants joining trade unions (which in the transition period led to the emergence of a large number of rival union organizations) has limited the capacity of the Spanish state to modernize the public services. In terms of personnel practice, the most visible tendency has been inertia.

The pattern of reform in France cannot be separated from the unique characteristics of the French administrative tradition: an especially elitist, centralized and unitary state and an administrative culture which has stifled attempts at modernization, despite a continuing public policy debate which provides strong rhetorical support for reform. The French republican tradition signified a central role for the state in fostering post-war economic growth. This has discouraged critical scrutiny of the role and scope of state action. There have been some initiatives to reform state structures, especially the decentralization of local government since 1982, and reforms within the health sector. These measures represent an attempt to lessen the dominance of national policy decisions and develop local decision making, but strong centralizing forces persist which contribute to the difficulties in reforming employment relations.

The structure of public service employment blends a deeply rooted system of legally regulated employment conditions and a highly centralized system of pay scales and job classifications. Attempts to reform a system which combines extreme centralization with a myriad of compartmentalized *corps* face great obstacles. Not only are the elite civil servants immersed in existing state values, which ensures that they retain a pivotal role in public policy, but they clearly have a material interest in retaining the *status quo* – a perspective supported by politicians, many of whom share the same elitist educational background.

The tradition of unilateral state regulation has only partially been altered in the last two decades because the legal status of collective bargaining does not preclude continuing unilateral state regulation. Similarly, despite some official interest in innovative private sector practice, the capacity to reform management structures and reinvigorate personnel practice has been hindered by the necessity to accommodate reform within existing rigid forms of legally regulated personnel management.

Public service trade unions have demonstrated an ambivalent attitude to reform, and this has reignited long-standing rivalries between the differing confederations. Trade unions have aired their members' frustration about inflexible pay and conditions but feared that reforms could be used to challenge their traditional 'privileges'. Successive governments, many of which have been short-lived coalitions, or have governed under conditions of *cohabitation*, have been wary of antagonizing trade unions. Their low membership levels belie a capacity to mobilize widespread support in resisting threats to their institutional status as participants in the management of the welfare state and their role in protecting the 'acquired rights' of citizens on whose behalf they claim to speak. Trade unions benefit also from their entrenched position within a web of co-determination structures across the public services which provides them with an effective veto over many aspects of management decision making.

In Denmark the modernization process has been shaped by strong emphasis on ensuring consensus in the development and implementation of proposals for reform. Reform measures have progressed furthest in terms of the process of administrative decentralization and management devolution. There has been an express willingness to experiment with forms of privatization, but experimentation has not progressed very far. The presence of coalition governments within a 'social democratic state' in which the welfare state has not been subject to serious challenge has diluted more far-reaching proposals for reform. Changes in the form and character of industrial relations have been modest, with the development of an elaborate system of co-ordinated coalition bargaining. It is the emphasis on consensus, with formal and informal systems of corporatism, in which the trade unions remain crucial and influential actors, which accounts for this pattern of public sector reform.

Until recently the decentralization of pay bargaining has been limited and experiments with local 'pay pools' had a marginal impact on pay determination. The pay reform of 1997 is more far-reaching. Basic pay decided at central level is being supplemented by local allowances which may constitute a sizeable proportion of pay. Considerable uncertainty surrounds this reform because it is not clear whether sufficient resources have been made available to facilitate decentralization and the necessary personnel expertise may be lacking. Moreover, decentralization opens up the prospect of more intense rivalry between trade unions and may encourage more far-reaching changes in working practices than hitherto.

The overall conclusions that can be drawn from the patterns of reform in these six countries can be assessed in relation to two propositions. First, that macroeconomic integration within the European Union and micro-economic concerns about efficiency and service quality are producing greater similarity in the structure and outcome of public service employment regulation within Europe. Second, that the restructuring process within each country and reforms in state, employer and trade union policy may partially erode the separation between public and private sector employment relations.

The schematic comparisons presented above suggest that a strong version of the convergence thesis can be rejected. All countries share a common concern to raise efficiency and curb public expenditure, but, as with the search for national competitiveness, state policies to further competitive advantage vary widely. If this is the case with nation states and their systems of employment relations, in which it may be expected that globalization, the policies of multinationals and European integration will exert strong pressure for convergence, it is even less likely that strong pressures for convergence will exist in the public services, in which such pressures are weaker or absent. For example, one potentially unifying force within the private sector – European-level social dialogue – is absent in the public services at European level (see Keller and Henneberger, 1997). The individual chapters provide an integrated account of the pattern of reform, the distinct characteristics of state policy and the continuing diversity of national experience.

There is stronger support for the second proposition, that there is growing convergence of practice between public and private sector employment relations in each country. The gap between public and private sector systems of employment relations has tended to be narrower than differences between countries, especially in the more recent past, but this fact has been partially disguised by the preoccupation within countries with comparisons between public and private sector pay levels.

It might be expected that the policies of employers would exhibit the strongest convergence with private sector practice. Such has been the case, with employers sharing the same concern as their private sector counterparts to reduce wage costs and increase the flexibility of the work force. There is widespread interest and some experimentation with human resource management techniques which have their origins in the private sector. This has arisen in part because there is the greatest scope for 'policy learning' and the diffusion of private sector practice among managerial groups. Governmental initiatives, policy and managerial networks, and the proselytizing role undertaken by management consultants and many educational institutions, such as business schools, all contribute to the diffusion process.

The other main signs of at least partial convergence relate to systems of pay determination, with the specificities of public sector pay determination being diluted. The coverage of collective bargaining is being extended in most countries and responsibility for setting some pay and non-pay conditions is being decentralized to lower levels of state structures. This overall picture needs to be qualified to take account of important differences between occupational groups arising from the segmentation of public sector labour markets. For predominantly low-paid occupational groups, with counterparts in the private sector, forms of marketization and privatization have exerted a downward pressure on wages and terms and conditions of employment. This 'downward' convergence needs to be contrasted with occupational groups such as teachers and nurses which have no equivalent in the private sector and whose pay determination arrangements have needed to continue to reflect their distinct occupational identities and labour market characteristics.

To conclude, although governments may face similar problems in different countries it is premature to predict a public services version of the 'End of History' with countries converging on a similar set of employment relations systems. National governments continue to shape their approach to the public services within a particular national configuration of political, economic and legal institutions. There is some evidence that individual countries are emulating practice in the private sector more closely, but convergence between countries remains a distant prospect.

References

Adema, W. (1998) 'Uncovering real social spending', *OECD Observer*, 211: 20–3.

Altenstetter, C. and Björkman, J-W. (eds) (1997) *Health Policy Reform, National Variations and Globalization*, Basingstoke: Macmillan.

Bach, S. (1998) 'Restructuring and privatization of health care services: selected cases in western Europe' in G. Ullrich (ed.) *Social and Economic Dimensions of Privatization: Health Care Services*, Geneva: International Labour Organization.

Bach, S. and Della Rocca, G. (1998) 'The management strategies of public service employers in western Europe', paper presented at the eleventh World Congress of the IIRA, Bologna, Italy.

Bamber, G. and Lansbury, R. (eds) (1998) *International and Comparative Employment Relations*, London: Sage.

Bekke, H., Perry, J. and Toonen, T. (eds) (1996) *Civil Service Systems in Comparative Perspective*, Bloomington: Indiana University Press.

Bordogna, L. and Winchester, D. (1998) 'Public sector collective bargaining in western Europe: recent trends and problems', paper presented at the eleventh World Congress of the IIRA, Bologna, Italy.

Clegg, H. (1976) *Trade Unionism under Collective Bargaining: A Theory based on Comparisons of Six Countries*, Oxford: Blackwell.

Dell'Aringa, C. (1997) 'Pay determination in the public service: an international comparison', Department of Economics Working Paper 16, Milan: Catholic University of Milan.

Ferlie, E., Ashburner, L., FitzGerald, L. and Pettigrew, A. (1996) *The New Public Management in Action*, Oxford: Oxford University Press.

Ferner, A. (1988) *Governments, Managers and Industrial Relations: Public Enterprises and their Political Environment*, Oxford: Blackwell.

—— (1994) 'The state as employer', in R. Hyman and A. Ferner (eds) *New Frontiers in European Industrial Relations*, Oxford: Blackwell.

Ferner, A. and Hyman, R. (eds) (1998) *Changing Industrial Relations in Europe*, Oxford: Blackwell.

Flynn, N. and Strehl, F. (eds) (1996) *Public Sector Management in Europe*, London: Prentice Hall.

Foster, C. and Plowden, F. (1996) *The State under Stress*, Buckingham: Open University Press.

Hegewisch, A., Van Ommeren, J., Brewster, C. and Kessler, I. (1998) *Direct Participation in the Social Public Services*, Dublin: European Foundation for the Improvement of Living and Working Conditions.

Hood, C. (1991) 'A public management for all seasons?' *Public Administration*, 69:1, 3–19.

Hood, C. and Guy Peters, B. (eds) (1994) *Rewards at the Top: A Comparative Study of High Public Office*, London: Sage.

Katz, H. (1993) 'The decentralization of collective bargaining: a literature review and comparative analysis', *Industrial and Labour Relations Review*, 47:1, 3–22.

Keller, B. and Henneberger, F. (1997) 'Prospects for social dialogue in the public sector', *Transfer*, 3:1, 119–46.

Keller, B., Due, J. and Anderson, S. (1998) 'The changing role of employers' associations and unions in public sector employment relations', paper presented at the eleventh World Congress of the IIRA, Bologna, Italy.

Kochan, T. (1974) 'A theory of multilateral bargaining in city governments', *Industrial and Labour Relations Review*, 27:4, 325–42.

Lane, J-E. (ed.) (1997) *Public Sector Reform: Rationale Trends and Problems*, London: Sage.

Lind, J. (1995) 'The modernization of trade unions in Denmark', *Transfer*, 1:1, 44–63.

Massey, A. (ed.) (1997) *Globalization and Marketization of Government Services*, Basingstoke: Macmillan.

Naschold, F. (1996) *New Frontiers in Public Sector Management*, Berlin: de Gruyter.

OECD (1992) *Historical Statistics*, Paris: OECD.

OECD (1995) *Governance in Transition: Public Management Reforms in OECD Countries*, Paris: OECD.

Olsen, T. (1996) *Industrial Relations Systems in the Public Sector in Europe*, Oslo: EPSC/FAFO.

Pollitt, C. and Summa, H. (1997) 'Trajectories of reform: public management in four countries', *Public Money and Management*, 17:1, 7–18.

Ridley, F. (1996) 'The new public management in Europe: comparative perspectives', *Public Policy and Administration*, 11:1, 16–29.

Rondinelli, D. and Iacono, M. (1996) *Policies and Institutions for Managing Privatization*, Geneva: International Labour Organization.

Streeck, W. (1992) *Social Institutions and Economic Performance: Studies of Industrial Relations in Advanced Capitalist Economies*, London: Sage.

Traxler, F. (1996) 'Collective bargaining and industrial change: a case of disorganization? A comparative analysis of eighteen OECD countries', *European Sociological Review*, 12:2, 271–87.

Treu, T. (ed.) (1987) *Public Service Labour Relations: Recent Trends and Future Prospects*, Geneva: International Labour Organization.

Van Ruysseveldt., J. and Visser, J. (eds) (1996) *Industrial Relations in Europe: Traditions and Transitions*, London: Sage.

Windmuller, J. (1987) *Collective Bargaining in Market Economies: A Reappraisal*, Geneva: International Labour Organization.

2 Britain

The transformation of public service employment relations

David Winchester and Stephen Bach

A large and complex public sector of employment developed in Britain during the three decades after 1945. In the immediate post-war period, major fuel, power and transport industries were nationalized and the reform of health, education and social security provisions established the basis of a substantial welfare state. Public sector employment increased continuously until the early 1980s, when it reached more than 7 million employees, nearly 30 per cent of the employed labour force. Since then it has declined to just over 5 million employees, or 20 per cent of the work force.

The declining size and scope of public sector employment resulted from the policies of Conservative governments in office continuously from 1979 to 1997. Almost all the nationalized industries were privatized and many public service functions were sub-contracted to private firms. These changes were shaped by a strong ideological commitment to strengthen management authority and reduce the power of trade unions, not least through the creation of competitive and market relations. Alongside strong central control of expenditure, the reforms led to the devolution of management authority, the fragmentation of previously unified organizations and structures, and increasing competition between public and private providers of services. Inevitably this organizational transformation challenged the centralized methods of collective bargaining and patterns of employment relations that had characterized the public sector for the last fifty years. Very few of these reforms have been reversed by the Labour government since its election in May 1997, but throughout the chapter reference will be made to new proposals designed to produce incremental change in public service organization and employment relations.

The boundaries between public and private sector employment, and between sub-groups within the public sector, have never been as clearly demarcated in Britain as in most other countries. This arises from the absence of a fundamental division between public and private sector employment legislation. Until thirty years ago, this was a consequence of the policy of legal abstentionism (or voluntarism) in industrial relations. Since then, the rapid development of individual and collective employment law has rarely differentiated between public and private sector employees in significant ways. The formal legal status of civil service employment was uncertain until the High Court decided that civil servants were employed by the Crown under contracts of employment in 1991, but the previous legal ambiguity had few important practical consequences. More generally, the absence of a clear legal distinction in the status of public and private sector employment has facilitated the programme of restructuring, privatization and market-led reforms.

Definitions of public service sectors

The national accounts divide the economy into institutional sectors covering organizations engaged in similar forms of economic activity. The threefold classification of different parts of the public sector is based on their legal and administrative responsibilities and their degree of financial independence from central government (Safford and MacGregor, 1998).

Central government covers all organizations for whose activities a government Minister (or other responsible person) is accountable to Parliament. Apart from the armed services, central government includes the civil service and its executive agencies, and other publicly constituted bodies financially dependent upon central government, such as research councils, national museums and district authorities of the National Health Services (NHS).

Public corporations are organizations with some degree of financial independence from central government. Whilst government Ministers directly or indirectly appoint most of the senior managers, public corporations are able to borrow and maintain financial reserves within limits set by Parliament. Until the mid-1980s, employment in public corporations was dominated by the nationalized industries and public utilities, but the radical programme of privatization, including telecommunications, air transport, gas, electricity, water, railways and coal mining, reduced the size of this sub-sector dramatically. Apart from the Post Office (the status of which is under ministerial review at the time of writing) and around forty other relatively small organizations, the majority of employees in public corporations are now in NHS trusts – that is, the hospitals and community health organizations that provide most health services in Britain.

Local authorities have the power to raise taxes and levies, and the statutory duty to provide a range of services defined in successive local government Acts passed by Parliament. Unlike other parts of the public sector, local authorities are governed by elected members or councillors whose political party affiliation may bring them into conflict with central government ministers. This tension has led to a gradual shift in the constitutional balance of power from local to central government. Since the early 1980s, central government has restricted the tax-raising powers of local authorities, regulated their policies more closely, and removed some of their functions. The latter has been achieved by creating new public corporations (e.g. municipal transport, airport and housing services), and by 'privatizing' some services. For example, polytechnics and higher education colleges were transferred from local authority control in 1989, and almost 10 per cent of teachers are employed in 'grant-maintained' schools which have opted out of local authority control. Despite these changes, local authorities still provide a wide range of services and employ more than half the public sector work force.

The focus of this chapter can be defined by modifying the above classification. First, central government will be viewed as synonymous with the civil service departments and executive agencies which currently employ 0.5 million staff in mainly non-manual occupations. Second, reference to local authorities will focus on 1.5 million manual and non-manual staff employed on a wide range of activities. In addition to these staff, most of the 0.5 million schoolteachers (and police and fire service staff) are also local authority employees, but they will be treated separately in the analysis where appropriate. This is because they comprise clearly defined and large occupational groups, with distinct employment conditions that are determined by separate systems of pay determination. Finally, the 1.2 million NHS staff will be treated as a separate category, and other public corporations will be excluded.

Organizational structure, employment and salaries

The composition of employment

The main changes in the sectoral composition of public service employment over the last seventeen years can be seen in Table 2.1. The decline in aggregate public sector employment since 1981 has arisen mainly from the privatization of nationalized industries. Privatization and subcontracting have also contributed to a decline of around 25 per cent in civil service employment and to a loss of manual workers' jobs throughout the public services. Aggregate employment in the NHS and in local authorities has been relatively stable.

Table 2.1 Work force in employment, by sector, 1981–97 (000)

Sector	1981	1986	1994	1997
Total work force in employment	24,489	24,739	25,548	25,526
Private sector	17,313	17,979	19,914	21,469
Public sector	7,185	6,534	5,332	5,057
Public corporations of which:	1,876	1,187	1,467	1,521
NHS trusts	–	–	1,000	1,121
Other	1,876	1,186	467	400
Central government of which:	2,419	2,337	1,213	941
Armed services	334	322	250	210
National Health Service	1,208	1,215	205	78
Other (mainly civil service)	878	800	758	653
Local authorities of which:	2,899	3,010	2,652	2,595
Education	1,454	1,452	1,182	1,187
Social services	350	387	408	400
Police	186	188	207	207
Construction	143	125	87	65
Other	766	770	768	736

Source: Safford and MacGregor (1998).

Table 2.2 Public sector employment, mid-year 1996 (000)

Sector	Total	Male	Female Total	Full-time	Part-time
Total public sector	5,150	2,127	3,022	1,477	1,545
Public corporations	410	348	61	50	11
Civil service	676	347	329	264	65
National Health Service	1,192	255	937	452	485
Local authorities	2,651	975	1,676	692	984
of which Education	1,183	233	950	357	593

Source: *Economic Trends*, March 1997.

Note
The figures for public corporations exclude NHS trusts, which appear in the NHS figures. The civil service figures include other public bodies funded by central government. The local authorities' education figures exclude grant-funded education no longer under local authority control.

These data, derived from the classification of the UK national accounts, exaggerate the decline in public service employment and the growth of the private sector. The reclassification of polytechnics, further education and sixth-form colleges, and grant-maintained schools as 'private non-profit-making bodies' (alongside the old universities) arose because they are no longer 'wholly dependent' on government funding, or subject to local authority control. None the less, these organizations are part of the public education system, highly dependent on expenditure decisions taken by central government, and covered by systems of pay determination and employment relations deeply rooted in public service traditions.

In the last decade, the proportion of women in the public sector work force has increased from 50.2 per cent to 58.7 per cent. This has resulted partly from the privatization of nationalized industries (which employed mainly men) and the growth of employment in social services. The education and health services have always employed a majority of women, not only in professional posts, such as teaching and nursing, but also in less qualified and lower status occupations (e.g. secretarial, cleaning and catering jobs). The data in Table 2.2 indicate that whilst the civil service still employs slightly more men than women, in the NHS and in local authority education services, women greatly outnumber men.

Table 2.2 also shows that more women work part-time than full-time in the public sector. Of the total of 1.7 million part-time employees in 1996, more than 90 per cent were women, concentrated mainly in the NHS and in local authorities rather than the civil service. Over the last decade, the proportion of public sector employees working part-time has increased from 25 per cent to 33 per cent. There is no simple explanation for this change – and there are wide variations in the use of part-time employees within different parts of the public services. The evidence suggests that both supply-side and demand factors are at work. Public service employers report that increases in part-time working arise from staff requests for job-sharing or reduced working hours, especially from women returning from maternity leave. Also, many employers have increased the use of part-time working to deal with labour shortages and budget constraints; the reorganization of working-time can offer increased flexibility in meeting service demands.

Since 1990 there has been an increase in the number of temporary employees in the British labour market. By 1996 there were 1.6 million temporary employees in total; around 10 per cent of all staff in the public sector, compared with 5 per cent in the private sector. The majority of public service temporary employees are on fixed-term contracts, and many work in professional occupations such as teaching (Sly and Stillwell, 1997). A smaller proportion obtain work through temporary employment agencies – for example, nurses and teachers in further education colleges. Case study evidence suggests that budget restrictions and uncertainties, as well as the need to provide cover for absent staff (e.g. on maternity leave), provide the main motives for the increase in temporary employment (IDS, 1996; Bach, 1998).

Labour markets and salaries

In comparison with most other countries, the labour market characteristics of the UK public services have been closer to those of the private sector for some time. None the less, until fairly recently many public service employees had a greater degree of job security, more clearly defined career prospects, and generally better pensions, sickness pay and other benefits than their private sector counterparts. These conditions of service were prescribed in national agreements and applied uniformly throughout each part of the public services alongside salary structures.

The Conservative governments of 1979–97, however, rejected the presumption that a 'good employer' obligation should prevail in the public services. Their policies encouraged greater diversity within the sector by weakening national systems of employment regulation and encouraging the devolution of management authority to the individual public service organization. Within nationally determined financial controls that limited employers' 'ability to pay', it was argued that employment policies should be based on a pragmatic labour market test: that is, they should enable managers to recruit, retain and motivate a sufficient number of appropriately qualified staff. As will be seen later, this objective has rarely been achieved fully, and its pursuit has led to conflicting assessments of the links between funding, employment relations and the quality of services.

These changes in public service employment policies have eroded many of the previous differences from private sector labour markets. Policies of competitive tendering and 'market testing' have encouraged convergence between public and private sector employment conditions and practices, especially those covering low-skilled manual workers and clerical staff. A degree of 'downward harmonization' has resulted from government policies of labour market deregulation, with many employees in the public services facing the same degree of job insecurity, work intensification and limited promotion prospects as their private sector equivalents.

The recruitment, compensation, appraisal, promotion and job security policies covering technical, professional and managerial staff in the public services also broadly reflect those found in the private sector. This is partly because the past practice of internal promotion to senior posts has been partially eroded by more open recruitment in recent years, especially in the civil service. Of the 131 agency chief executives in post in 1996, almost 70 per cent had been recruited by open competition, and nearly 40 per cent were outside appointments. All were appointed on limited-term, renewable contracts, and some had to reapply for their post at the end of the period of their appointment (House of Lords, 1998). There is now greater mobility of staff between the private and public sector, and within the public services, than in the past. Equally important, the constant exhortations of government ministers for public services to emulate the policies and practices of the private sector have been influential in the area of personnel management. The new 'human resource management' policies of the last decade (e.g. flexible employment practices, performance-related pay and quality management) have been pursued actively throughout many parts of the public services.

There are, of course, exceptions to this broad pattern of convergence between public and private sector labour markets and employment practices. Where the state directly or indirectly employs the overwhelming majority of any professional group, and takes some responsibility for regulating entry standards, funding training, and monitoring the quality of service provision, the character of public service labour markets is likely to retain distinct differences from that of the private sector. The obvious examples are doctors, nurses and schoolteachers. The qualifications, specialist experience and membership of professional associations and trade unions all influence the occupational identity and labour market position of employees.

Whilst attempts have been made to subject the pay and conditions of service of these groups to local 'labour market pressures', national salary structures, grading, and employment practices have survived the pressures towards devolution and fragmentation. Each of these professional groups retains distinct forms of recruitment, job classification schemes and patterns of mobility within defined career structures. Trade unions and professional associations have strongly resisted the introduction of performance-related pay, arguing that individual 'merit' pay is inappropriate in a work environment that requires effective team working to maintain professional standards of service. Similarly, they have defended the national pay review bodies and influenced their recommendations, which have often produced pay increases above the rate of inflation and the level of settlements elsewhere in the public services (see p. 50). They have been less successful, however, in preventing job losses, greater use of part-time and temporary staff, skill dilution and increasing work loads.

Employers and employers' associations

State policies

The Conservative governments of 1979–97 pursued a continuous programme of reform in the public sector. Whilst the most visible feature of their policies was their attack on trade union power, they also developed a strong critique of management values and policies. It was argued that managers had been too submissive in their dealings with trade unions and professional groups; the interests of 'producers' had prevailed over those of the 'consumers' of public services. The governments' strategy involved an ideological and practical prescription that emphasized the superiority of market relations, competition and private sector management expertise. It had three main components: management reforms; compulsory competitive tendering; and the creation of 'internal markets'.

First, the government intervened more actively to reshape the organization and management of public services. This involved the devolution of management authority, and clear lines of accountability for controlling expenditure and monitoring performance. To ensure the active support of a cadre of senior managers, the government recruited a number of private sector managers to high-profile public service posts, in the expectation that they would introduce private sector 'best practice'. Senior public service managers, who remained the majority, harboured few illusions about the role they were expected to play in changing the culture of a restructured public service sector.

Second, the introduction of compulsory competitive tendering emphasized the ways in which competition and new contractual relations would reinforce the managerial revolution. By the mid-1980s, managers in local authorities and the NHS were required (by law or administrative fiat respectively) to invite bids from the private sector for specified service contracts and, in most circumstances, to accept the lowest cost bid. Despite strong trade union opposition and management ambivalence, the policy was rigorously pursued and monitored. In local authorities, compulsory competitive tendering was gradually extended to cover more services, including specialist functions, such as personnel services and information management. The leaders of the most enthusiastic Conservative-controlled authorities envisaged a transformation in their role; their ideal was the 'enabling authority', which would employ few staff, and manage contracts with numerous private sector providers (Colling, 1993). In the NHS, hospitals were encouraged (but not forced) to invite tenders for an ever wider range of functions, such as pathology services. In the civil service, where central government had the most direct influence, 'market testing' was developed and, often, managers were not allowed to make an in-house bid to retain direct provision of services.

Compulsory competitive tendering led to a substantial reduction in employment in the public services. Critics have argued that most of the cost reductions arose from job losses, worse pay and conditions and work intensification – especially, but not only, when contracts were won by private sector organizations. Even when basic pay rates were protected, hours of work were often reduced, and bonuses, holiday and sick pay entitlements were eroded. The deterioration in pay and conditions was invariably greater for women workers; private contractors rarely pursued the equal opportunity policies typically found in the public sector. This erosion of the terms and conditions of employment was facilitated by the way in which the European Union's 1977 Acquired Rights Directive was transposed into law in Britain. The 1981 Transfer of Undertakings (Protection of Employment) regulations (TUPE) excluded the public sector for the first twelve years of its operation, until the judgement in a major court case reversed this presumption in 1993. Subsequent legal judgements, and the lengthy process of revising the EU directive, generated further uncertainties, but these should be clarified in 1999 when the Labour government plans to rewrite the general TUPE regulations and issue guidelines specifically relating to the public sector (Cavalier, 1997).

Notwithstanding the problems arising from the exploitation of employees and legal uncertainties, compulsory competitive tendering had many supporters among private and public sector employers. They argued that it contributed significantly to the reform of management practice and the measurement and control of work: some cost savings arose from genuine efficiency improvements; service standards were more clearly defined and monitored; and improvements in the quality of services were achieved (IRS, 1998).

The third part of the government reform strategy focused on the creation of a system of 'internal markets' in the 1990s, intended to mimic the competitive relations found in the private sector. In the NHS, and to a lesser extent in schools, the provision of services by semi-autonomous organizations was separated from funding by purchasing authorities. The scope of internal markets varied considerably, but they were based on the rationale that providers (e.g. hospitals or grant-maintained schools) had to compete for the funding allocated for the treatment of patients or school places. In many hospitals, managers faced year-by-year financial uncertainties; they could not guarantee the volume or the price of service contracts negotiated with the purchasers of health care (health authorities and GP fundholders). This encouraged tighter control of labour costs and extended the use of fixed-term and temporary contracts.

Since its election victory the Labour government has enthusiastically endorsed the broad policy of public service management reform and development but has indicated that it will end compulsory competitive tendering in local authorities and reform the NHS 'internal market'. In place of the legal compulsion to seek tenders for specific services, the government has proposed that all services should be subject to periodic review to ensure 'best value'; that is, performance targets, based on benchmark comparisons with similar public and private services, should be set and monitored. Trade union officials' concern that the new policy will lead to some of the same problems as competitive tendering have been partially allayed by the greater stress on service quality, as well as efficiency, and by their involvement in a series of pilot studies. Proposals for the reform of the NHS also outline new procedures for setting and monitoring quality standards, combined with a reorganization of the contracting process between purchasers and providers; new 'primary care groups' will replace smaller groups of GP fundholders and, in co-operation with health authorities, NHS trusts and other providers, will develop long-term agreements in place of the previous annual contracting process.

The characteristics of public service employers

Over the last decade, the policies of central government have combined a very high level of influence over the funding and management of public service providers with a commitment to devolve authority to managers within separately constituted 'business units'. Drawing on organizational forms and practice in the private sector, the government has invoked the model of the multi-divisional company. The centre ('head office') makes most of the strategic decisions and monitors the financial performance and service standards of separate organizational units whose senior managers are responsible for operational efficiency. The attempt to impose organizational and political change on this scale has been facilitated by the unitary nature of the British state and the absence of a written constitution. In comparison with many other countries, there are few formal limits on the power of central government; parliamentary majorities allow a form of 'elected dictatorship', in the words of a Conservative government minister and senior law official in the 1960s. The implications of this constitutional position are different for organizational change and the employers' role in each part of the public services.

The civil service

Until the 1980s, the civil service was financed wholly by central government revenues allocated by Parliament, and each department was headed by a minister, or secretary of state, who was directly accountable to Parliament for its business. The Treasury (ministry of finance) controlled public expenditure. Following a review of the piecemeal changes introduced by government in the early 1980s (Ibbs, 1988), radical reforms have been implemented. The report argued that the civil service was too big and too diverse to manage as a single entity; too little attention had been paid to management and service delivery in comparison with policy-making. The solution was to reorganize the executive activities of government, as distinct from its policy advice, into separate agencies.

Each agency has its responsibilities, aims and objectives defined in a published framework document. Key performance targets covering finance, efficiency and quality of service are set by government ministers annually, and performance against these targets has to be reported in each agency's published annual report and accounts. By 1997 76 per cent of all civil servants worked in 138 executive agencies (or executive offices and units managed in a similar way), and the annual report of their activities outlined the progress made in achieving 1,244 performance targets (Cabinet Office, 1998).

There are important variations between the agencies in terms of their size, functions, financial regimes and links with sponsoring departments. It is thus difficult to assess the overall impact of the reforms, but it is clear that they have undermined the old unified civil service and encouraged divergent personnel policies and management styles. Trade union negotiators and senior managers have been forced into a new system of devolved collective bargaining, but report that the Treasury still exerts a strong influence on their agreements. The redefined relationship between chief executives, ministers and parliamentary accountability also has proved to be problematical, not least when senior managers have been dismissed. Despite these tensions, the Labour government is committed to building on these reforms: the minister noted in his first annual report that 'agency status has had a transforming effect on the way in which executive parts of the civil service have carried out the tasks for which they are responsible' (Cabinet Office, 1998: iv).

The National Health Service

Since it was founded in 1948, the NHS has been viewed as a component part of central government. With the exception of general practitioners (GPs), who are self-employed contractors with the NHS, until 1992 most staff were employed by district or regional health authorities. The reforms of the mid-1980s introduced a more corporate-style management structure. At the centre, there was a chief executive and a management board, presided over by the Secretary of State for Health and, below, regional, district and unit level general managers. Since the introduction of the 'internal market' in the 1990s, the majority of NHS staff are now employed by more than 400 individual NHS trusts that provide hospital and community health services; a relatively small number work for the district health authorities responsible for purchasing health care. At the centre, the NHS Executive functions as both an integral part of the civil service and corporate head office of the NHS.

Thus, in a similar manner to the civil service, the NHS has become more fragmented in its organization. The board of each trust has the discretion to seek external funding within agreed limits, has considerable freedom in its recruitment and staffing policies, and can devise its own local bargaining and consultation arrangements. None the less, it is directly accountable to the Secretary of State for Health and subject to many administrative and political controls by government. First, the government establishes national health policy priorities and the financial targets that trust managers must meet. Second, the NHS Executive retains direct control over key appointments and has to be consulted if a trust board wishes to dismiss a chief executive. It also audits the business plans, financial returns and performance targets (e.g. financial and manpower). Finally, apart from the close scrutiny of government officials, trusts have to sustain the support of the local health authority and GP fundholders, as well as powerful professional interest groups. Thus the nominal independence of 'self-governing' trusts is heavily circumscribed. The Labour government's reforms (noted above) will not erode the centralization of power significantly, whatever other effects they may have.

Local authorities

In contrast to the civil service and the NHS, local authorities have the capacity to raise taxes, and are governed by councillors subject to periodic election. They also provide a wide range of local services, some of which are prescribed by legislation. In combination, these features of local government allow more than 460 local authorities some freedom in interpreting national policies in the light of their local population needs, and in raising resources to pursue their priorities. This discretion has given rise to greater variation in the implementation of national pay and conditions agreements than is found in other public services; indeed, around 10 per cent of local authorities had opted out of the national bargaining machinery and negotiated or imposed local agreements by the early 1990s.

As noted earlier, the conflict between mainly Labour Party-controlled local authorities and the Conservative central governments of 1979–97 led to severe restrictions on the financial freedom of local authorities, the loss of some functions and new forms of accountability: 'the aim was to weaken and bypass local authorities and empower consumers' (Wilson and Game, 1998: 125). Local taxation now accounts for only 20 per cent of total income and central government directly limits local authority expenditure plans. Local authorities have to work alongside a plethora of other agencies which have been given responsibilities which previously belonged to them. It has been estimated that there are 5,000 quasi-autonomous non-governmental organizations (quangos), run by 50,000 appointed members, compared with 23,000 elected local councillors. In the mid-1990s they received £37 billion annually, or two-thirds of the central government grant to local authorities (Stoker, 1996). Apart from the imposition of compulsory competitive tendering discussed earlier, managers in local authorities have faced additional forms of accountability. External financial accountability was placed under the jurisdiction of the Audit Commission in 1983, and it has subsequently developed an active role in promoting 'value for money' audits and performance indicators for most services. These changes have stimulated the wider use of judicial review of local authority decisions – a further retreat from the old model of political accountability through elections.

The above discussion indicates some of the common changes in employers' accountability and constraints on management, as well as the main differences between the three sub-sectors. Despite government ministers' desire that public service management should mimic best practice in the private sector, it is clear that the context, objectives and constraints on management in the 'public domain' remain very different (Ransom and Stewart, 1994). Public service managers are frequently confronted by difficult, if not incompatible, objectives such as the provision of better-quality services with diminishing real resources. The 'internal market' in the NHS does not offer unambiguous market signals for the determination of policies; the contract income of trusts is influenced far more by historical patterns of funding and provision, and the micro-politics of local health provision. There is no 'consumer sovereignty'; a multitude of intermediary processes and political uncertainties impact on measures of performance and the success or failure in competing for scarce resources.

Finally, and most important for the purposes of this chapter, managers are confronted by the distinctive nature of employment relations in the public services. In comparison with the private sector, trade union membership and density remain high, even among managers, and many public service employees have a distinct occupational or professional identity that is in conflict with the new language of competitive and market relations, and the fragmented organization of services. In health, education and social services, professional associations and trade unions often intervene in public policy debates in opposition to the proposals of senior general managers and their government allies. At the organizational level, they may have the influence to inhibit management initiatives in the name of service standards, as well as in defence of their own interests.

The status and role of managers

The above discussion suggests that a brief summary of the status and role of public service managers in Britain is not possible. The absence of a strong and legally bound tradition of public administration of the kind that persists in many other countries, and the enormous scope and scale of organizational change that has been implemented in the last decade, have led to a widespread but inconclusive debate on the impact of 'new managerialism' – or 'New Public Management' (NPM) in most parts of the public services (Ridley, 1996). The management process has always been dispersed among 'professions' with considerable autonomy in defining and monitoring service standards, senior 'administrators' exercising hierarchical responsibilities for budgets and political accountability, and a wide range of 'functional' managers – and the reforms have affected these groups in different ways.

A few general points can, however, be made. First, many public service managers seem to be receptive to the rhetoric of devolution, cultural change, quality management, entrepreneurial and customer orientations and other aspects of NPM, and some have been able to overcome the constraints on their freedom to implement policies espousing these values. Second, many have benefited from the complex changes introduced in the last decade; their visibility, status and pay have increased, the latter often substantially in comparison with lower graded staff in their sectors. Third, the recruitment, appraisal and rewards of managers have moved much closer to those found in many parts of the private sector.

It was noted earlier that senior civil service staff are increasingly recruited through open competition and, more generally, recruitment procedures have been delegated to departments and agencies. Whilst the rules and procedures of recruitment must conform with the Civil Service Commissioners' Code, agencies do not have to consult Recruitment and Assessment Services – part of the civil service until 1996, when it was privatized – and their procedures are audited by another private sector company. More open and competitive recruitment methods have thus diminished the previous importance of the internal labour market. At the senior level especially, the desire to import private sector skills and experience has reduced the promotion prospects of many middle-ranking managers. Also, given the pace and scope of the restructuring process, the job security of many managers in the civil service has diminished.

The level and form of compensation for public service managers has changed radically to reflect the greater emphasis on performance and labour market factors. Salary levels and increases have become more variable as a result of merit- or performance-related pay (PRP), or in order to fill vacancies where skills or experience are in short supply – a trend facilitated by the erosion of collective agreements covering managerial pay. The most extensive development of PRP has occurred in the civil service. A decade ago it was introduced for senior staff, and by 1995 a form of PRP had been extended to cover most other staff for whom pay increases depend partly on an annual assessment of their performance against agreed objectives. Elsewhere in the public services, the coverage of PRP has been restricted mainly to senior management.

The difficulties associated with the introduction and maintenance of public service PRP schemes have been widely publicized, not least by trade union representatives of professional staff who believe that the individualist assumptions of PRP are antithetical to team-work values and workplace practices. Moreover, tight budgetary constraints often make it difficult to reward good performance adequately, so small pay increases are typically distributed to a large number of staff and account for only a small proportion of total pay. When forced distribution procedures are introduced to accommodate financial constraints, they risk demotivating staff who believe that they have been unfairly denied a higher rating.

The research findings of Marsden and French (1998), based on surveys of the views of line managers and employees in two civil service agencies, two NHS hospital trusts and head teachers in schools, offer qualified support for these negative views whilst revealing some more positive results. On the latter, the research revealed a high degree of support for the principle of linking pay with performance (except in the case of primary school head teachers), and almost half the managers believed that PRP had helped to raise productivity, mainly because it had improved goal setting. The other findings supported a negative view of the pay system. Most staff did not believe that it had increased their motivation, not least because it was divisive and inhibited co-operation, and they believed that managers restricted performance pay through quotas, and further undermined the scheme through favouritism. Many of the line managers had negative views on PRP because staff had insufficient control in their jobs, and a substantial minority believed that it had reduced co-operation between staff and management.

Employers' associations

Employers' associations try to articulate and represent their members' interests on a variety of policy issues. They are consulted by government on proposals for reorganization and significant shifts in public policy, and in the annual cycle of expenditure planning and allocations. As in the private sector, they combine this broad policy and finance function with the representation of their members' interests in negotiations, and in the 'arm's length' bargaining of the pay review process. Their part in the pay determination process has always been complicated by the dispersion of power and the potential conflict between central government and public employers, and various expressions of intra-organizational conflict among employers. This has been exacerbated by the institutional fragmentation of market-style reforms, and the pressures towards the decentralization of collective bargaining. These representational problems, and attempts to solve them, take different forms in each part of the public services.

The civil service offers the least complex illustration of the representational problems of employers. As the direct employer, the government (mainly the Treasury), has been able to develop policies on public expenditure and play a direct role in negotiations with the trade unions. Until the mid-1980s, this sustained a detailed set of conditions of service for all civil servants within a unified salary structure. In the 1990s, the fragmentation of the service into more than a hundred executive agencies, and the implementation of devolved bargaining, have complicated the position. Although civil service union negotiations with agency chief executives have produced greater diversity in salary structures and conditions of service, the Treasury continues to play a very powerful role.

In the case of the health service, whilst the influence of the Treasury on negotiations has always been strong, the representation of the interests of the employers has been more problematical. More than twenty years ago, McCarthy noted that the management side of the negotiations consisted of 'employers who do not pay and paymasters who do not employ' (1976: 11). Senior civil servants from the Department of Health outnumbered representatives of health authorities, and rarely won arguments with the formally absent Treasury. The new internal market and moves towards devolved bargaining have complicated this process further. Initially the split between purchasers and providers of services led to the development of rival employers' organizations. The weakness of both, and their inability to influence the NHS Executive, which leads negotiations, led to a merger in 1997 to form the NHS Confederation. The absence of a strong and coherent voice among senior managers has contributed to the slow and uneven process of bargaining and human resource management reforms in the NHS.

The representation of local authority employers in national collective bargaining has proved to be the most difficult. First, the employer role is divided between elected councillors and senior managers, with the leading position in negotiations taken by representatives of the former. Second, until they merged recently, separate local authority associations reflected the overlapping divisions between higher- and lower-tier authorities, and between rural and urban councils. Also, the party political leadership of the associations fluctuated over time, affecting the intra-organizational conflict between and within the associations, and conflict with central government. Despite these problems, by the 1990s local authority employers had developed a coherent bargaining strategy and an effective negotiating role through their specialist bargaining agency, the Local Government Management Board. In 1997 this facilitated a major innovation in collective bargaining; a new 'single status' national agreement covering 1.5 million manual and non-manual staff (see p. 48).

Trade unions

The legal framework

For most of this century, there have been few legal obstacles to trade union organization and representation for most public service employees. The public and private sectors were part of a 'voluntarist' system of industrial relations in which the law was virtually silent on the freedom of association and the recognition of trade unions for negotiation and consultation. Within this abstentionist legal framework, however, government policies encouraged public service employees to join unions and participate in their activities from 1919 to 1979. This resulted in generally high levels of membership, especially among non-manual and management grades, in sharp contrast to the private sector.

Civil servants were organized in a large number of separate associations based on grade, occupation and service. The Trade Disputes and Trade Unions Act of 1927, introduced the year after the only 'general strike' in British history, influenced the character of civil service trade unions by insisting that they could not affiliate to the sole national union confederation – the Trades Union Congress (TUC) or take part in political activities. Trade unions organizing non-manual employees elsewhere in the public services chose to follow this model; until the 1970s most had relatively moderate policies and were outside the political mainstream of the labour movement.

The main exception to the official endorsement of trade unionism focused on the police and the armed forces. Following extensive union organization and a strike in London, the Police Act of 1919 prohibited trade union membership but introduced an alternative channel of collective representation through the Police Federation. In the amended legislation of 1964, membership of the Federation was made compulsory and, although the regulations covering its activities place it outside the legal definition of a trade union, the Federation acts as a powerful pressure group for the 'welfare and efficiency' of its members. In contrast, whilst members of the armed forces are not prohibited from joining a trade union, very few do so, as there is no form of collective representation, nor the right to strike.

The Conservative government of 1979 was elected after a period of unprecedented industrial conflict in the public services. It embarked on a series of legislative and administrative reforms that were designed to weaken trade unions in general, and public service unions in particular. The most drastic intervention occurred in 1984 when the government announced that 4,000 civil servants working at General Communications Headquarters (GCHQ), a communications and intelligence centre, would no longer be allowed to be a member of a national trade union. Despite widespread opposition and an offer from the unions to negotiate a *de facto* 'no strike agreement', the government insisted on the new conditions of employment and offered a payment of £1,000 as compensation for the loss of employment rights. Within a few months, 98 per cent of the staff had accepted the imposed change and, four years later, the eighteen staff who had refused to relinquish their union membership were dismissed or transferred

(Fredman and Morris, 1989). The symbolic importance of this case was under-lined when the new Labour government announced that it would restore the right of GCHQ staff to join an independent civil service union in 1997.

Trade union structure and organization

The structure of trade unionism has evolved over the past 150 years without any fundamental reforms stimulated by war or political crisis. For most of that time, the single national union confederation (the TUC) has lacked the authority to pre-vent competitive recruitment, inter-union rivalry or multi-union representation in many workplaces. The mid-nineteenth-century craft unions of skilled workers offered a partial model for the later growth of occupational (non-manual) unions, and both survived the development of two large general unions formed through amalgamations in the 1920s. The organizational principle of industrial or sectoral trade unionism never became firmly established in Britain. Whilst trade union struc-ture has been rationalized through amalgamations in the last few decades (there were 543 unions with 11.1 million members in 1970, compared with 245 unions with 7.9 million members at the end of 1996; see Cully and Woodland, 1998), there are still areas of severe inter-union competition and organizational inefficiency. The structure of public service trade unionism reflects this overall national pattern, but it also exhibits distinctive characteristics in each of the sub-sectors.

Until recently, civil service trade unions were structured mainly on the organiza-tional principle of grade: five unions represented the separate interests of manual workers, clerical staff, middle-ranking executive officers, professional and scient-ific staff, and a small élite group of senior staff. The main exception to this model of grade-based organization was the separate union for all grades in the Inland Revenue (tax collectors). Each of the unions participated in a council (or federa-tion) to discuss general issues, and each benefited from a strong degree of man-agement support. In the last decade or so, the structure of civil service trade unionism has changed considerably in response to the dramatic shift in public policy. The previously unified service and salary structure has been fragmented through organizational change, market testing, some privatization and devolved collective bargaining. Some agencies have developed more aggressive HRM policies that discourage trade union organization by eroding the previous facilities for recruitment and workplace union participation. These changes encouraged a series of union amalgamations in the mid-1990s. At the beginning of 1998 four unions completed a series of mergers to form the union for Public and Commer-cial Services (PCS). Also the union for professional and scientific staff (IPMS) were in inconclusive discussions with the fifth largest union, the Manufacturing Science and Finance Union (MSF). These amalgamations were an attempt to attain economies of scale in servicing a declining and more dispersed membership and, as their new names suggest, to retain members in recently privatized services.

The main characteristic of trade union structure in the health services is the tension within, and between, two groups of organizations. The first comprises TUC-affiliated unions, which compete for members within the NHS, but also outside it.

The second group is composed of a large number of non-TUC organizations that combine the functions of trade unions and professional associations, and recruit only within the health service. Until recently, more than forty separate organizations were recognised in the national bargaining machinery. The decline in membership of some grades, as well as the organizational fragmentation of the service into more than 400 separate units, has led to some rationalization of trade union structure.

The three TUC unions with a large health service membership (NALGO, NUPE and COHSE) merged in 1993 to form Unison, the largest trade union in the UK. It organizes most of the union members among clerical and administrative staff, the majority of ancillary staff members, many of the members among unqualified nurses (auxiliaries and health care assistants) and some highly qualified nurses. None the less, Unison still has to compete with other TUC-affiliated unions for these grades and faces intense competition from the non-affiliated Royal College of Nursing (RCN) for qualified nursing staff. The smaller health service professional associations face an organizational dilemma in representing their members in a more fragmented service; some are contemplating affiliation to the TUC, and others will probably join MSF, consolidating its current NHS membership among laboratory staff, health visitors and scientists. These changes may be insufficient to overcome the present difficulties of defending narrow professional interests in a more devolved system of bargaining.

Trade union structure in local authorities has been simplified by the creation of Unison. The union can justify its claim to be 'The Public Service Trade Union', as it represents the majority of both manual and non-manual employees of local authorities. It has to compete with non-TUC unions representing senior managers, and the two general unions (TGWU and GMB), which have significant manual membership in some locations. Within the local authority sector, however, the structure of teachers' trade unionism offers the most significant expression of inter-union rivalry and conflict. Six separate unions partly reflect traditional status distinctions between types of school (primary and secondary, public and private), gender, qualifications, and the differing roles of classroom teachers and senior staff. The widespread disputes of the mid-1980s also revealed continuing divisions between 'professional' and 'militant' union practice, and between TUC unions and non-affiliated staff associations. In the 1980s and 1990s, the largest union (the National Union of Teachers) lost its claim to be 'the union for all teachers', and its rivalry with the second largest union in the sector (the NAS/UWT) remains intense.

Trade union membership

There can be little doubt that the structure of public service trade unionism has undermined its overall capacity to respond effectively to the challenges posed by restructuring, hostile government policies and more assertive management over the last decade or so. It is not so clear, however, whether union structure – and its associated expressions of inter-union rivalry and conflict – has helped or hindered the recruitment and retention of union members. In a period in which overall trade union membership declined for an unprecedented seventeen consecutive years a few public service unions increased their membership.

Table 2.3 Membership of the eleven largest unions in 1979, 1992 and 1996 (000)

Union	1979	1992	1996	% women
Unison – the Public Services Union[a]	1,658	1,487	1,375	72
Transport and General Workers Union (TGWU)	2,086	1,037	885	19
Amalgamated Engineering and Electrical Union (AEEU)	1,310	884	726	6
GMB – General Union	967	799	740	36
Manufacturing Science and Finance (MSF)	691	552	425	31
Royal College of Nursing (RCN)	162	299	307	92
Union of Shop Distributive and Allied Workers (USDAW)	470	316	290	58
Communication Workers Union (CWU)	203	179	275	58
National Union of Teachers (NUT)	291	214	271	75
Public and Commercial Services (PCS)[a]	397	295	266	
Schoolmasters and Women Teachers (NAS/UWT)	152	191	234	53

Source: *Annual Reports of the Certification Officer.*

Note

a The 1979 and 1992 figures for Unison and the PCS are the aggregate of the membership of the unions involved in the mergers.

As Table 2.3 indicates, five of the eleven largest unions in Britain are based in the public services. Moreover, in comparison with the large general unions recruiting mainly in the private sector, their membership has been sustained fairly successfully; indeed, the Royal College of Nursing almost doubled its membership in the 1980s and 1990s, and the combined membership of the two largest teachers' unions has increased. The difference in the relative strength of public and private sector union membership can, of course, be explained partly by changes in employment in the two sectors (see Table 2.1). It arises also from the much greater success of public service unions in recruiting part-time employees (usually women) into membership than trade unions in the private sector.

It is difficult to produce accurate union membership data disaggregated by sector or occupation from the two sources of data that are available. The first source, provided by trade unions in their annual returns to the Certification Officer, presents two problems: first, the figures may include retired or unemployed persons who retain membership; second, it is not easy to allocate the membership of some trade unions to specific industrial, sectoral or occupational categories. Despite these limitations, Table 2.4 indicates the significant growth of membership and increases in union density (union membership as a proportion of those in employment, excluding the unemployed) across the three main subsectors of the public services between 1948 and 1979. The substantial increase in union density in national government and the health services took place in the 1960s and 1970s, when employers' support for trade unionism was most apparent. Table 2.4 also shows the beginning of the decline in membership and, in the case of national and local government, the decrease in union density in the 1980s.

Table 2.4 Trade union membership and density, 1948–87

Service	1948 UM (000)	D (%)	1979 UM (000)	D (%)	1982 UM (000)	D (%)	1987 UM (000)	D (%)
National government	375	54	589	96	519	90	459	76
Local authorities[a]	885	72	2,186	78	2,347	88	2,333	83
Health services	204	39	982	76	987	71	1,008	73

Source: Waddington and Whitston (1995: 164–5).

Notes
a Including education.
b *UM* union membership, *D* density.

Table 2.5 Trade union density by sector in 1997 (%)

Sectors	All	Private sector	Public sector
All employees	30	20	61
Manufacturing	30	30	–
Construction	22	13	77
Transport/Communications	45	39	75
Public administration	62	29	63
Education	54	27	58
Health	47	15	63

Source: Cully and Woodland (1998).

The second source of union membership data comes from the quarterly Labour Force Survey (LFS), which covers around 60,000 households. As the LFS covers only those in employment, it excludes union members who are economically inactive during the survey period or retired. Its estimates of union membership and density are thus lower than those arising from trade union sources. The value of the survey arises from its size and the range of information collected on respondents' individual and workplace characteristics. It thus facilitates more detailed analysis of patterns and changes in membership. The selective summary of the data from the 1997 LFS in Table 2.5 shows that, whilst overall union density was 30 per cent, the figure for the public sector was much higher than that for the private sector – 61 per cent in comparison with 20 per cent. It also shows that the small 'privatized' parts of public administration, education and health services have a much lower union density than that of the main segment of direct public provision. Previous surveys have shown that, in the public services, the gap between male and female union density is relatively small, that the union density of part-time employees is above that of full-time employees in the private sector, and that the union density of non-manual (managerial and professional) employees is much higher than that for manual workers.

Workplace organization and representation

The two previous sections have suggested that the public services' trade union structure has been partially reformed, and the decline of membership has been much less severe than in the private sector. None the less, the organizational capacity of trade unions to articulate and protect their members' interests has been threatened by the pace and scope of public services' organizational fragmentation. In the absence of legally regulated procedures for consultation and negotiation (such as works councils), trade unions offer the only channel of collective representation in Britain.

Public service trade unionism has been rooted in centralized and bureaucratic organization, reflecting the national structures of collective bargaining. Relatively few national officials, located mainly in London, were responsible for negotiations, and the involvement of local officials and activists in policy-making procedures was focused mainly on national policies. After the emergence of widespread industrial conflict in the 1970s, trade unions developed a more extensive network of staff representatives and shop stewards. But attempts to decentralize union organization were limited and uneven, reflecting the narrow scope of local bargaining issues. They also depended on a degree of management support or 'sponsorship' – that is, the offer of facilities for meetings, and the granting of time off for representatives to carry out union duties.

In recent years, all public service unions have implemented some changes in organization and services – for example, the reorganization of local branches, training for staff representatives and the relocation of some officials from national to regional or local offices. It is difficult to assess the effectiveness of such changes and to generalize about the overall strength of public service trade unionism. Some case studies have identified areas of union strength and confidence that support the argument that 'union renewal' may develop from more active and participative forms of workplace trade unionism (Fairbrother, 1996). Other research findings have indicated enormous variations in the strength of local union organization within a more general pattern of uncertainty or weakness (Colling, 1995; Lloyd, 1997).

This is partly because the 'balance of power' between trade unions and employers has shifted decisively in favour of the latter. The severity of budget constraints, the demand for 'efficiency savings', and the creation of 'market competition', have forced managers to review their relations with trade unions. In some cases, this has led to a more abrasive style of management designed to marginalize trade union influence, sometimes accompanied by the implementation of new HRM techniques. In other cases, where managers retain a commitment to 'consensus management', and continue to support a degree of joint regulation, the constraints under which they operate require concessions from unions, with the threat of imposed changes where they do not agree with management proposals. In either case, it is clear that multi-unionism and inter-union rivalry remain obstacles to effective union representation in many of the public services.

Public sector labour relations

Historical overview

Collective bargaining has been the most important method of determining the public services' pay and conditions of employment, and regulating the relationship between employers and trade unions, for the last fifty years. The essentially 'voluntary' system, with very little direct legal regulation, covered both the private sector and most of the public services. In contrast to the position in many other countries, there has been no general legal obligation on employers to engage in collective bargaining, and collective agreements are not legally binding between the parties; they are recommendations to central government or public employers.

In the exceptional case of schoolteachers, legislation from 1944 required the secretary of state to establish a negotiating committee to consider teachers' remuneration. Also, the agreements were given statutory force so that local education authorities had to pay teachers in accordance with the salary scales contained in the order. In the NHS, recommendations of the negotiating committees required the consent of the secretary of state and, until the early 1990s, hospitals required ministerial approval if they wished to depart from the agreed rates of pay. In other parts of the public services, 'voluntary' agreements have been applied almost universally in practice.

The establishment of collective bargaining machinery, and the evolution of its distinctive features in each sector, were shaped primarily by the voluntary agreements of trade unions and employers. As noted above, however, governments promoted and endorsed collective bargaining as a crucial element in the ideal of the state as a 'good employer' in the sixty years from 1919 to 1979 (Fredman and Morris, 1989: 142). One of the clearest expressions of the governments' commitment could be found, between 1891 and 1983, in a series of Fair Wages Resolutions that required subcontracting firms to observe the generally accepted rates of pay (in practice, found in collective agreements) if they wished to win contracts from government departments. The centralized structure of collective bargaining that developed originally in the civil service had been extended to all parts of the public services by the 1950s. The scope of collective bargaining was fairly wide, including many issues excluded from national agreements in the private sector, and its coverage was almost universal. Collective agreements typically established national wage and salary structures, and specified a wide range of terms and conditions of employment, often in a detailed and prescriptive manner.

Until the late 1960s, the system of collective bargaining produced relatively few industrial disputes: the bargaining principle of 'fair comparison' with the levels and increases of pay in the rest of the economy was widely accepted; and third-party arbitration provided a satisfactory method of avoiding disputes. In retrospect, the stability of public service labour relations in the 1950s and 1960s depended upon the unusually favourable political and economic circumstances. Successive Labour and Conservative governments accepted the post-war settlement of a mixed economy, and were committed to an expansion of the welfare state, requiring increases in public expenditure and public service employment more or less continuously. Unemployment and inflation were low, and the aspirations of employees and the demands of their trade unions were modest in comparison with those found in many parts of the private sector.

In the years of high and fluctuating inflation from the mid-1960s onwards, the central problem of public service labour relations concerned the compatibility of collective bargaining with governments' anti-inflation policies. The principle of 'fair comparison' with pay movements in the private sector led to a cyclical pattern of pay movements linked with periodic episodes of intense industrial conflict. Government incomes policy norms were imposed more rigorously on public service negotiations than on those in the private sector for several reasons: government ministers could directly influence the employers' side of the negotiations; the centralized bargaining units were very large; and, in contrast to the more decentralized private sector negotiations, it was not possible to conceal the size of pay agreements from the agencies responsible for incomes policy compliance, or to allow wage drift to increase earnings through bonus payments or other pay supplements.

In this context, the traditional wage moderation of public service trade unions and professional associations was tested and eventually broken. The erosion of pay relativities with the private sector, and the proliferation of pay anomalies within the public services, produced widespread grievances and a series of protracted disputes. These nationally co-ordinated disputes involved almost all groups of public service employees in the 1970s. They were invariably resolved by large 'catch-up' pay increases, often legitimized by public inquiries or independent arbitration awards. The restoration of previous pay relativities with the private sector often took place in the period before, or soon after, a general election, reflecting the desire of politicians to boost their electoral prospects by rewarding – or promising to reward later – a large group of electors employed in the public services. When the Labour Prime Minister ignored this elementary political rule in the winter of 1978/79, he precipitated the most widespread series of public service disputes in British history and lost the general election. This 'winter of discontent' paved the way for a decisive shift in government policy on public services' collective bargaining; the planning and control of public expenditure and the structure, process and outcomes of collective bargaining were altered significantly (Winchester, 1983).

The forms and principles of pay determination

The Conservative government inherited an economy with double-digit inflation and a public services' pay determination system with two recent institutional innovations. First, fire service workers, after a prolonged strike, and police, after a public inquiry that was set up to avert a dispute, achieved large pay increases and an indexation formula to preserve their new pay relativities. These arrangements were unique in the public services and have survived subsequent attempts to remove them. The indexation formula was the source of a protracted dispute in the ambulance service in the late l980s when, in a very different labour relations climate, the government resisted the argument that the 'third emergency service' should benefit from a similar arrangement (Nichol, 1992).

Second, the Standing Commission on Pay Comparability (chaired by Professor Hugh Clegg) had been set up in the last months of the Labour government with two functions: a short-term role in resolving a number of disputes by acting as an arbitration body; and a longer-term task to report on the possibility of establishing acceptable 'bases of comparison' for most of the public services (Clegg, 1982). In its two years' existence, the commission made recommendations on the pay grievances of twenty-five groups of public service workers covering 2.5 million employees before it was abolished. The Conservative government soon demonstrated its priorities for the reform of pay determination. It sought to erode the principle of 'fair comparison' and replace it with the criterion of 'affordability', defined by strict cash limits on expenditure. It also encouraged employers to resist trade union pay demands, and showed unusual willingness to accept the political risks and financial costs of protracted disputes. For example, the government precipitated a twenty-week dispute with civil service unions when it withdrew from its pay agreement in 1981 and, a year later, allowed few concessions to health service unions during a sustained nine-month pay campaign backed by demonstrations and selective strike action.

The NHS dispute was eventually resolved by the establishment of an independent pay review body for nurses and other health service professional staff. More than half a million nurses were removed from the traditional system of pay bargaining in the expectation that they would never again join other health service unions in sector-wide pay campaigns. Government ministers no doubt also assumed that those they appointed to the 'independent' review body would be sympathetic to their arguments about affordability and labour market flexibility. Both expectations have been realised only partly since then.

The nurses' pay review body, as well as the others which cover top state officials, doctors and dentists, the armed services and, since 1991, schoolteachers, receives detailed written and oral evidence from government, employers and trade unions. It also commissions its own research and data analysis, and makes recommendations to the government. It is presumed that the government will accept the recommendations unless there are 'clear and compelling reasons for not doing so'. In practice, no government has ever rejected a pay review body's report totally, but frequently the implementation of the recommended pay increases has been staged in order to reduce the annual paybill costs.

The methodology and impact of the pay review system have influenced wider debates on pay determination in the public services. The review process has encouraged a much more systematic analysis of the parties' arguments, and the evidence on which they are based, than is usually found in traditional collective bargaining. The reports typically assess conflicting arguments on affordability and comparability, develop detailed analysis of vacancies, retention, turnover and other labour market data, and consider evidence and arguments on employees' motivation, morale and work loads. Although the pay review system formally removes around 1.3 million public service employees from the coverage of collective bargaining on pay, the process is far removed from unilateral government decision-making. It is better viewed as a form of 'arm's length bargaining', in which the arguments of government ministers and senior civil servants, as well as those of employers and trade union officials, are scrutinised and often criticised in published reports. The extension of the pay review system to nurses and school-teachers has also undermined the apparent preference of government ministers for more decentralized pay determination (Bach and Winchester, 1994).

Levels of collective bargaining

Britain has had a highly decentralized system of collective bargaining in the private sector for more than two decades, so it is scarcely surprising that Conservative government ministers and employers questioned the relevance and efficacy of the national pay and conditions arrangements that characterized public service industrial relations since the 1950s. They consistently advocated more decentralized collective bargaining, arguing that it would be more responsive to the needs of managerial efficiency and labour market conditions, and more sensitive to employee performance. Public service employers gradually accepted most of these arguments, but were critical of the inconsistencies in government policies, arguing that the Treasury found it more convenient to control pay and expenditure through its influence on national negotiations. Trade unions generally resisted the pressure towards decentralization and sought to retain national wage and salary structures and standardized conditions of employment to protect their more vulnerable members. The decentralization of collective bargaining has developed in a piecemeal and uneven manner, as can be shown by an analysis of changes in each sector.

The civil service

From the mid-1950s until a decade ago, the civil service had a highly centralized structure of collective bargaining. Also, it had the most elaborate institutionalized process for determining pay levels and increases based on the principle of 'fair comparison with the current remuneration of outside staffs employed in broadly comparable work'. This arrangement was rejected by the government before the 1981 strike, and over the next decade trade unions and Treasury negotiators struggled to reach compromise agreements that retained a modified version of 'fair comparison' alongside the managerial concern for increased flexibility. The latter was pursued in a piecemeal manner; performance-related pay for senior grades, and the more flexible interpretation of broader pay spines for other staff, reflected the government's desire for a system that was more responsive to individual merit and local labour market conditions (Kessler, 1993).

In the last few years, the second phase of reform has been consolidated. First, the Civil Service (Management Functions) Act of 1992 enabled the Treasury to delegate its responsibility for negotiating pay and conditions to individual departments and executive agencies. After a slow start, the Conservative government announced that service-wide pay bargaining would be terminated in 1996, and would be replaced by 'delegated bargaining': each agency or departmental unit would be expected to develop its own grading, appraisal, promotion, training and performance-related pay schemes. The government also initiated a radical review of senior management structures and policy-making machinery. This has led to 'delayering' and job losses, more emphasis on team working and the use of job titles rather than grades (IRS, 1996). Taken together, the changes have led to increasing variation in the procedures and outcomes of negotiations, reflecting variations in the size, functions and financial circumstances of agencies; and produced the most decisive shift in the level of bargaining within the public services.

The health service

The government has been much less successful in encouraging such a clear-cut move away from national pay bargaining in the NHS. Its overall policies of strict cash limits and competitive tendering, and its more aggressive response to trade union wage demands, gradually weakened the regulatory effect of national agreements for many groups of staff. By the early 1990s, most of the national agreements had reformed wage and salary structures to produce less rigid job definitions and to facilitate local pay supplements. These changes, and the selective introduction of performance-related pay schemes, were designed mainly to deal with the recruitment and retention problems of particular occupations in the early 1990s. Managers also had some success in negotiating, or imposing, changes in working practices and in the development of 're-profiling' exercises or skill-mix reviews. These changes often reduced the ratio of highly qualified to less qualified staff, and altered the division of labour between occupational groups (e.g. nurses and health care assistants). When faced with severe financial constraints, managers were more likely to achieve short-term savings by reorganizing working practices, limiting overtime and premium rate payments, or exerting tighter control over absenteeism than through the lengthy process of negotiating a comprehensive local pay and conditions agreement. Although the creation of the 'internal market', and the fragmentation of the service into independent trusts, raised expectations of a more rapid and extensive development of devolved pay bargaining, this did not take place.

The limited and piecemeal nature of bargaining reform can be explained partly by the extension of the pay review process to nurses. From 1983, nearly half the NHS work force was removed from traditional collective bargaining, and since then the trade unions and professional associations have fought a long campaign to retain this modified system of national pay determination. Their efforts were threatened in 1995 when the nurses' review body adopted a two-tier approach to pay determination. It recommended a national pay increase of only 1.0 per cent, to encourage local bargaining over efficiency and flexibility, and in the expectation that a range of overall pay increases of between 1.5 per cent and 3.0 per cent might result. Over the next seven months, the trade unions threatened industrial action and demanded (and in most cases, achieved) unconditional local pay increases of 2.0 per cent. In a compromise agreement reached at the end of 1996, a majority of the unions reluctantly accepted the principle of local pay determination in return for a 'safety net' procedure, whereby national salary scales would be up-rated annually to reflect the outcome of local negotiations in the preceding year.

In 1996 the review body recommended a 2.0 per cent increase in the up-rated national scales, 'as a basis for further local pay determination', but again this did not generate the response it sought. As the review body's 1997 report noted, hardly any serious negotiation took place, and decisions were delayed and severely restricted by financial constraints. Whilst confirming its support for the principle of local pay determination, the review body recommended a 3.3 per cent increase in the national up-rated scales, providing 'a "breathing space" for those Trusts where management and staff have not yet implemented innovative approaches to local pay strategies' (NPRB, 1997: 4). A year later, the review body extended the 'breathing space' by recommending an increase of 3.8 per cent on the national scales, reporting that it had been informed by the parties that they wanted to design 'a new pay system which would command the confidence of all interested parties and would combine national pay and local flexibility' (NPRB, 1998: iv).

The 1997 Labour government retained the overall public expenditure plans of its predecessor for two years, and angered health service trade unions by staging the 1998 nurses' pay award. It was able to create a more favourable climate for discussions on the reform of the pay system, however, by distancing itself from the previous government's ideological commitment to pay devolution, and by increasing significantly the planned growth in NHS expenditure over the following three years in its 'comprehensive spending review'. It is possible that radical changes in the pay system will be agreed in the next few years, but serious obstacles have to be overcome.

Whilst most of the unions agree that a strong national framework of pay and grading must be preserved, especially for professionally qualified staff, there are significant policy differences concerning the future relationship between the review bodies and national collective agreements. Also, there are conflicting views on the ways in which grading structures for different occupational groups can be integrated, not least to avoid the threat of further 'equal value' pay claims and legal actions. Health service managers share some of these concerns, and many lack the expertise and resources to design and implement comprehensive local pay agreements. Whatever progress is made in creating a new pay determination system, it is certain that the recent trend towards local negotiations on an increasing range of conditions of employment affecting working-time and work organization will continue, and probably accelerate, to realize management's objective of 'local flexibility' (Winchester and Bach, 1995).

Local authorities

In local government the scope and pace of bargaining reform have been greater than in the health service since the 1980s. The two national agreements covering the largest groups (manual workers and administrative, professional and technical staff) became less prescriptive and more flexible for several reasons. First, they embraced a large and occupationally diverse work force, employed in a complex structure of authorities varying in size (from more than 20,000 staff to a few hundred) and in their functions. Second, although the main trade unions generally supported the continuation of national agreements, strongly organized union branches in urban areas had considerable experience of local bargaining. Where labour market conditions and the authorities' financial position allowed, they have negotiated improvements in benefits and increases in pay through 'soft' bonus schemes and 'grading drift' for many years. These opportunities diminished significantly in the 1980s as tighter budgets and compulsory competitive tendering exerted a downward pressure on labour costs.

The third pressure towards greater flexibility arose from the political dimension of employers' policies, expressed in the conflict within the national negotiating machinery, as well as in the strategies developed by managers within each authority. The greatest change came from Conservative-controlled authorities in south-east England, struggling to recruit and retain qualified technical and professional staff in the tight labour markets of the late 1980s. These employers exerted most pressure for a looser framework of national agreements and, unsatisfied with the outcome of a prolonged dispute in 1989, more than thirty authorities had opted out of national bargaining and developed their own collective agreements by the early 1990s (Bryson *et al.*, 1993).

In the late 1990s, local government trade unions and employers developed a radical reform of the bargaining structure. A new 'single status' agreement was reached in 1997, covering 1.5 million manual and non-manual employees, which will create a single national bargaining council, a unified national terms and conditions handbook, and a single national pay spine. The enthusiasm of the union negotiators for the agreement was based on the principle of 'equality' in conditions of employment, especially the harmonization of working hours, which removes the historical status division between manual and non-manual employees. The employers wanted the agreement because it clarifies the relationship between national and local bargaining. It is essentially a 'national scheme for local application': a new job evaluation scheme may be used by authorities but is not mandatory; local grading reviews will allow authorities to move away from national grades; and it will be possible to modify some conditions of service through local negotiations. It will be several years before the agreement is fully implemented and its impact can be assessed. It is likely, however, to increase the variations in terms and conditions of employment and offer greater legitimacy to local bargaining, albeit within a national framework agreement.

These developments contrast vividly with the structure of pay determination for schoolteachers, most of whom are still employed by local authorities. After the widespread industrial conflict of the mid-1980s, the government first abolished the collective bargaining machinery and, second, established a statutory School Teachers' Review Body in 1991. Its remit was to make recommendations on pay and conditions of service 'which relate to schoolteachers' professional duties and working-time' (STRB, 1993: 1). Even though the annual terms of reference of the secretary of state have directed the attention of the review body towards performance-related pay within a more flexible structure of pay determination, relatively few schools have used their nominal discretion to increase pay to deal with recruitment problems or to reward excellent teachers. Apart from the opposition of teachers' unions, based, like that of the nurses, on the defence of national salary structures and uniform conditions of service, the organizational prerequisites for local bargaining are entirely absent. Neither the 153 local education authorities (in England and Wales), nor the 26,000 schools, offer an ideal level for pay bargaining, and the 'management' role is dispersed between head teachers, school governors, local authorities and government ministers. It is likely that a fairly strong national framework of pay and conditions will persist and that greater devolution of pay bargaining will emerge only if 'the funding of schools is at a level which enables school management to use the pay and related discretions available to them' (STRB, 1998: 40).

Pay outcomes and trends

Elliott and Duffus (1996) provide a comprehensive analysis of public service pay movements from 1970 to 1992 that facilitates an assessment of the impact of government policies and bargaining reforms. First, it shows that there has been considerable variation in the pattern of earnings growth. Between 1981 and 1992 doctors, qualified nurses, schoolteachers, police and fire officers had real earnings increases of more than 30 per cent. In contrast, the real earnings of male scientists in the civil service and of male further education teachers and university academics increased by less than 10 per cent (1996: 58). More generally, women working full-time had a higher growth of earnings than men, and non-manual employees' earnings increased more than those of manual workers. These variations in real earnings growth did not arise solely because of higher annual pay settlements. Some groups of public service non-manual employees benefited more than others from 'wage drift', that is, progression up incremental scales, regrading or discretionary awards. Annual wage drift for nurses and schoolteachers was equal to the size of the annual pay settlement, and it accounted for a significant part of earnings growth for non-manual employees in the civil service and local authorities. In contrast, manual workers received lower annual pay settlements than non-manual employees in their sector and faced declining opportunities for wage drift as managers tightened their control of overtime pay and bonus schemes.

Second, Elliott and Duffus show that there is a strong cyclical pattern in public service pay relativities with the private sector. Over the last twenty years, improvements in relative pay, especially for professional staff, have often followed from *ad hoc* inquiries, or from infrequent reforms of salary structures. In contrast, the short-term relative improvement in manual workers' pay has usually reflected the sharper deceleration of earnings growth in the private sector – for example, during the deep recession in the early 1990s. They argue that the typical pattern is one of 'discrete and sometimes substantial improvements in relative pay followed by a steady, often protracted, erosion of relative pay . . . the relative earnings of public sector employees generally exhibit a distinct anti-cyclical pattern' (1996: 75). With few exceptions, pay relativities with the private sector declined from 1981 to 1992, but there were large variations and fluctuations. For example, the relative pay of university lecturers deteriorated much more than that of schoolteachers, whilst nurses' pay declined throughout the 1980s until the implementation of a new clinical grading structure greatly improved their relative pay in 1989.

Third, Elliott and Duffus explore whether these diverse patterns of earnings growth and relative pay changes can be linked with the different institutional mechanisms of pay determination found in the public services. They note that the pay review system has produced more favourable pay outcomes for doctors, nurses and schoolteachers than the system of 'free collective bargaining' has achieved for most employees. They reject the argument that this is because the review bodies have been 'captured' by their client groups, arguing instead that the demand for the services of these groups has been increasing, and that they are represented by influential professional associations, able to protect their members' pay by stressing the quality and importance of their work.

The above analysis suggests that the Conservative government was fairly successful in regulating public service pay over the decade from 1981. The greater diversity of pay settlements, and the increasing dispersion of pay between unqualified and professional staff, reflected more general forms of segmentation and the government's wider policies of labour market deregulation. Since 1992 pay relativities with the private sector have probably deteriorated further, not least because the government introduced an additional constraint on public service pay increases. After an absence of more than a decade, incomes policies returned to the public services, in the form of a pay bill freeze, under which pay increases had to be offset by efficiency gains or productivity improvements. In practice, pay increases have been awarded at around the level of price inflation, but below the level of settlements in many parts of the private sector. These increases have been accompanied by strict cash limits on budgets so that the pay bill freeze has often led to job losses, even tighter control of 'wage drift', and increasing work loads in many public services.

The Labour government, elected in 1997, retained the existing pay policy and spending limits for two years, even though there was increasing survey evidence of recruitment and retention problems in the education and health services, and declining employee morale elsewhere. The future of the pay restraint policy is uncertain: on the one hand, the increased expenditure plans announced in 1998 may allow more generous pay settlements in the next few years, especially for staff in schools and hospitals; on the other hand, the end of a sustained period of economic growth and low unemployment may weaken the labour market pressures

on public service managers, enabling the government to achieve its stated objective – to use additional resources to improve the quality of services by increasing the
number of staff rather than increasing their pay.

Industrial conflict

Earlier in the chapter, it was noted that an unprecedented wave of industrial
conflict spread throughout the public services in the 1970s and early 1980s. The
combination of high levels of inflation and government incomes policies that
discriminated against public sector employees led previously moderate public
service trade unions and their members to embark on a sustained period of
wage militancy. Strikes in the public sector contributed significantly to an overall
pattern of industrial conflict in Britain in which the number of recorded strikes
fluctuated between 2,000 and 3,000 in the 1970s, and the number of 'working
days lost' through strikes peaked at almost 30 million in 1979. Over the next
decade, there were on average 1,271 strikes each year and the 'days lost' through
strikes averaged just under 10 million. In sharp contrast, since 1990 the number
of strikes has averaged 307 and an average of 800,000 days have been lost through
strikes each year.

This dramatic decline in the overall pattern of strikes since 1980 can be explained by a combination of factors: higher levels of unemployment; a more
hostile political context and a much more restrictive legal framework; the decline
in employment in traditionally strike-prone industries such as coal mining, docks
and manufacturing (Edwards, 1995). The legal restrictions on strikes introduced
by Conservative governments – especially compulsory strike ballots, the wider
definition of unlawful 'political' disputes, and the increasing liability of union
officials and vulnerability of union funds to employers' litigation – covered both
the private and the public sector of employment. The impact of the law, however,
may have been greater in the public service sector: first, the government was able
to encourage public sector employers to use (or threaten to use) the legislation;
second, the centralized structure of bargaining made it difficult for unions to meet
the stringent administrative demands of the legislation on strike ballots. This may
explain why Conservative governments did not introduce legislation specifically
targeted on disputes in the public services – despite frequents threats to do so –
except in the case of prison officers, whose right to take disruptive action was
removed in the Criminal Justice and Public Order Act 1994.

Despite these legal and other constraints, public service disputes still contribute significantly to the overall pattern of strikes in Britain. Since 1990 an
average of 35 per cent of the days lost through strikes, and around 40 per cent of
strikes resulting in more than 5,000 days lost, have been located in the public
services. There have been far fewer of the national pay disputes that characterized the 1970s and early 1980s and, whilst local pay disputes have taken place,
most disputes were a response to the restructuring of employment relations –
for example, market testing, job losses and the imposition of new contracts affecting work loads and hours of work. There is also considerable survey evidence of

an increase in other, less organized, expressions of conflict: absence rates are higher than in the private sector and, as noted earlier, low morale and high rates of labour turnover have contributed to staff shortages in many of the public services.

Conclusions

The title of this chapter indicates that a 'transformation' of public service employment relations took place over the 1980s and 1990s. During most of the period a succession of Conservative governments were able to develop policies that restructured the organizational forms of public administration, strengthened management authority and accountability, undermined the organization and confidence of trade unions, and threatened long-established methods and principles of pay determination. Upon its landslide election victory in 1997 the 'New Labour' government had to decide whether it would accept the main parameters of the previous reforms or attempt to change them. At the end of 1998 it can be concluded that the most important reforms in public service organization and employment relations will survive, perhaps in a modified form.

When elected in 1979 the first of four Conservative administrations had not developed a coherent strategy for reform, but it was able to use the widespread public unease arising from the 'winter of discontent' to develop more rigorous public expenditure controls and more aggressive bargaining tactics that cumulatively weakened trade unions. By the mid-1980s the government had initiated a privatization programme that eventually embraced almost all the nationalized industries, and had introduced legislation and executive guidelines on compulsory competitive tendering in local authorities and the health service respectively.

In retrospect, it can be argued that the policies on competitive tendering, and incremental initiatives on the reform of management structures, paved the way to the more radical reorganization of public services in the early 1990s. Competitive tendering required a more systematic approach to work organization and the costing of services, a methodology to monitor and evaluate contract performance, closer contact with the private service sector, and forms of organizational fragmentation between clients and contractors, and purchasers and providers of public services. Management reforms clarified, and often devolved, lines of accountability, and encouraged a shift from traditional models of hierarchical administration towards private sector 'best practice'.

These reforms were, of course, uneven and often inconsistent, but they prepared managers for the more comprehensive reorganization of all parts of the public services in the 1990s. The 'transformation' thesis is perhaps strongest in this area of reform than in most others. The Labour government would face severe difficulties if it wished to turn the clock back to a previous era when the organization of public services was more unified and its management relatively immune from the influence of private sector practice and market influences. It is clear, however, that the Labour government embraces most aspects of the new 'managerialism', especially in its commitment to evaluate organizational and individual performance and to develop a closer partnership between the public and private sectors in the funding and delivery of services.

In comparison with the radical programme of organizational restructuring, the scope and pace of collective bargaining reform over the last twenty years have been rather more modest. Outside the civil service, national structures of pay determination survived the ideological exhortations of Conservative ministers in favour of devolved bargaining, arguing that the latter would be more sensitive to local labour market conditions, organizational efficency and individual employee performance. None the less, the regulative effect of national agreements has been weakened and employers now have more freedom in applying salary structures and pay systems to achieve greater flexibility at local level. Moreover, under the pressure of budget constraints and the injunction to achieve annual efficiency gains, employers have negotiated – or imposed – widespread changes in work organization and in patterns of working-time. And despite the hostility of trade union leaders and activists, performance-related pay has become established in the civil service, and may be extended significantly in the education sector, if the Labour government's proposals for a radical reform of the career structure of schoolteachers survives a period of consultation and is implemented in 2000.

In this area, as in many others, the Labour government has aroused the criticism of public service trade union leaders and activists. After the undisguised hostility of four Conservative governments they celebrated the election of a Labour government, albeit a self-styled 'New Labour' government that had campaigned on a programme that was 'business-friendly' and contained only a few commitments that might reverse the declining power and influence of trade unions. Indeed, the proposals in the 1998 White Paper *Fairness at Work* and the details of the national minimum wage (to be implemented in 1999), disappointed most union leaders and, in any event, were expected to have a greater impact on the private sector than in the public services.

The decision to retain for two years the Conservatives' spending plans and public service pay restraint policies (including the staging of pay review body awards) was accompanied, however, by much more frequent consultation with trade union leaders and the rhetoric of 'social partnership'. In practice, the relationship between the unions and the government – as well as the success of the government's commitment to improve the quality of public services and the quality of employment relations – will depend largely on the credibility of the public expediture plans. The July 1998 'comprehensive spending review' outlined the government's spending plans for 1999–2002. Alongside aggregate current expenditure growth of 2.25 per cent in real terms, with 50 per cent of the increase targeted on education and health services, the Prime Minister insisted that it was 'money for modernisation . . . in return for investment there must be reform'. There can be little doubt that the political and financial context of public service employment relations will encourage further reforms in a system that has changed dramatically over the last few decades.

References

Bach, S. (1998) 'The Management of Employment Relations in the NHS: Pay, Work Organisation and the Internal Market', unpublished Ph.D. thesis, University of Warwick.

Bach, S. and Winchester, D. (1994) 'Opting out of pay devolution? Prospects for local pay bargaining in UK public services', *British Journal of Industrial Relations*, 32,2: 263–82.

Bryson, C., Gallagher, J., Jackson, M., Leopold, J. and Tuck, K. (1993) 'Decentralisation of collective bargaining: local authority opt-outs', *Local Government Studies*, 19,4: 558–3.

Cabinet Office (1998) *Next Steps Report 1997*, Cm 3889, London: HMSO.

Cavalier, S. (1997) *Transfer Rights: TUPE in Perspective*, London: Institute of Employment Rights.

Clegg, H. (1982) 'Reflections on incomes policy and the public sector in Britain', *Labour and Society*, VII: 3–12.

Colling, T. (1993) 'Contracting public services: the management of competitive tendering in two county councils', *Human Resource Management Journal*, 3,4: 1–15.

Colling, T. (1995) 'Renewal or rigor mortis? Union responses to contracting in local government', *Industrial Relations Journal*, 26,2: 134–45.

Cully, M. and Woodland, S. (1998) 'Trade union membership and recognition 1996–97: an analysis of data from the Certification Officer and the LFS', *Labour Market Trends* (July), 353–64.

Economic Trends (1997) 'Employment in the Public and Private Sectors', No. 520: (March), 15–25.

Edwards, P. (1995) 'Strikes and industrial conflict', in P. K. Edwards (ed.) *Industrial Relations: Theory and Practice in Britain*, Oxford: Blackwell.

Elliott, R. and Duffus, K. (1996) 'What has been happening to pay in the public-service sector of the British economy? Developments over the period 1970–92', *British Journal of Industrial Relations*, 34,1: 51–85.

Fairbrother, P. (1996) 'Workplace trade unionism in the state sector', in P. Ackers, C. Smith and P. Smith (eds) *The New Workplace and Trade Unionism*, London: Routledge.

Fredman, S. and Morris, G. (1989) *The State as Employer: Labour Law in the Public Services*, London: Mansell.

House of Lords (1998) *Report*, Select Committee on the Public Service, Session 1997–98, HL Paper 55, London: Stationery Office.

Ibbs, R. (1988) *Improving Management in Government: The Next Steps*. London: HMSO.

Incomes Data Services (1996) 'Public sector labour market survey 1996', *IDS Report*, No. 725 (November), 25–30.

Industrial Relations Services (1996) 'A new Senior Civil Service is born', *Employment Trends*, No. 610 (June), 11–16.

Industrial Relations Services (1997) 'Historic single-status deal in local government', *Employment Trends*, No. 639 (September), 5–10.

Industrial Relations Services (1998) 'Goodbye CCT', *Employment Trends*, No. 647 (January), 5–11.

Institute of Health Service Management (1997) *Pay for Senior Managers in the NHS*, London: IHSM and the Reward Group.

Kessler, I. (1993) 'Pay determination in the British civil service since 1979', *Public Administration*, 71,3: 1–31.

Lloyd, C. (1997) 'Decentralization in the NHS: prospects for workplace unionism', *British Journal of Industrial Relations*, 35,3: 427–46.

Marsden, D. and French, S. (1998) *What a Performance: Performance-related Pay in the Public Services*, London: Centre for Economic Performance, LSE.

McCarthy, W. (1976) *Making Whitley Work*, London: HMSO.

Nichol, D. (1992) 'Unnecessary conflict: NHS management's view of the 1989–90 ambulance dispute', *British Journal of Industrial Relations*, 30,1: 145–54.

Nurses' Pay Review Body (1997) *Fourteenth Report*, Cm 3538, London: HMSO.

Nurses' Pay Review Body (1998) *Fifteenth Report*, Cm 3832, London: HMSO.

Ransom, S. and Stewart, J. (1994) *Management for the Public Domain*, London: Macmillan.

Ridley, F. (1996) 'The New Public Management in Europe: comparative perspectives', *Public Policy and Administration*, 11,1: 16–29.

Safford, J. and MacGregor, D. (1998) 'Employment in the public and private sectors', *Economic Trends*, No. 532 (March), 22–33.

School Teachers' Review Body (1991) *Third Report*, Cm 2466, London: HMSO.

School Teachers' Review Body (1993) *Second Report*, Cm 2151, London: HMSO.

School Teachers' Review Body (1998) *Seventh Report*, Cm 3836, London: HMSO.

Sly, F. and Stillwell, D. (1997) 'Temporary workers in Great Britain', *Labour Market Trends* (September), 347–54.

Stoker, G. (1996) 'The struggle to reform local government, 1970–79', *Public Money and Management* (January–March), 17–22.

Waddington, J. and Whitston, C. (1995) 'Trade unions: growth, structure and policy', in P. K. Edwards (ed.) *Industrial Relations: Theory and Practice in Britain*, Oxford: Blackwell.

Wilson, D. and Game, C. (1998) *Local Government in the United Kingdom*, London: Macmillan.

Winchester, D. (1983) 'Industrial relations in the public sector', in G. S. Bain (ed.) *Industrial Relations in Britain*, Oxford: Blackwell.

Winchester, D. and Bach, S. (1995) 'The state: the public sector', in P. K. Edwards (ed.) *Industrial Relations: Theory and Practice in Britain*, Oxford: Blackwell.

3 Germany

Negotiated change, modernization and the challenge of unification

Berndt K. Keller

The public sector in Germany includes all individuals employed at the federal (*Bund*), federal state (*Bundesländer*), or local (*Gemeinden/Gemeindeverbände*) level. This organizational structure reflects the political constitution of a federalist state, providing the federal states with encompassing autonomous rights in different policy areas and a sophisticated division of political power strictly defined in the Basic Law (*Grundgesetz*).

The public sector in Germany is confronted with similar problems to those facing other Western European countries, especially the need to improve efficiency, contain costs, and the important, but widely neglected question of organizing interests at the EU level (Beaumont, 1996). There is the additional and unique problem of coping with the long-term consequences of unification. Change and adaptation within a traditional, highly juridified and well established system have been piecemeal and not based on encompassing and long-term objectives; hence management policies are diverse. The public sector, however, is not the centre of radical changes within the German system of employment relations. Despite budget restraints and privatization measures, the public sector has been characterized by a considerable degree of stability and continuity.

Until recently, official employment data used to include the railway system (*Bundesbahn*) and the postal service (*Bundespost*), although privatization measures have been under way for some years. All interpretations of the most recent figures should take into account the importance of unification. To avoid misunderstanding, all time series for the 1990s should be given for both parts of the country. Also the following analysis will, with the exception of only one section on the new federal states (*neue Bundesländer*), be limited to major developments in the western part of the country. Finally, in contrast to countries such as Italy or France, state-owned public industries and companies are much less relevant in the case of Germany (Mosley and Schmid, 1992) and will not be discussed here.

Differences between the legal status of the three groups of public employees are of fundamental importance because they give the German public sector its peculiar structure. According to the 1949 Basic Law (Article 33), the reconstruction of the public service had to be regulated with due regard to the traditional principles of the professional civil service, which can be traced back to the nineteenth

Table 3.1 Development of overall, full-time and part-time employment (000)

Year	Overall	Full-time	Part-time	Part-time % of overall
1960	3,002	2,808	194	6.5
1965	3,351	3,080	271	8.1
1970	3,644	3,266	378	10.4
1975	4,184	3,669	515	12.3
1980	4,420	3,802	618	14.0
1981	4,498	3,846	652	14.5
1982	4,532	3,851	681	15.0
1983	4,540	3,838	702	15.5
1984	4,554	3,821	733	16.1
1985	4,594	3,824	770	16.8
1986	4,625	3,827	798	17.3
1987	4,634	3,838	796	17.2
1988	4,626	3,809	817	17.7
1989	4,617	3,774	843	18.3
1990	4,676	3,803	873	18.7
1991	4,718	3,818	900	19.1
1992	4,750	3,820	930	19.6
1993	4,759	3,814	945	19.9
1994	4,622	3,680	942	20.4

Source: Henneberger (1997: 39).

century and the Bismarck constitution. All civil servants (*Beamte*) are, independent of their individual tasks and jobs, excluded from some basic rights because of their special legal status (see Merten, 1994). They have, like all other employees, the right to join unions or form interest associations of their choice. But according to the majority interpretation of the Basic Law, they are, in contrast to all salaried employees (*Angestellte*) and wage earners (*Arbeiter*), not allowed to bargain collectively or to go on strike (Weiss, 1995).

It has been argued that these legal differences in employment rights can hardly be justified by reference to the duties involved. The decision whether newly hired personnel should be employed as *Beamte* or salaried employees is arbitrary and accidental in many cases. Employees doing exactly the same job can have a different status; teachers are just one prominent example. In general, this special status, which is not restricted to certain (higher) ranks of administrative officials or to specific sub-sectors, is typical not only of certain core groups (like the police, tax officials or judges) but also for various groups within the general public administration (Keller, 1983). The necessity and usefulness of the special status of *Beamte* have been the subject of controversy for almost three decades. A central question has been whether it should be preserved, changed in some detail or in principle, or abolished completely. Despite the criticisms no major structural reforms have been initiated.

The focus of the analysis

The clear division of political power mentioned above includes a corresponding division of public services. For example, the education sector and the police are the responsibility of the federal states. This division of tasks is the decisive factor in explaining the distribution of public employees according to the three levels. At the federal level, increases occurred in the 1950s and early 1960s because of the reconstruction of the armed forces. Since the mid-1970s the number of employees has decreased. About 80 per cent of all employees at this level work in defence. At the federal state level, increases occurred mainly in the late 1960s and early 1970s in different sub-sectors, including education and science. Currently about 50 per cent are employed in the area of education. In quantitative terms, the federal states are the most important public employers. At the local/municipal level increases have been more evenly distributed over time. The most important areas are public health (about 30 per cent) and general administration (about 20 per cent).

Three-quarters of the growth in personnel in the 1960s and 1970s was concentrated in the above-mentioned areas. This resulted from political decisions on the increased importance of certain sub-sectors (for example, defence, education, health or security) and was not an uncontrolled growth of bureaucracy. In absolute terms: in the mid-1990s there were 0.46 million at the federal, 1.91 million at the federal state, and 1.26 million at the local/municipal level. Public employers are clearly characterized by pro-cyclical behaviour: when unemployment was very low in the 1960s and 1970s, they hired many new employees, whereas in the 1980s, when unemployment rose steadily, growth rates were much lower. In the 1990s, the long-term trend of increasing public employment has been reversed (DIW, 1998; IWD, 1998).

These overall employment figures are significant because they indicate the percentage of public budgets needed for personnel expenditures alone. The ratios, which differ greatly because of the legally defined distribution of public tasks, are about 14 per cent at the federal level, about 41 per cent at the federal state and about 31 per cent at the local/municipal level. In the 1990s, sharply increasing deficits of all public budgets (up to more than 60 per cent of GDP), the unexpectedly high and continuing costs of unification and the need to fulfil the convergence criteria for European Monetary Union created enormous pressure not only to stabilize public employment levels, but to decrease gradually the number of public employees, especially at the local/municipal level, and to introduce public sector reform plans. Notwithstanding these reform pressures, Germany occupies, in contrast to public statements and popular belief, only an intermediate position in public sector employment (as a percentage of total employment) among OECD countries (Mosley and Schmid, 1992; Beaumont, 1996). In the mid-1990s about 15 per cent of total employment was within the public sector.

Organizational structure, employment and wages

Organizational structure of the main sectors

Arising from the legal framework mentioned above, there are two sub-systems of labour relations with unilateral and bilateral processes of decision making; that is, the so-called dualism of the private law employee status of salaried employees and wage earners, and the public law employment status of *Beamte*. These subsets have influenced each other to a considerable degree; however, the empirical meaning of the legal difference should not be exaggerated (Keller, 1989).

The system of labour relations, or, to be more precise, of collective bargaining, has traditionally been fairly centralized and its different components have been highly integrated. This is surprising, considering the political constitution, which might lead us to expect major differences between the federal, federal state and local/municipal levels. The degree of centralization is even higher in the public sector than in private industry, where sectoral contracts, negotiated at the regional level, are widespread (see Jacobi *et al.*, 1998).

The result of this public sector bargaining structure is a surprisingly high degree of uniformity in all working conditions. This conformity includes rather small pay differentials within groups, a relatively stable wage structure between groups over time and, with very few exceptions, identical working hours for all public employees. These trends at the sectoral level are reinforced by the fact that all public employees are covered by basically the same rules of co-determination by staff councils at the 'enterprise' level. Because separate negotiations for particular groups are not the rule but a rare exception, group-specific bargaining power can, in contrast to more decentralized systems, hardly be exploited to its full extent; comparisons of pay between groups aiming at group-specific increases are also less relevant. All group-specific problems of working conditions (like teaching loads in education or patient/nurse ratios in the health sector) have to be solved within the existing general frame of reference. As a result, studies of specific working conditions in various sub-sectors or occupational groups are rare and are relatively unimportant for understanding the German system.

In the past, there were so-called structural improvements (*Strukturverbesserungen*) comparable to a bonus system, but they were purely collective rewards and egalitarian in nature. If there was a bonus everybody belonging to the particular group received this special reward irrespective of individual performance. In the 1960s and 1970s, unions and interest organizations increased the income of particular groups by negotiating these collective bonuses. Improvements achieved for one particular group often created strong incentives for other groups to apply the same strategy (Keller, 1989). These group-specific negotiations used to be independent from regular annual bargaining rounds so their visibility for the general public was rather low. Since the early 1980s such opportunities, which created additional expenditure, have been curtailed substantially.

There is neither a clear distinction of overall working conditions between sub-sectors nor a strict separation between different levels of government. The local/

Table 3.2 Development of female employment (overall and according to status)

		Percentage of full-time employed women in relation to		
		Full-time employed		
Year	All full-time employees	Beamte	Salaried employees	Wage earners
1960	22.7	12.3	48.3	17.2
1966	25.4	14.2	50.5	18.3
1969	26.7	16.1	51.2	18.1
1974	29.2	18.2	53.9	18.4
1977	29.8	19.9	53.9	17.9
1980	30.5	20.4	54.8	17.7
1983	30.5	20.5	55.3	16.8
1986	30.6	20.4	55.5	16.3
1987	31.0	20.6	55.8	16.6
1988	31.1	20.7	55.8	16.4
1989	31.3	20.7	56.0	16.6
1990	31.8	21.3	56.3	16.8
1991	32.2	21.8	56.6	16.6
1992	32.8	22.5	56.8	16.8
1993	33.0	23.2	56.3	16.9
1994	34.1	23.9	56.5	18.4

Source: Henneberger (1997: 54).

municipal level is a legally autonomous but closely co-ordinated and completely integrated part of the labour relations system. The federal state level, which should not be confused with regional governments in other countries, is autonomous in legal terms, but in reality it is also highly integrated.

The composition of employment

The most important legal distinction is between the three already mentioned groups of public employees. In quantitative terms: about 40 per cent of all public employees have the traditional status of *Beamte*, about 37 per cent are salaried employees, and about 23 per cent are wage earners. In an historical perspective the percentage of *Beamte* has remained fairly stable, the percentage of salaried employees has increased to a considerable degree, and the percentage of wage earners has decreased. These long-term trends will almost certainly continue, because the number of jobs for wage earners will decrease and *Beamte* will try to prevent any major change in their status.

The percentage of female employment (as part of overall public employment excluding soldiers), which was approximately 20 per cent in the 1950s, has increased to almost 45 per cent in the mid-1990s (Breidenstein, 1996). The principle of equal pay for equal work does apply. There are, however, still significant differences between full-time and part-time employment; about one third of all full-time, but between 85 per cent and 90 per cent of all part-time, employees are female. In other words, any discussion of part-time employment across the economy can be equated with female employment. One explanatory factor is the traditional division of labour between the sexes.

Improved opportunities of access for women are not correlated with improved chances of promotion, and they are concentrated in education, public health and the postal service, which provide 'typical' jobs for women. Moreover, women are substantially overrepresented in the lower career groups (Keller, 1993; Henneberger, 1997). Different public sector labour markets are vertically segregated according to sex. These differences cannot be completely explained by human capital theories; other explanations include the impact of temporary interruptions of work within a promotion system which rewards permanent employment.

The introduction of different forms of labour market flexibility into a highly legalized, bureaucratic, and fairly rigid system of labour relations is of increasing importance. Various forms of 'flexibility' – external/internal, numerical and functional – have quite different connotations. An increase in numerical flexibility may be considered important in an employment system with a traditionally high degree of job security and few dismissals. An increase in functional flexibility may mean that employees can be given different or enlarged jobs.

The more or less systematic use of the following policies and procedures can be seen (Keller and Henneberger, 1998; *Statistisches Bundesamt*, 1996). First, part-time work, which has spread from salaried employees and wage earners to *Beamte*, has grown steadily from 6 per cent of the work force in the late 1960s to about 20 per cent in the mid-1990s. This compares with about 16 per cent in the private sector. The proportion of part-time workers remains higher among wage earners and salaried employees than among *Beamte*. This strategy has been adopted at the federal state and local/municipal level. Part-time work has considerable advantages for both sides and it increases the total number of employees at times of high unemployment.

Second, since the 1970s, the legal and contractual opportunities for long-term leave for labour-market and family-related reasons have been extended several times (up to fifteen years) for all public employees. Third, more short-term and fixed-term contracts have been used, not only within vocational training schemes, but also in education, the postal service and elsewhere. Thus public employers have increased their numerical flexibility and reduced their long-term commitment to job security. This strategy has been applied in the local/municipal and federal state sectors, but rarely at the federal level.

Fourth, greater use has been made of other forms of contingent work and atypical employment (*atypische Beschäftigung*) instead of the traditional pattern of full-time, permanent employment. In social services, hospitals and education many positions are designated 'temporary', because they are short-term or because they are seen as 'training posts', or posts for which it is desirable to have a turnover of personnel to ensure a continual influx of new ideas. Finally, most non-conscript members of the armed forces are committed to serve for strictly defined periods, and they too count as temporary workers (Casey *et al.*, 1989).

Consequently, full-time, permanent employment with employment security is no longer the norm. But the emergence of new patterns of contingent work does not necessarily imply that patterns of precarious employment have spread. Some full-time jobs have been replaced by part-time opportunities, and nominal increases in overall public employment in the 1980s are largely explained by significant increases in part-time employment. General tendencies are difficult to discern because different public employers follow different strategies of flexibilization and employment reduction.

Public sector labour markets

The obvious result of these developments is further segmentation within the employment structure, between good and bad jobs, and between well protected and more marginal groups, resulting in growing inequality. Arguing from perspectives taken by the school of segmentation theory, as well as other labour market theories (DiPrete, 1989), public sector labour markets are not, in contrast to neoclassical assumptions, homogeneous entities. They constitute different prototypical internal markets with a strictly limited number of points of entry, a series of structured job ladders, clearly defined channels and rules of vertical mobility, internal promotion instead of external hiring, including plans for career development, reduced opportunities for horizontal interdepartmental mobility, the elimination of wage competition, a high degree of employment security or tenure, protection against and isolation from pure market forces, etc. (Brandes *et al.*, 1990; Henneberger, 1997). The remuneration and other working conditions of the 'ins' are much better protected than those of the 'outs', entrants face more difficulties than ever before in finding adequate jobs, and later in achieving job security or promotion. Increasing lines of segmentation within the public sector, not just between sectors, are more difficult to bridge than in the past; the disadvantages of flexibility are externalized whereas the advantages are internalized. (For similar developments in other countries see Marsden, 1993; Wise, 1996).

Despite these changes, there still exists the traditional, strictly hierarchical system of different career groups with specific job classification and salary groups, which has been heavily criticized for many years. These rules, which have to be applied at the decentralized workplace level, are uniform across the public sector. There are four different career groups (*Laufbahngruppen*) for *Beamte*, all with jobs graded according to the level of qualifications required. A legally different but functionally equivalent hierarchical system exists for salaried employees and wage earners. Each path or career group consists of four interrelated groups so that the complete system includes, with a few exceptions for specific groups like judges and professors, sixteen not strictly interrelated grades. Horizontal mobility is very rare because of the specific qualifications required. Over the last couple of decades there has been a continuous trend towards higher proportions of employees in the upper career groups (Keller, 1993).

All entrants have to start in the lowest group of their particular path. The higher positions are filled by promotion from within. It is basically length of service rather than individual performance that has always been the decisive factor in promotion decisions. Individual opportunities for promotion within career groups do exist, but have been limited because the percentage of higher positions within the four groups has been strictly curtailed since the mid-1970s for budgetary reasons (see Keller, 1993). Demotions are legally possible but, in reality, very unlikely.

Germany belongs, with France and Italy, among the countries with 'an intensive use of pay practices that are typical of internal labour markets and of bureaucratic organizations' (Dell'Aringa, 1997). All *Beamte* are guaranteed lifelong job security at the very start of their career as an integrated part of their special status. Under collective bargaining arrangements, salaried employees and wage earners are protected against dismissal after fifteen years of employment.

Wages and salaries

Traditionally, wages and salaries have been determined by three main components (see also p. 85). First, the career group (or grade) and the corresponding salary group, to which public employees actually belong, are one major determinant. Second, within pay schemes, which have to date had a strictly seniority-based component, length of service is the second crucial factor: wages and salaries increase automatically every other year according to length of service up to a certain age, which differs as between career groups. Individual performance has been of almost no importance within these different, but rather uniform, pay scales. Since the introduction of the reform package in 1997 (see below), individual performance is supposed to have more influence in the future. Third, regular increases in wages and salaries are the result of collective bargaining (for salaried employees and wage earners) or of legislation (for *Beamte*).

This system has been criticized as being highly inflexible because of its purely collective and uniform character, its independence from individual performance on the job and its high degree of job security (Tondorf, 1995a). Across-the-board wage increases are rarely differentiated by grade. But an increase of *x* per cent for all public employees means higher money increases for higher grades, so widening the gap between different groups in absolute terms. Over recent decades, there have been very few exceptions, with either flat-rate pay increases or so-called 'mixed demands', with percentage and absolute components, which favoured the interests of lower grades more than others. Solidaristic wage policies which have been the rule in different, more egalitarian Scandinavian societies for decades (Keller, 1997a), have been rare exceptions in Germany. Flatter wage structures are not acceptable either to public employers or to higher-ranking employees.

Employers and employers' associations

State policies and public sector regulation

Privatization has been a controversial political issue in most West European countries since the mid-1980s (Martin, 1993). In Germany, major technological changes, economic pressure and political decisions that have been taken since the late 1980s, include the deregulation and restructuring of the 'natural monopolies' of railways and the postal service and their transfer into joint-stock companies (*Aktiengesellschaft*). In both cases, privatization means a change of ownership and a shift in labour relations towards private sector patterns. Deutsche Bahn AG Holding, the successor of the old Federal Railway System, has been reorganized into three business units: railways; passenger transport; and freight-traffic. After two reforms in 1989 (deregulation as the first step) and 1995 (privatization as the final goal), the formerly unitary postal service consists of three parts: Deutsche Post AG, the postal service in the narrower sense; Deutsche Telekom AG, whose monopoly was abolished at the beginning of 1998; and the postal bank, Deutsche Postbank, a rather small organization, which will also be partially privatized in the near future.

Newly emerging problems from this politically motivated marketization have been, among others, the very complicated transition of former public employees (especially *Beamte*) into the completely different employment patterns and principles of private industry. This is, first of all, a difficult legal problem, but also a question of proportions, because *Beamte* constituted more than 50 per cent of all employees in these former parts of the public sector. The protracted legal problem includes the encompassing protection of their former status by additional agreements, plus the definition and implementation of new, private sector-style mechanisms for the determination of pay and other working conditions. The so-called *Beleihungsmodell*, which includes a necessary change in the Basic Law (Article 143), allows *Beamte* to be carried over into private sector employment relations without losing their special status rights. In contrast to these complicated legal questions, the transition of salaried employees and wage earners has been much easier.

Massive redundancies were considered to be necessary, various programmes of retraining had to be developed, more flexible forms of work organization were implemented, and favourable early retirement schemes were introduced. Despite considerable improvements in productivity, retrenchment will continue alongside new investment and some growth in employment. Other measures have included the federal state withdrawing from industrial corporation ownership since the 1980s. In the 1990s, when concepts of the 'lean state' gained in importance, further steps towards privatization were initiated (e.g. airports) or completed (e.g. *Deutsche Lufthansa*).

At the federal state and local/municipal level, some services have also been privatized, among others rubbish collection and street cleaning, creating major problems for the unions involved. Different public agencies have tried to reduce some voluntary components of their services (public libraries, museums, theatres and opera houses, indoor swimming pools) and the number of their employees to some degree. This strategy has been pursued especially by public sector managers at the local level, where, as mentioned above, budgetary problems have been most urgent, and because their scope for raising taxes is limited by the general fiscal constitution. Similar policies have been pursued at the federal state level, where officials face the highest percentage of labour costs. None the less, public sector deregulation has been more cautious and less ideologically motivated than in other countries, such as the UK (Martin, 1993). A key difference is that these measures of privatization were introduced relatively late in Germany and were negotiated in a consensual corporatist spirit (Esser, 1998). Steps actually taken are, in contrast to conservative and liberal programmes, very pragmatic and lack a strategic coherence. We have to take into consideration:

> that public ownership of industrial corporations was relatively insignificant. Unlike the situation that applied in a number of other European countries, a policy of privatization was not, from an economic standpoint, of paramount importance in making sure that Germany remained competitive in world markets.
>
> (Esser, 1998: 118)

The political debate about privatization for fiscal and efficiency reasons was launched, somewhat half-heartedly, in the mid-1970s. But the financial pressures were not very strong, public sector unions in particular were definitely not in favour of such ideas, and social democrats were not alone in trying to defend the achievements of the welfare state for the majority of citizens. Therefore, the political costs of privatization measures were viewed as disproportionately high.

More recently, however, some public authorities, and even some unions, have started thinking about alternative modes of regulation such as public-private partnerships, and outsourcing, instead of 'pure' privatization, which is associated with some disadvantages (Eichhorn and von Loesch, 1989). These measures have consequences for employment relations which have received little attention in the literature. They have caused stricter segmentation of labour markets because the privatized and deregulated segments are directed by private sector-style rules. Within labour relations they have caused problems for employees and their interest organizations; for example, less favourable collective contracts, change of co-determination rules, and changes in work organization; 'the trade union influence will typically be reduced by privatization' (Bös, 1998: 60). The advantages for employers are supposed to be greater 'flexibility' as far as status (including pensions), salaries and working conditions are concerned. The borderline between the public sector and the private sector has shifted because of the new definition and is less clear.

In marked contrast to the 1960s and 1970s, management, and not the unions, has been the prime mover over the last decade or so, prompted by budgetary difficulties. Public sector employers are no longer the model employers they used to be up to the 1970s, when positive examples of social employers were also set for private industry, in addition to the ideal of the state as 'employer of last resort', which was supposed to create job opportunities for the least qualified applicants (Keller and Henneberger, 1998).

It is fair to conclude that the federal state and other public agencies behave more or less like any other private employer, taking advantage of prevailing general regional or local labour market conditions. Public employers do not accept more responsibility for labour market developments than their private counterparts; the use of so-called 'natural wastage' in order to reduce the number of employees has been a frequently applied strategy that has had destabilizing effects on the labour market. But Treu (1987: 270) suggests that:

> The traditional orientation of the state as a good employer is insufficient; it might be counterproductive if 'good' is equated with 'protective'. To face this challenge implies a growth in professional know-how of those in charge of personnel management. It also requires greater political consistency on the part of the governing bodies vis-à-vis the pressures coming from public opinion and from public employees themselves.

The consequences of restructuring and modernization processes have been rarely explored in the literature; the implicit assumption is that there will be no distributional effects. In practice there are, especially at the local or municipal level, signs of altered forms of interest representation (Oppen *et al.*, 1997). These include: the introduction of individual, workplace-related forms of participation; a diminished role for unions as organized interest representatives in tasks of steering and control; a shift of interest representation from centralized towards decentralized bargaining; the emergence of senior management and politicians as 'prime movers', and increasing plurality within the system of labour relations. There are certain trends towards the destabilization of traditional collectivized-centralized systems of interest representation and tendencies towards more individualistic-decentralized human resource management in deregulated environments. However, there are still major differences between English-speaking and Continental as well as Northern European developments (ibid., 1997).

Since the early 1990s, there has been much debate about modernization as a permanent task, with criticism of bureaucracy and the tentative introduction of different forms and methods of new public management (Budäus, 1994; Damkowski and Precht, 1995). This approach incorporates a more strategic orientation, using principles of organization derived from private industry. In contrast to its predecessor in the early 1970s (Studienkommission, 1973), this current discussion will have major consequences for several reasons. First, permanent fiscal crisis, aggravated by the vast, largely unexpected financial demands of unification, will continue to exert an enormous strain on all public budgets in both parts of the country. Second, a growing percentage of public budgets has to be spent on interest payments because state borrowing has been fairly high historically – and not only since unification. Third, in a highly bureaucratic system with a considerable degree of job security, more individual incentives are essential to achieve greater flexibility.

Finally, expenditure on the pensions of retired *Beamte* will increase significantly in the medium to long term, especially at the federal state level, taking up a growing share of public expenditure. A key factor is the 'deteriorating' age structure of public employees, because their numbers increased significantly in the 1960s and 1970s, and they have shorter periods of active service, earlier retirement, and longer life expectancy. This general problem also exists within all other pension funds but is more difficult to solve in the public services because neither public servants nor their employers have contributed to such funds. In contrast, funds for all wage earners and salaried employees were established many years ago (Färber, 1996). One popular recent demand has been that *Beamte* should also pay their own contributions to pension funds at the federal and federal state levels. In 1998 it was decided that between 1999 and 2013 all *Beamte* will have to contribute 0.2 per cent of all regular pay increases. A potential problem of this strategy will be protecting these funds from being used for other purposes, for example, public consumption, or the reduction of public deficits (see Färber, 1997).

In 1995, following the announcement that it planned a major overhaul of public sector regulation, the federal government published its basis for a reform of the public sector legal framework. This requires broad political consensus between the major political parties, including the Social Democrats because of their majority in the Council of Federal States (*Bundesrat*), the second chamber. The reform package is supposed to include the federal states but not automatically the local/municipal level.

The political controversy about the necessity of major public sector reforms has focused on *Beamte*. The implementation of measures is assumed to be easier for this particular group because its special legal status allows more scope for unilateral decision making by public authorities. But ultimately salaried employees and wage earners will have to be included, not only because they constitute the majority of public employees but also because fundamental differences between the three groups will not be acceptable. Any changes will need the explicit consent of the unions in collective bargaining, which will be difficult to attain, so variations in the outcome for different groups of employees are likely. Explicit co-operation between the government, unions and other interest organizations will also be necessary during the implementation process, but coherent and consistent policies will be difficult to define and implement.

Overall, this reform is likely to be only the first step in a sequence of modernization strategies. Instruments of reform to change existing regulations will include the following (see Siedentopf, 1997; Beus 1998): first, promotions to executive positions will take place for a limited period of time instead of for the rest of the individual's career; second, probation periods before promotion and final appointment to higher-level positions will be introduced from the beginning of the individual's career, and not just for a limited period of time; third, *Beamte* will be appointed on a part-time basis; fourth, the strictly seniority-based system of automatic pay increases will be changed and will include indicators of individual performance; finally, a proportional reduction of pensions in cases of early retirement will be gradually introduced.

The impact of these changes is not yet clear. One open question focuses on the scope of restructuring and reorganization of management. Another difficulty is that the systematic difference between structural reforms and modernization of the public sector, and purely fiscal measures, is not very clear; consequently, criticism by the trade unions has been fairly harsh. This reform, the first of its kind for decades, does not, in spite of frequent claims by non-conservative parties and some unions, signify a fundamental change of the special status of *Beamte* in particular or institutional restructuring in general. If it succeeded at the federal level, positive incentives would also be set for the federal states. Some initiatives towards modernization of the state have been partially implemented at this level, but they have been poorly co-ordinated between the independent federal states. Instead, a process of trial and error continues, with uncertain results. Some of the new strategies for market-led restructuring of the public sector and market testing, like compulsory competitive tendering in the UK, are completely unknown in Germany. The influence of the federal level is limited because all improvements have to be implemented on a decentralized basis. These reform processes started relatively late and are therefore less advanced than in other OECD countries (OECD, 1990, 1993).

In recent years, numerous modernization initiatives have been started at the local/municipal levels. They refer, primarily, to financial management, rather than to policies of quality or competition measures (Naschold *et al.*, 1997). They do not include, in contrast to the federal level, legal changes and their results are uncertain. A tentative conclusion is that modernization policies show differing degrees of intensity according to levels of public administration, as well as variations between regions. Activities intensify from the top – federal and federal state level – to the bottom – local/municipal level (Damkowski and Precht, 1998).

The conservative-liberal coalition government that came into power in 1982 has been more cautious than conservative governments in other countries in 'rolling back the state'. Financial pressures seem to be the most important trigger rather than political beliefs. Germany belongs (together with Japan, the United States and Australia) to a heterogeneous group of countries which 'have in common the clear predominance of administrative rule steering, having largely rejected results steering . . . and the selective reduction in the scope of state activity by means of competitive instruments and privatization programs' (Naschold and Arnkil, 1997: 285).

Status and role of public managers

The recruitment of public managers follows the same selection principles as for other public personnel. Direct appointments by politicians are very rare and limited to a few senior positions, but informal relationships do exist. The compensation of managers follows the overall principles valid in the public sector, with performance-related pay virtually unknown. In the majority of cases of conflicting interests, 'managerial prerogatives' are limited because of the existence of fairly elaborate rights of co-determination by elected staff councils with decisions influenced by employees' representatives (see below). Public managers are subject to regular, formal and legal controls over their behaviour, but not to control of results, quality or output. Thus the problem of defining and exerting management prerogatives, which is of primary importance in other countries, has basically been solved by legal enactment, enforcing bilateral instead of unilateral decision making in areas of potential conflict.

In contrast to many other countries, managers do not have separate bargaining units of their own; they are allowed to (and do) join the same unions and interest organizations as other public employees. Their pay schemes are, with very few exceptions, part of the general schemes. The bilateral or unilateral regulation of their employment relationship depends on their status as salaried employees or *Beamte* and they do not play a special role in collective bargaining activities. All general rules concerning job security are also valid for the vast majority of managers. The whole issue of 'managerialism' has definitely never been, and probably never will be, a high priority.

There has been growing debate about changes in management strategies in almost all West European countries since the 1980s (Lane, 1995). New public management, with its emphasis on results and markets, alongside human resource management strategies, was developed and politically tested in the English-speaking countries. In practice, however, there are no homogeneous trends of modernization; different national regimes and trajectories of development prevail. In Germany, public managers' decisions about the introduction of new, more private sector-style strategies are primarily motivated by fiscal constraints, but homogeneous concepts of public management reform hardly exist (Budäus, 1994; Damkowski and Precht, 1995). Legal problems are numerous and difficult to solve (Blanke, 1998). In contrast to many other countries, the scope of new policies will be limited by the existing rules of co-determination granting staff councils major rights of participation in almost all managerial decision making (see below). These rights are, of course, open to some form of flexible interpretation but they definitely define certain limits.

The *Kommunale Gemeinschaftsstelle für Verwaltungsvereinfachung* (KGSt), a joint establishment of German cities and municipalities for the transformation and modernization of local administration, plays an important role in initiating and promoting these processes of internal modernization (KGSt, 1993). Since the early 1990s, the KGSt has developed new, more private sector-orientated principles of organization. These new 'guiding concepts' (*neue Steuerungsmodelle*) include the decentralization of responsibility for resources, budgeting, definition of products, external competition and internal comparisons, quality management, participation by citizens, contract management, and personnel and organizational development.

The KGSt has stimulated a controversial discussion about new public management and initiated some decentralizing trends, especially at the local/municipal level. Regardless of existing deficiencies and internal contradictions there is currently no competing concept of public sector modernization (Jann, 1998). It is the German variant of the well known new public management model. Unions have criticized these concepts as one-dimensional and stressed the importance not only of consultation but also of active, continuous participation by staff councils and unions in the processes of modernization (ÖTV, 1997). The present controversy is primarily concerned with different cost reduction measures and much less with the quality and improvement of public services, changed consumer interests, client orientation and steps towards democratization of public administration by the participation of citizens and employees. Fundamental differences between public and private sectors, such as constitutional law, or the requirements of the social state, are misrepresented (Bogumil and Kißler, 1997, 1998).

Overall, innovative changes towards more competition and client orientation have not happened very fast and have been isolated events. Public managers' decisions about the introduction of new strategies are hesitant and not always sustainable. Furthermore, measures taken are not very well co-ordinated between different levels of administration. The restructuring of local/municipal service provision has been the focal point of reform (Oppen and Wegener, 1997). One fundamental problem is the limited room for manoeuvre because structural reforms are being advocated in a period of major cutbacks and severe cost pressures. In a period of unpredictable change, discussion has focused on further decentralization and more experimentation with new strategies of human resource management; for example, more systematic training, better motivation and more direct participation by employees, expansion of team work, and increasing vertical mobility of employees. As in private industry, new, more individualized employee relations are supposed to complement, but not replace, the old collective labour relations. Overall there have been very few fundamental changes.

Furthermore, there has not been a strategic discussion about a 'lean government' model at different levels, or about the future role of the public sector. The political debate about the model of the future state continues, but necessary decisions about political priorities, such as core competences and new modes of regulation, have not been made. Interventionist state policies are unlikely because they are difficult to implement in a federal state with a sophisticated division of political power. Finally, the sequence of events is important. Major political decisions about the direction of structural reform, including the future scope of services, the relationship between private and public provision, the shape of flattened hierarchies, and the modernized structures of different parts of the public sector have to be made before individual measures can be introduced. Otherwise, the present structure of working conditions and labour relations will be preserved (Tondorf, 1996).

Employers' associations

German public employers are organized according to the three levels of public administration. At the local/municipal level, there are different employers' associations within all federal states; their national, or peak, association is the Federation of Local Government Employers Associations (VkA), founded in 1949. At the federal state level, the Bargaining Association of German States (TdL), which was also founded in 1949, has as its goal uniformity of working conditions in all federal states, as well as safeguarding wages and employers' interests. At the federal level, since 1960 the Minister of the Interior has been responsible for safeguarding the public interest, and must formally approve collective agreements. The Minister not only leads the employers' bargaining committee in collective negotiations for wage earners and salaried employees, but also prepares legislation on remuneration and other working conditions for *Beamte*. This double function places the Minister in a focal position in the negotiation and determination of income for all public employees.

The employers' associations are legally independent of their private sector counterparts, but have a similar internal structure. The density ratio at the local and federal state level is very high. The distinction between 'single employer representation' and 'separate representation' is hardly applicable in the German case of close co-ordination and high centralization, where the safeguarding of public functions is clearly regulated by law. The bargaining leaders are empowered to decide upon all issues subject to negotiation. Through this centralization of competence, the problems of arriving at decisions are obviously simplified, with bargaining responsibilities clarified early on. None the less, conflicts of interest of a general nature (lower settlements *v.* political survival), as well as conflicts between the representatives of the different levels, do arise. A degree of hetero-geneity of interests complicates internal policy making. A characteristic feature of these processes is that they take place within and between groups of employers. The representatives of the federal level take the lead on an informal basis and try to achieve the necessary internal and external consensus before and during the bargaining process. Some differences of interest arise from the special conditions at the local/municipal level – a weak financial situation and a greater susceptibil-ity to strikes.

Public employers and their organizations from all three levels have always bargained together; representatives from all three levels of government meet and reach a common position. Despite growing difficulties of interest aggregation and intermediation, especially at the local level because of the larger number of employers, all employers maintain and preserve this peculiar form of coalition bargaining, which is a result of the idea of uniformity of terms and conditions of work. They have always argued that it is in their long-term self-interest to stick together instead of searching for short-term advantages outside the coalition. Thus the problem of control over decentralized bargaining and the impact of pay settlements on macro-economic stability does not exist. Questions of the fiscal and financial autonomy of certain employers and authorities are eased. All prob-lems resulting from formal or informal comparisons between different groups are less urgent than in other decentralized systems. This structure has remained stable without experiencing major recent changes.

Trade unions

Since the end of the First World War all employees in Germany have had the right to join unions and interest groups. After the hiatus of the Third Reich, these rights were restored. The Basic Law guarantees, in Article 9 section 3, the right to positive and negative freedom of association. Compulsory membership clauses are therefore illegal.

Trade union structure and organization

Unions have the right to bargain collectively and to strike, not only in private industry, but also on behalf of all wage earners and salaried employees in the public sector. In contrast to the established organizational principle of industrial unionism in private industry, the principle of multi-industry unions was not established in the public sector. Instead, a certain diversity of organizations developed, and some groups of employees formed independent professional associations based on status or ideology.

The German Trade Union Federation (*Deutscher Gewerkschaftsbund*, DGB), the dominant union central confederation, has its organizational focus in the private sector, but several of its affiliated unions have members in the public sector. The Public Services, Transport and Communication Union (*Gewerkschaft Öffentliche Dienste, Transport und Verkehr*, ÖTV) with 1.6 million members is the second largest industrial union after IG Metall. The organizational focus of ÖTV is clearly on public employees, who comprise more than 90 per cent of its membership. As ÖTV has a large and heterogeneous membership, its bargaining on behalf of wage earners and salaried employees in the public sector is of particular national interest. The other public sector unions affiliated to the DGB are much smaller. The Union of German Railway Employees (GdED) with about 370,000 members, and the German Postal Union (DPG) with about 490,000 members, have been seriously affected by privatization. The Union for Education and Science (GEW) with 290,000 members and the Police Union (GdP) with about 197,000 members are also important.

The other peak association, the German Civil Servants' Association (*Deutscher Beamtenbund*, DBB), has more than fifty member associations with 1.1 million members and organizes only in the public sector, mostly *Beamte* (DBB, 1995). It subscribes to the tradition and principles of German officialdom, whose professional and political interests it serves. The DBB does not claim the right to strike for *Beamte* and is therefore not a trade union in the usual sense of the term (Keller, 1993). The two umbrella organizations, the DGB and DBB, have only autonomous associations and no individuals as members.

Apart from the member unions of these two peak organizations, the independent German Union of Salaried Employees (*Deutsche Angestelltengewerkschaft*, DAG) also organizes in the public sector, where about a quarter of its 500,000 members are employed. The DAG organizes and represents the special interests of salaried employees, competing with DGB-affiliated unions – but not with the DBB – for these staff. There are relatively few independent unions outside the confederations.

For a long time the DGB had a stable structure consisting of sixteen, mostly industrial, affiliated unions. Since the mid-1990s, however, there have been some

Table 3.3 Membership of public sector unions (000)

Union	1989	1991	1993	1995	1996	1997	1991–97
DGB	7,861	11,800	10,290	9,355	8,973	8,624	−26.9
IG BCE	1,040	1,425	1,209	1,123	1,052	1,012	−29.0
GdED	320	527	450	398	382	368	−30.3
GEW	189	360	330	306	296	289	−19.7
ÖTV	1,235	2,138	1,996	1,771	1,712	1,644	−23.1
GdP	161	201	198	199	199	197	−2.2
DPG	472	612	578	529	513	488	−20.3

Source: http://www.eiro.eurofound.ie.

mergers of private sector unions, reducing the overall number to eleven, and clustering around two merger blocs, Mining, Chemicals and Energy and IG Metall (Streeck and Visser, 1997). Mergers have arisen because of significant losses of membership and decreasing density, especially in the new federal states. These losses led to financial problems and a gradual loss of power. Within the public sector, restructuring has also played a major role.

First, all public sector unions affiliated to the DGB announced their willingness to co-operate more closely but ruled out mergers. Later on, however, six unions (ÖTV, IG Medien, HBV, DPG, GEW, DAG), organizing in the private as well as the public service sector, expressed their common view that organizational changes and the creation of a single large service sector union would be necessary. Whether this change of strategy towards the principle of 'general unionism in the service sector' will create a viable solution to organizational and financial problems, and the blurring of sectoral demarcations, is difficult to predict. None the less, the well preserved independent status of DAG will probably come to an end in the foreseeable future. The internal organizational structure of a union with about 3.7 million members is difficult to define and implement. Moreover, after these mergers, the status of the union confederations will have to change, and currrent organizational reforms within individual unions may develop further (von Alemann and Schmid, 1998).

As in many other countries, union density has been considerably higher in the public than in the private sector, and this gap widened in the early 1990s (Beaumont and Harris, 1998). Overall union density is about 30 per cent, and while data on the public sector are imprecise, estimates of more than 60 per cent seem to be realistic if DGB-affiliated and other unions are taken together. The explanation of higher union density in the public sector is well known (ILO, 1997). Density increases with organization size, and the units of public administration are larger than private sector organizations on average. Second, the public sector has a high degree of homogeneity of occupational status. Third, management and government attitudes have been less hostile and often favourable towards union organization, and managers can be members of the same union as their subordinates.

These factors, alongside legal protection for union membership, have not prevented significant membership losses since 1992 which are likely to continue.

Union confederations

The DGB and the DBB are not only the largest but also, because of their organizational power, the most important peak organizations. On issues such as incomes policy and general improvements in working conditions it has been possible to establish some sort of consensus between them. There are important differences between them, but this does not affect day-to-day activities; co-operation makes interest representation easier and more effective. Controversy arises mainly from the question of the right to strike of *Beamte* and the problem of standardization of the employment rights of the three different groups of employees. The DBB is interested in preserving the *status quo* whereas the DGB has demanded the introduction of unified employment status for decades. The fundamental difference is that the vast majority of members of DBB-affiliated organizations are *Beamte*, whereas different DGB unions organize mainly wage earners and salaried employees. Demarcation disputes between unions belonging to different peak organizations do occur, but the degree of co-operation between DGB affiliated unions has been fairly high. The dispersed representational structure minimizes the degree of competition or rivalry at the workplace level and the amount of conflict at the sectoral level.

Urgent problems are related not to the coexistence of confederations, but to management strategies. Privatization of the railway network and the postal service has created turbulence within the system of collective bargaining, and threatened the formerly 'stable pattern of co-operation' (Rosenboom, 1996). The small but independent DGB unions, the German Postal Union and the Union of German Railway Employees, have traditionally had very high density ratios (about 85 per cent in the postal service). Other smaller unions have not been of much importance. These unions will have to change from a form of enterprise unionism to private industry-style sectoral organizations co-ordinating more heterogeneous interests and coping with additional questions of interest representation. They will face representatives of three different employers instead of just one, a weakened ability to strike as a result of the restructuring process, and some new competition from other unions, such as the Banking, Commerce, Insurance Union (HBV), and IG Metall in the case of Telekom AG. The continuing process of deregulation and demonopolization is having a significant impact on employment relations.

Workplace representation

The dual system of labour relations combines two levels and forms of representation at sectoral/regional and enterprise/workplace level. Within the dual structure, which is characteristic of both private industry and the public sector, there are special laws for the lower level which can be traced back to the Weimar Republic in the 1920s. In the public sector, the Federal Staff Representation Act is mirrored by similar legislation covering the federal state and local/municipal levels. They follow, with some specific adjustments, the principles of the Works Constitution Act, which applies to the private sector only. The hierarchical organ- ization of public administration is mirrored by the pattern of representation at different levels (Altvater *et al.*, 1996).

Staff councils, the equivalent of works councils in private industry, are elected by all employees. Following proportional representation principles, they are composed of representatives of the three different groups of employees (i.e. *Beamte* are included). Joint elections of group representatives are possible after a majority decision of all three groups. Government departments and staff councils work together, in a spirit of mutual trust, 'for the benefit of the employees and in fulfilment of the obligatory functions of the government departments'. Staff coun- cils have statutory rights of co-determination covering a wide range of powers, from an effective veto to full informational rights in social and personnel affairs (e.g. hiring, promotion, transfers), but not economic matters. These rights are strictly defined by law and can, therefore, never be the subject of collective bar- gaining. In comparison with private industry, these 'voice mechanisms' are more restricted. There is no equivalent of private sector models of employee representa- tion on company boards, that is, the management board (*Vorstand*) and supervisory board (*Aufsichtsrat*). This strict separation avoids open conflict and stimulates co-operation at the enterprise level by participation in decision-making. As in private industry staff councils are essentially co-operative elements of labour rela- tions; they are not allowed to call a strike because of the strict 'peace obligation'. All conflicts of rights that cannot be solved by voluntary agreement between management and the staff representatives are always settled by an Arbitration Committee. Within the 'dual system' of interest representation, only unions are allowed to initiate strike action.

In contrast to some other Western European countries, patterns of co- operation continue to dominate labour relations in the public sector. This is partly due to the unique and peculiar system of legally institutionalized co-determination. Staff councils are widely recognized by all employers and managers as interest representatives and negotiation partners. Both institutions, unions and staff councils, are legally separate organizations, but informal ties between unions and staff council members are frequent, and usually closer at the local/municipal level than at the federal state level. There are no other forms of interest representation outside this dual system.

One peculiarity of German co-determination is its legalistic, representative and collective character as against the contractual, direct and individual set-up found elsewhere. This may change in the future as new and more direct forms of employee participation, like quality circles or semi-autonomous work groups, become more important with the restructuring of work organization. Public management will try to improve productivity by introducing more direct forms of participation. Empirical evidence on the diffusion and impact of direct par- ticipation for the public sector, in contrast to private industry, is scarce. However, one recent survey shows that 'the share of workplaces with direct participation was greater in services, notably public services, than in industry or construction' (EPOC, 1997).

As in private industry, the established patterns and procedures of institutionalized co-determination may no longer adequately represent changing conditions, and the relationship between direct participation and representative co-determination will have to be redefined. Because of the high degree of juridification and formalization of conventional administrative action, traditional co-determination rights of staff councils focus on individual cases and personnel issues, such as promotion. However, processes of organizational development are integral to modernization, changing the opportunities for participation and co-determination (Sperling, 1998). Within the processes of restructuring staff councils become co-managers with an altered role. Their co-operation will be, like direct participation of individual employees, indispensable for the successful implementation of reforms at different levels within the German system of labour relations.

If the overall labour relations environment and climate are of major importance in the success of public sector modernization, then conditions in Germany (the existence of a fairly co-operative system of labour relations with rather sophisticated 'voice mechanisms') seem to be more favourable than in other West European countries. The early and complete inclusion of the unions in the processes of redesigning public services could even contribute to more sustainable results. One of the open strategic questions is, of course, whether and, if so, how the established patterns of co-determination and the new, experimental forms of direct participation can fit together.

Public sector labour relations

Overview

International comparative analysis shows that there are three different modes of employment regulation in the public sector (Traxler, 1997). First, as in private industry, collective bargaining can be the sole or dominant mode of regulation (as in Belgium, Denmark, Italy or Sweden). Alternatively, employment conditions can be unilaterally defined by public authorities, with unions having only consultative rights (as in Austria, Spain or the Netherlands). Finally, a mixed pattern of collective bargaining and unilateral regulation may be established. Germany belongs to the third group as two sub-systems have developed.

The legal base for the collective bargaining system is the Collective Agreement Act of 1949, which applies not only to the private sector but also to wage earners and salaried employees in the public sector. This law guarantees free collective bargaining, that is, the right of the parties involved to negotiate pay and all other working conditions without the intervention of the state. Autonomous unions and employers' associations negotiate for wage earners and salaried employees and are able, like corporate actors in private industry, to use measures of industrial action.

The subject matter of collective bargaining is remuneration and conditions of work. Both sides negotiate two types of collective agreements. Master agreements

(*Manteltarifverträge*) are in force for several years and govern mostly non-pay issues (e.g. working hours), whilst pay agreements (*Tarifverträge*) are in force for about one year. Negotiated employment conditions apply to all employees, because of a ban on 'differentiation clauses' in favour of union members. Some benefits and conditions, such as pensions, health insurance, and maximum hours of work, are contained in legislation, thus limiting potential areas of disagreement within the collective bargaining system. There is no difference in the scope of bargaining between sub-sectors, and no distinctions are made between mandatory, voluntary or other categories of bargaining.

In contrast to the above, the Federal Civil Servants Law (*Bundesbeamtengesetz*) represents an independent legal system. *Beamte* do not have collective bargaining and strike rights. Unlike the limits on strike action covering employees engaged in 'essential services' in some countries, in Germany the strike ban covers all *Beamte* because of their collective status. Furthermore, it applies to the whole of the country, does not differ according to federal states or within local governments, and has not been changed in the recent past.

For *Beamte* there is, from a purely legal point of view, a unilateral decision-making process by the Federal Parliament (*Bundestag*). The DBB and DGB have a legally guaranteed right of formal participation, but not of collective bargaining and equal partnership. In practice this legal definition is not as restrictive as it may appear. Interest organizations and unions have ample opportunity to influence relevant decisions taken by the Federal Parliament by means of intensive lobbying. These activities are facilitated by the attitudes of members of parliament and the ministerial bureaucracy, many of whom are also *Beamte*, and sometimes reinforced by political threats to withdraw votes (Keller, 1983).

Legal distinctions which are striking at first glance do not necessarily exert a crucial influence. Looking at the results of these informal processes, one could even argue that both systems of interest representation, despite major legal differences, led to basically the same results, at least throughout the 1970s and 1980s (Keller, 1993). Pay increases and changes in working conditions for *Beamte* have been closely correlated to those for salaried employees and wage earners. In most years, the bargaining procedure has fixed the agenda for the rest of the public sector, thus resolving the potential problem of equal treatment of different groups. This is by no means an automatic sequence of events because of the existence of two legally independent sub-systems of labour relations.

This traditional sequence of pattern setting and pattern following has been subject to some recent changes because it is still easier to introduce slightly different conditions for *Beamte* unilaterally, instead of bargaining with unions whose consent may be difficult to obtain. The established mode of regulation has not changed in principle but some recent results have been different (e.g. the postponement of salary increases for some months or the reintroduction of longer working hours for *Beamte* in some federal states). These events could presage a more general shift in the future.

Different arguments about comparability between public and private sector pay have been put forward by both sides for many years. Exact comparisons are extremely difficult and the results cannot always claim to be valid (Belman and Heywood, 1996). In a long-term perspective, the public sector as a whole has held a position in the middle and has not been detached from pay movements in the rest of the economy; different studies indicate that structural or permanent under- or over-payment did not occur (Keller, 1993). The average incomes of public sector employees are, because of differences in the degree of formal education and qualification, slightly higher than those of private sector employees.

The traditional pattern has changed to a certain degree. Settlements in the public sector since the late 1980s have consistently been below the average increases in major sectors of private industry and the rate of inflation (Bispinck and WSI-Tarifarchiv, 1997). In relation to the growth of incomes in private industry, the public sector has lost in relative terms. Public employers' associations have kept arguing that in times of high and growing unemployment, the job security of public employees in general, and of *Beamte* in particular, should be taken into account. Within the public sector, increases for *Beamte* in general, or particular high-ranked groups, have sometimes been delayed for months. It is likely that these trends will continue, applied strategically by public employers because of persistent high structural unemployment and ailing public budgets.

Another frequently discussed problem is the gender issue. It is correct to argue that public employers discriminate less than their private counterparts in different segments of the labour markets because there is political pressure towards equal pay for equal work. Differences in male and female earnings are generally smaller in the public sector than in private industry and in cases of discrimination sanctions can be applied. Problems of equal opportunity have been on the political agenda since the mid-1980s and there have been some improvements. Employers at all levels have developed and tried to implement equal opportunity acts or female promotion programmes, either in legal and binding forms, or through contractual and voluntary means, in order to overcome different forms of gender segregation in the labour market (Bednarz-Braun and Bruhns, 1997). The public sector has contributed to the integration of women into the labour market, despite the fact that women are still underrepresented in senior positions and among *Beamte*, and face greater employment risks, such as limited contracts. Their participation rate is relatively unchanged at about 50 per cent in the mid-1990s. As in other countries, the public sector has been more successful than private industry in creating and implementing equal employment opportunities for men and women.

Collective bargaining structure

There are two legally separate but closely interrelated layers of labour relations, the enterprise and the sectoral or branch level. The upper layer consists of a centralized and encompassing system of collective bargaining which covers the state, federal state and all local government employers' associations on the one side, and different unions on the other. Problems about the selection or representativeness of negotiators on the union side do not exist. Strategies of pay restraint, indexation or independent pay review bodies have not been discussed. Collective bargaining is the only form of pay determination for wage earners and salaried employees. The comparatively high degree of centralization produces a non-dispersed, rather unitary wage structure and provides a high degree of internal equity. ÖTV always takes the lead and co-ordinates the demands of smaller DGB unions; thus the ÖTV is the pattern setter for the rest of the public sector, though definitely not for private industry. Wages and all other working conditions are, with few exceptions, still settled in one annual round of negotiations for all public employees at the national, federal state and local levels.

Before privatization took place, both the German Postal Union and the Union of German Railway Employees had negotiated independently but co-ordinated their bargaining activities with ÖTV. They had always copied the wage increases negotiated by ÖTV, but had developed independent strategies on more qualitative issues, such as protection against rationalization, supplementary benefits and shift work. The result of these informal processes of co-ordination had been the creation and maintenance of the most encompassing bargaining unit in the German system, despite the existence of different unions within the public sector.

This informal coalition will end after privatization. Telekom AG, favouring strategies of outsourcing, will probably be the first candidate to leave the old coalition, setting a new agenda for more flexible management strategies and for working conditions, including wages and salaries. A less centralized and more fragmented bargaining structure is the likely outcome. There will be independent collective contracts concluded between the unions and different employers for each of the three separate parts of the old postal service. The development of new patterns of employment more akin to those of private industry, and lower density ratios on both sides of the bargaining table, could create additional problems and strains. If the logic of decentralization and the delegation of authority makes sense in the German context, it refers to these privatized services.

Since the mid-1980s the issue of working time, especially weekly working hours, has become the major qualitative bargaining issue. In the public sector, it became more important only after a period of hesitation by public employers, and after the average weekly working time had been cut in engineering from 1995. The general pattern has been that a certain reduction of working time (being in the unions' interest) has been accompanied by more and further flexibilization (being favoured by employers) (Keller, 1997b). The other proposal has been for some form of voluntary early retirement, which was rejected by public employers and did not find favour among the union membership. The major reason why unions pushed hard for these reductions was their convinction that they could save existing jobs and create additional employment opportunities in times of rising unemployment.

The average working week of public sector employees was gradually reduced from 40 to 39 (April 1989), then to 38.5 hours (April 1990). Further reductions in working time (towards the 35 hour week) were intended but never agreed. The overall number of new jobs created has been difficult to estimate. The employment effects of this strategy of solidarity with the unemployed were not overwhelming; results differed significantly according to area of employment (with health, public transport, energy and water supply, local administration being above the average), but overall results were modest (Keller, 1993). Not all public employers co-operated, but instead have used cost savings for other purposes, mainly for reducing budget deficits. In formal terms, basic pay was not changed after the working time reductions of the late 1980s, but in practice it is clear that wage increases were lower.

Further reductions in working time have not been an issue. Since the mid-1990s, some public employers have even successfully tried to increase the number of working hours up to the old level of 40 hours per week, at least for *Beamte* or some sub-groups, but not for wage earners and salaried employees, whose unions flatly refused to bargain about this issue. When the topic of working time made it back to the public agenda in the new version of an alliance for work (*Bündnis für Arbeit*), the discussion was initially limited to private industry, where unions tried to bargain not only over wages but also over employment (Keller, 1997b). More recently, unions in both sectors started demanding further reductions even with some loss in real wages. These demands will be difficult to achieve for two reasons: employers' associations will resist further reductions; and union members may be unwilling to sacrifice part of their salaries. Therefore, general employment pacts are unlikely in the public sector.

Public sector labour relations have shown no clear trend towards decentralization since the mid-1980s. Wages and salaries are still settled at the national level for all employees and none of the major corporate actors has been explicitly interested in structural changes towards less regulation, and a downward shift of power and influence. In this regard, Germany fits very well into the overall international pattern:

> Countries which favour the continuation of centralized, relatively uniform pay arrangements tend to take a more monolithic view of the public sector than those that have moved to more flexible systems. Issues of mobility and internal equity . . . loom large in the arguments against flexibility, and motivation tends to be viewed from a long-term perspective linked to career management and job security.
>
> (Dell'Aringa and Murlis, 1993: 228)

There have been some recent developments, however, which may indicate gradual movement towards a more decentralized and flexible system. First, as noted above, steps towards deregulation and privatization have led to some fragmentation of the formerly unified bargaining system (Bispinck, 1995a). Second, new working time arrangements in the late 1980s had to be implemented at the local level through additional subordinate agreements; local managers and staff councils could choose between the different options of daily or weekly reductions in hours. Third, whilst the recent controversy about the erosion of sectoral collective bargaining has been focused mainly on private industry (Bispinck, 1995b), opening clauses (*Öffnungsklauseln*) favouring tendencies towards less uniformity and more decentralization have been introduced in some collective contracts at the local and regional levels. This has been the case not only in the new federal states but also in the west in areas where public ownership and private ownership overlap. In local and regional systems of mass transport in particular, employers have threatened to leave their organizations and joined private employers' associations in order to become subject to more favourable collective contracts. Outsourcing of some functions (e.g. catering, cleaning, printing) has been a related strategy used in other areas.

ÖTV had to react and, while protecting the wages of existing staff, accepted lower wages for entrants, thus creating what in other contexts have been called 'two tier wage systems'. Similar trends have been observed at airports in response to EU directives on liberalization which opened all ground services to international competition. Even some insiders have concluded that the erosion of sectoral bargaining, in at least some parts of the public sector, is more advanced than is usually assumed (Wendl, 1998). Recent experiments concerning the introduction of performance-related pay (discussed later) provide further evidence pointing in the same direction of decentralization. The introduction of new technologies and the reorganization of work may also change the established structure in the future. There are increasing demands for more flexibility and competence in the public sector as well, including longer and later opening hours of public offices, and faster and better quality services for clients, if possible at lower cost. Recent developments in the new federal states, where subordinate additional contracts have been concluded at the county and local level to save jobs, could be interpreted as additional evidence of decentralization (see p. 88).

Overall, this partial delegation of authority and competence, and the accompanying shift of centralized power and decision-making, constitute processes of trial and error in a period of gradual change. It has neither been politically motivated nor simultaneously introduced in different parts of public administration. Established institutions, like unions and staff councils, legal rules, informally agreed customs and practices, collective bargaining and other forms of interest representation, still matter. Employers' associations, in contrast to some of their counterparts in private industry, have not shown any strong interest in decentralizing the structure of collective bargaining. The emerging tendencies towards decentralization of the collective bargaining system are of a rather moderate nature; they threaten not to abolish the existing system, but rather to adjust it to changing conditions.

It is possible that a devolution of management authority, but not of collective bargaining, will take place. Individual employers and their managers may become more of a driving force in the future, although their employers' associations or the state will not strictly co-ordinate these isolated activities. This development could first arise in experiments to reform and modernize parts of the public sector rather than traditional collective bargaining issues. Trends towards individualization of pay are not very likely to happen. A widening gap between forms of interest representation in different policy areas could be one possible result. The local level, where the majority of agreements have been signed with unions, would be more heavily influenced than the federal level. It is likely that trends towards decentralization do not embrace all components of labour relations systems but some parts only, and unilateral developments are not necessarily to be expected.

Industrial disputes

Comments on patterns of industrial conflict can be brief because the public sector in Germany has never been very strike-prone (Keller, 1989, 1993). The first major strike after World War II took place in 1974 and lasted only three to four days. The second and last strike occurred in 1992. Occasionally, especially in the 1960s and 1970s, some groups of *Beamte* made use of industrial action equivalent to a strike, such as sick-ins, go-slows or work-to-rules. There were also some unofficial, but minor, strikes of salaried employees and wage earners in this period (Keller, 1983). Unofficial 'warning strikes' happen occasionally during bargaining rounds and are considered more or less routine practices, informally influenced by trade unions. Participants could face sanctions, but rarely do. In contrast to some other OECD countries (Shalev, 1992), industrial unrest did not increase in the 1980s. In times of high and continuous unemployment, increasing tax levels and losses in real wages across the economy, the whole strike issue would be difficult to sell to the public. Overall, fundamental differences of interest between employers and employees are rarely apparent.

The comparatively small number of strikes can be explained partly by the fact that all unions have the right to bargain collectively and to strike, so have no 'recognition' problem. International comparison shows that in highly centralized systems of collective bargaining relatively few strikes can be expected, with Germany fitting this pattern. Furthermore, civil servants' organizations have, with the above-mentioned very few exceptions, observed the ban on strikes. This was possible, above all, because they could defend their members' interests through political means.

The settlement of disputes

For more than twenty years after World War II, no formal mechanism of conflict resolution for collective disputes existed. The mediation agreement concluded by the autonomous social partners after the first major strike in 1974 has been used several times, preventing more frequent strikes. In contrast to this voluntary mediation procedure, any arbitration arrangements would be illegal and incompatible with the principle of free collective bargaining. Formal or informal state interference is unknown. In other words, the results of mediation procedures are not automatically binding on the parties; instead, they require their explicit consent if they are to become valid. Because of the high degree of centralization of the bargaining system, there is only one mediation agreement for the whole public sector.

There has never been an intensive public debate about different forms and mechanisms of impasse procedures. The mediation services have not become highly professionalized. Within a fairly legalistic system, including a functional division of special labour jurisdiction, individual and collective conflicts over the interpretation of existing contracts are solved not by strike action but only by decisions of the courts. Conflicts over new contracts are controlled by collective bargaining mechanisms. Grievance procedures in collective agreements are thus unnecessary.

Relations between the parties

The system of interest representation has been fairly stable; that is, so far, there have been no new unions or mergers, and no increase in levels of industrial unrest. In the mid-1990s, the coverage rate of the various systems regulating employment conditions was 100 per cent (Kohaut and Bellmann, 1997). Thus decollectivization is not an issue. The most surprising recent event was that an old bargaining coalition, which had been dissolved in the late 1970s, was revived in the early 1990s. The largest public sector union, the DGB-affiliated ÖTV, and the independent DAG managed to end their long-running differences which had been caused by their conflicting principles of organization; DAG represented the comparatively narrow interests of salaried employees, whereas the industrial union ÖTV had to represent a much broader range. The basic reason for this unexpected change was that, to exert some influence, both organizations had to co-operate at the European level; that is, within the European Public Service Union (EPSU), one of fourteen organizations at the sectoral level (Keller and Henneberger, 1998). The need to co-operate at the supranational level terminated the long-lasting conflict at the national level and led to a renewal of their coalition bargaining. This reshuffle will have significant implications for the smaller unions and all interest associations, especially the DBB, the umbrella association of *Beamte*. It can be argued that the relationship between DGB-affiliated unions and DBB organizations will become more pragmatic and less conflictual because of the common problem of mutual survival, especially in the European context. Despite historical and ideological differences, forms of intensified co-operation are likely.

As consumers and taxpayers, citizens are interested not only in the development of costs and constraints on public expenditure, but also in better quality and more responsive welfare services. Traditionally, different consumer interests have been widely neglected in the public sector. Since the late 1980s, the ÖTV has taken the lead in discussions about the processes of public sector modernization instead of purely defending the *status quo*. ÖTV has tried to form a broader strategic alliance with the interests of service users to experiment with new strategies of co-management, and to improve the quality and productivity of services, instead of simply demanding new resources from taxpayers.

The motivation behind the ÖTV initiative has been to strengthen the organization, protect its members' interests and recruit new members (Wulf-Mathies, 1991–4). Its involvement in the processes of modernization was designed to influence – or even shape – basic managerial decisions about restructuring instead of having such strategies developed by management alone, and merely demanding new resources (Simon, 1998a, b). The local/municipal level, not the federal state level, was supposed to be of primary importance, because issues of reform were different, financial constraints were more severe, and that level was the most important for overall employment. Some experimental projects of modernization have been carried out, but they have not been closely co-ordinated and they achieved differing degrees of success (Kißler *et al.*, 1993).

The basic problem of the whole campaign 'Shaping the future through public services', launched at the end of the 1980s, but interrupted by the unexpected process of unification, has been twofold: neither the general public, nor the majority of ordinary union members, have been really involved. The triangle of interests between service users, staff and the union is less integrated than is often assumed. Democratization has not been the focal point of the campaign, and it is clear that its results could be risky for the union as an organization because it will produce winners and losers among the membership; there will be few, if any, new jobs and it is likely that not all existing jobs will be preserved.

Opinion is divided about these initiatives. Union officials consider the new policies a success in turning the ÖTV into a 'learning organization' and in the development of new forms of active co-operation and strategic co-management (Dickhausen, 1995). A second phase of the (now more decentralized) campaign of modernization was started by the end of 1995. A sympathetic foreign observer disagrees:

> ÖTV's first round of reforms generated a long series of largely irrelevant reports, but otherwise left only negative traces on the organization itself ... ÖTV's financial crisis has forced the union to attempt internal reform once again, and this time, top union officials are talking about strengthening the intermediate level of the union and delegating new duties to it at the expense of the union headquarters. This switch in strategy is a clear reaction to the failure of the first reform.
>
> (Silvia, 1993: 44)

The idea of performance-related pay, or merit-related bonuses, is not entirely new; the Committee of Inquiry into the Civil Service proposed the introduction of PRP in its final report in the early 1970s, but little happened during the following two decades. In the early 1990s, employers and managers started pushing harder than ever before to introduce different mechanisms of performance-related components in public employees' wages and salaries. They are supposed to supplement, but not replace, the traditional system of strict seniority and job-rank principles of remuneration.

Public employers want to increase organizational performance by systems of individual bonuses, designed to motivate employees to improve their individual performance and prevent different forms of shirking. Bonuses have not yet been introduced on a very wide scale; new mechanisms for the introduction of market-type incentives complementing the old forms of collective incentives are thought to be necessary. The crucial question is who has the power to define and implement such measures?

The question of how to measure output or efficiency objectively is a highly controversial issue (Naschold and Pröhl, 1994, 1995). Indicators will have to be defined not only for different sub-sectors but also for a huge number of hetero-geneous jobs (Tondorf, 1996; Reichert *et al.*, 1995). The basic problem of finding a new balance between winners and losers is also fairly difficult to resolve. Imple-mentation will most likely have the character of a zero sum game; because of severe budgetary constraints, there will be no additional funds for distribution, so only a limited number of employees will have the opportunity to earn more.

After a period of controversial discussion among the membership, the ÖTV changed its official position on this issue. In 1994, ÖTV declared its general readiness to co-operate despite the difficulties in coping with the situation. The potential for unilateral implementation by management is very limited by the specific circumstances of the system of co-determination in the public sector (Tondorf, 1997a). Public managers will not be able, and employers' organizations will probably not even try, to achieve their goals without the explicit general consent of the unions.

The continuing negotiations over procedures of implementation for this kind of merit pay have not led to any definite results. In early 1997, a framework agree-ment on the principles of granting performance-related bonuses and premiums was signed by a coalition of unions led by ÖTV and the Federation of Local Employers Associations. Payments can be agreed only on the basis of additional regional or local contracts (Tondorf, 1997b). So far, there are very few such contracts, and the existing contracts have not been implemented yet. The intro-duction of negotiated change and conflict avoidance will be a protracted process of trial and error. Further risks associated with these new forms of productivity agreements include the following: employees may compete for individual bonuses instead of co-operating; employees' representatives would become co-managers even more than they already are; the role and behaviour of managers would have to be transformed; and resources, especially the time needed for negotiation and administration, could be very costly and used more efficiently elsewhere. Promotion systems, which could have been a possible substitute for PRP, have been running out of steam for fiscal reasons. The rather controversial discus-sion lacks a coherent theoretical base and seems to overestimate the significance and potential of PRP in comparison with general conditions and organization of work.

Conclusion

Coping with unification

Unification in October 1990, less than a year after the collapse of the Berlin wall, meant that an independent public sector had to be constructed in the new federal states within a very short period of time. The local/municipal level and the fed-eral states that had been abolished in the early 1950s by the German Democratic Republic (GDR) had to be reorganized from scratch and needed the financial capacity to fulfil their tasks. In the first years after unification, experienced public employees from the west worked in the east for limited periods of time to support the process of reconstruction (Henneberger and Keller, 1992).

Co-operation with the old unions, the transmission belts of the communist regime, proved to be impossible; the peak association, the Free German Union Confederation (FDGB), and its member unions had completely lost their credibility and ceased to exist in 1990. Like their counterparts in private industry, all West German public sector unions organized a substantial transfer of financial and human resources and expanded their organizational domains into the east at a very early stage. Some DGB-affiliated organizations were more successful than others, e.g. DAG and DBB. They even urged public employers to launch associations of their own in order to ensure a reliable partner for collective bargaining and other forms of co-operation. Overall, patterns of organization on both sides copied exactly the structure of their well established counterparts in the west – with all the advantages and disadvantages this complete transfer of organizations proved to have.

As in the case of unions, the organizational pattern in the west was copied at the regional and the federal state levels. The density ratio of employers at the local and federal state levels, in clear contrast to private industry, is very close to 100 per cent. If problems were to occur because of diverging interests they would probably be of more relevance to the Federation of Local Government Employers Associations and not for its new regional members (Rosdücher, 1994).

After some initial success in recruiting new members and increasing density ratios, the unions have been facing serious organizational difficulties; they have lost many of their members since 1992 (see Table 3.3). The expectations of the new members were unrealistically high; unions could not save jobs within the process of transformation. Furthermore, unions' options to fight unemployment are rather limited. The job losses have started a process of gradual erosion of the unions' power, undermined their precarious financial situation and increased

Table 3.4 Development of employment in the public sector (new federal states)

Year	BODS (000)	BODO (000)	DLBODO versus previous year (%)	DLBODO 1991–96 (%)
				−23.0
1991	1,780.5	1,429.1		
1992	1,685.0	1,385.0	−9.54	
1993	1,534.9	1,252.9	−2.40	
1994	1,282.3	1,186.9	−5.27	
1995	1,138.9	1,138.6	−4.07	
1996	1,102.2	1,101.1	−3.29	

Source: Statistisches Bundesamt; own calculations (for 1996 preliminary results).

Notes: *BODS* overall figures of employment in the public sector (including soldiers). *BODO* overall figures of employment in the public sector (including soldiers, excluding railways/Bundes-/Reichsbahn and postal service, excluding *Beamte* of Deutsche Post AG, Postband AG, Telekom AG. *DLBODO* yearly rates of change.

their annual deficits because the expenses of newly hired personnel and different services for individual members are much greater than the dues paid by a shrinking number of members.

One significant difference between the two parts of the country is that the new federal states and their local/municipal counterparts have been reluctant to adopt and implement the special status of *Beamte*. There are comparatively few exceptions within the 'core' roles (the police and the state and federal state ministries are the major examples). Public authorities continue to employ the vast majority of their employees (teachers, among others) as salaried employees, because they want to gain additional numerical flexibility. It is not likely that this strategy will alter in the future. Despite frequent public and political intervention, the DBB has been unable to change the situation in its favour (DBB, 1995), and towards the end of the 1990s only 16 per cent of public employees had *Beamte* status, compared with 44 per cent in the west (IWD, 1998).

The new system of collective bargaining in the east has been more stable in the public sector than in private industry. The coverage rate is similar to that in the west but, in contrast to private industry, very high. There are joint negotiations for both parts of the public sector, despite continuing differences in pay and working conditions. By the end of 1997, wages and salaries in the public sector in the east had reached 85 per cent of the level in the west, working hours were longer (40 compared with 38.5 per week), and some benefits (like Christmas or holiday bonuses) were lower than in the west (Bispinck and WSI, 1998). The overall direction of these developments is in line with general trends in private industry. One continuing problem is that, despite large increases, wages are still considerably lower in the east, and the process of equalization has slowed down after major initial increases. It will clearly take much longer than originally expected to eliminate differences in wages and working conditions.

The German Democratic Republic had employed about 2.2 million people (including the police and the secret service) in what could be called the equivalent of the 'public sector'. This rather high figure had to be reduced considerably. It is fairly obvious that job losses have taken place for structural reasons as well as political considerations. Political affiliation with the old communist regime was grounds for dismissal and, overall, dismissals were highest in 1991 and 1992 (Henneberger and Keller, 1992).

One major problem for the foreseeable future will be that the public sector in the east is still considered by outside observers (IWD, 1998) to be overstaffed by comparison with western standards. Criticism of staffing levels is focused especially on local and municipal services, including kindergartens, day centres and parts of the health service. Nevertheless, some core parts of local government are understaffed and attempts to reallocate personnel have proved difficult to implement. Furthermore, training measures continue to be necessary at all levels of public administration.

Recently, new collective contracts have created the opportunity to bargain not only over wages but also over employment. The most prominent example of this job-conserving bargaining policy is at Volkswagen, which has been copied elsewhere. The framework agreement in the public sector in the east signed in 1994 was also inspired by the idea of saving jobs. Working hours and corresponding salaries can be cut for either some or all employees (from the regular forty down to thirty-two hours per week with either partial wage compensation or none); otherwise, conventional measures like lay-offs would be used. The centralized framework agreement on the solidaristic 'social distribution of working time' is not like other collective contracts of a binding nature. It needs as a basic prerequisite an opening clause in the National Master Agreement for Salaried Employees. It has to be implemented at the county and local/municipal levels by additional subordinate agreements (Grafe, 1995).

The empirical evidence is not yet clear. The overall number of voluntary, additional agreements at the county and local/municipal level has been rather low; optional agreements for teachers in some of the new federal states are the most prominent example. Others have been concluded for employees in local administration (Rosdücher, 1995; Tondorf, 1995b). Employees in kindergartens, in particular, and in education, in general, are the most frequent examples (Haller and Shea, 1997). These examples seem to indicate that the experiment of conserving employment, and of 'regulated flexibility of the bargaining system', will be used only in a minority of cases and will therefore be of limited significance. These new options do not create a general new trend in bargaining policy (Rosdücher, 1997).

Future challenges

The title of this chapter indicates several trends that were expected to undermine the stability of employment relations in the public sector. Strategies of change and modernization have been initiated, but the changes have been slow and uneven. Unification happened unexpectedly without, however, revolutionizing the public sector, but delaying the processes of transformation. The process of Europeanization has started to have some long-term impact at least on some parts of the public sector, but less than in private industry (Henneberger and Keller, 1997). The tentative conclusion is that changes have occurred without being far-reaching. Key reasons for the rather slow pace of change include the high degree of juridification, the federal structure of the state with a clear division of power, and the strong impact of the established, traditional structure.

What will public sector employment relations be like in a decade or so? Incremental transformation will probably happen more frequently than in the past, but it will not be very rapid. The most likely scenario includes a high degree of continuity and the evolution of a system which in at least some of its major components (not necessarily its institutional settings) is more decentralized than at present. However, it will still be more centralized than that of private industry, probably not very fragmented or dispersed in contrast to some parts of private industry, but more flexible in quantitative as well as qualitative terms. The privatized parts of the former public sector will be governed by principles derived from private industry.

References

Alemann, U.von. and Schmid, J. (eds) (1998) *Die Gewerkschaft ÖTV. Reformen im Dickicht gewerkschaftlicher Organisationspolitik*, Baden-Baden.

Altvater, L., Bacher, E., Hörter, G., Sabottig, G., Schneider, W. and Vohs, G. (1996) *BPersVG. Bundespersonalvertretungsgesetz mit Wahlordnung und ergänzenden Vorschriften. Kommentar für die Praxis*, third edition, Cologne.

Beaumont, P. (1996) 'Public sector industrial relations in Europe', in D. Belman, M. Gunderson and D. Hyatt (eds) *Public Sector Employment in a Time of Transition*, Madison WI.

Beaumont, P. B. and Harris, R. (1998) 'Trends in public sector union membership', *European Industrial Relations Review* 293: 21–3.

Bednarz-Braun, I. and Bruhns, K. (1997) *Personalpolitik und Frauenförderung im öffentlichen Dienst. Gleichberechtigungsgesetze zwischen Anspruch und Alltag*, Munich.

Belman, D. and Heywood, J. (1996) 'The structure of compensation in the public sector', in D. Belman, M. Gunderson and D. Hyatt (eds) *Public Sector Employment in a Time of Transition*, Madison WI.

Beus, H.-B. (1998) 'Public management auf Bundesebene', in W. Damkowski and C. Precht (eds) *Moderne Verwaltung in Deutschland. Public Management in der Praxis*, Stuttgart.

Bispinck, R. (1995a) 'Stabil oder fragil? Die bundesdeutschen Arbeitsbeziehungen im Umbruch', in M. Mesch (ed.) *Sozialpartnerschaft. Arbeitsbeziehungen in Europa*, Vienna.

Bispinck, R. (ed.) (1995b) *Tarifpolitik der Zukunft. Was wird aus dem Flächentarifvertrag?* Hamburg.

Bispinck, R. and WSI-Tarifarchiv (1996) 'Vom Lohnstreik zum "Bündnis für Arbeit". Tarifpolitik im Umbruch – Eine Bilanz des Jahres 1995', *WSI-Mitteilungen* 49: 141–65.

Bispinck, R. and WSI-Tarifarchiv (1998) *WSI-Tarifhandbuch 1998*, Cologne.

Blanke, T. (1998) *Verwaltungsmodernisierung. Direktionsrecht des Arbeitgebers, Mitwirkungsrechte des Personalrats und Tarifautonomie*, Baden-Baden.

Bogumil, J. and Kißler, L. (1998) 'Verwaltungsmodernisierung auf dem Prüfstand der Partizipationspraxis. Erfahrungen mit Beschäftigtenbeteiligung in den Kommunalverwaltungen Hagen, Saarbrücken und Wuppertal', *WSI-Mitteilungen* 51: 54–60.

Bogumil, J. and Kißler, L. (eds) (1997) *Verwaltungsmodernisierung und lokale Demokratie. Risiken und Chancen eines Neuen Steuerungsmodells für die lokale Demokratie*, Baden-Baden.

Bös, D. (1998) 'Theoretical perspectives on privatization: some outstanding issues', in D. Parker (ed.) *Privatization in the European Union: Theory and Policy Perspectives*, London and New York.

Brandes, W. and Buttler, F. (1990) *Der Staat als Arbeitgeber. Daten und Analysen zum öffentlichen Dienst in der Bundesrepublik*, Frankfurt and New York.

Breidenstein, W. (1996) 'Personal im öffentichen Dienst am 30 Juni 1994', *Wirtschaft und Statistik*, 3: 181–6.

Budäus, D. (1994) *Public Management. Konzepte und Verfahren zur Modernisierung öffentlicher Verwaltungen*, Berlin.

Casey, B., Dragendorf, R., Heering, W. and John, G. (1989) 'Temporary employment in Great Britain and the Federal Republic of Germany: an overview', *International Labour Review*, 128: 449–66.

Damkowski, W. and Precht, C. (1995) *Public Management. Neue Steuerungsmodelle für den öffentlichen Sektor*, Stuttgart and Berlin.

Damkowski, W. and Precht, C. (1998) *Moderne Verwaltung in Deutschland. Public Management in der Praxis*, Stuttgart.

Dell'Aringa, C. (1997) 'Pay determination in the public service: an international comparison', Milan. Università Cattolica del Sacro Cuore.

Dell'Aringa, C. and Murlis, H. (1993) 'Agenda for the future public sector pay policies in the 1990s', in OECD *Pay Flexibility in the Public Sector*, Paris.

DBB (1995) *Bundesvertretertag 1995. Geschäftsbericht der Bundesleitung*, Bonn.

Dickhausen, G. (1995) ' "Gewerkschaftsreform und Zukunftsgestaltung". Die Erfahrungen der ÖTV', in U.von. Alemann and J. Schmid (eds) *Die Organisation der Reform. Ein Werkstattbericht zum ÖTV-Projekt*, Polis. Arbeitspapiere aus der FernUniversität Hagen 33.

DiPrete, T. (1989) *The Bureaucratic Labor Market: The Case of the Federal Civil Service*, New York.

DIW (1998) 'Öffentlicher Dienst. Starker Personalabbau trotz moderater Tarifanhebungen. Entwicklungstendenzen in den neunziger Jahren', *DIW-Wochenbericht* 5: 87–97.

Eichhorn, P. and von Loesch, A. (1989) 'Privatisierung', in K. Chmielewicz and P. Eichhorn (eds) *Handwörterbuch der öffentlichen Betriebswirtschaft*, Stuttgart.

EPOC Research Group (1997) *New Forms of Work Organization: Can Europe Realize its Potential? Results of a Survey of Direct Employee Participation in Europe*, Dublin.

Esser, J. (1998) 'Privatisation in Germany: symbolism in the social market economy?' in D. Parker (ed.) *Privatisation in the European Union: Theory and Policy Perspectives*, London and New York.

Färber, G. (1996) 'Projektion der Personalausgaben im öffentlichen Dienst. Empfehlungen und Konsequenzen', in R. Görner (ed.) *Beamtenversorgung. Daten, Fakten, Perspektiven*, Düsseldorf.

Färber, G. (1997) 'Zur Entwicklung der Personal- und Versorgungsausgaben im öffentlichen Dienst', *WSI-Mitteilungen* 50: 426–38.

Grafe, F. (1995) 'Die Umsetzung des §15c BAT–O im Land Brandenburg', *Arbeit und Arbeitsrecht* 50: 190–3.

Haller, R. and Shea, D. (1997) 'Arbeitsrechtliche Probleme beim Lehrer–Personalkonzept', *Arbeit und Arbeitsrecht* 52: 47–50.

Hassel, A. (1997) 'Mitbestimmung und industrielle Beziehungen in Behörden der Europäischen Union', in O. Jacobi and B. Keller (eds) *Arbeitsbeziehungen im öffentlichen Dienst Europas. Interessenvertretung und Mitbestimmung in der EU*, Berlin.

Hebdon, R. (1996) 'Public sector dispute resolution in transition', in D. Belman, M. Gunderson and D. Hyatt (eds) *Public Sector Employment in a Time of Transition*, Madison WI.

Henneberger, F. (1997) *Arbeitsmärkte und Beschäftigung im öffentlichen Dienst. Eine theoretische und empirische Analyse für die Bundesrepublik Deutschland*, Bern and Stuttgart.

Henneberger, F. and Keller, B. (1992) 'Der öffentliche Dienst in den neuen Bundesländern. Beschäftigung, Interessenverbände und Tarifpolitik im Übergang', in V. Eichener, Kleinfeld, R., Pollack, D., Schmid, J., Schubert, K. and Voelzkow, H. (eds) *Organisierte Interessen in Ostdeutschland*, Marburg.

Henneberger, F. and Keller, B. (1997) 'Freizügigkeitsregelungen und Arbeitskräftemobilität im öffentlichen Dienst', in O. Jacobi and B. Keller (eds) *Arbeitsbeziehungen im öffentlichen Dienst Europas. Interessenvertretung und Mitbestimmung in der EU*, Berlin.

ILO (1997) *World Labour Report 1998–98: Industrial Relations, Democracy and Social Stability*, Geneva.

IWD (1998) 'Ostdeutschland. Fette Zeiten sind vorbei', *Informationsdienst des Instituts der deutschen Wirtschaft* 24: 6–7.

Jacobi, O., Keller, B. and Müller-Jentsch, W. (1998) 'Germany: facing new challenges', in A. Ferner and R. Hyman (eds) *Industrial Relations in the New Europe*, second edition, Oxford: Blackwell.

Jann, W. (1998) 'Neues Steuerungsmodell', in B. Blanke, St von Bandemer, F. Nullmeier and G. Wewer (eds) *Handbuch zur Verwaltungsreform*, Opladen.

Keller, B. (1983) *Arbeitsbeziehungen im öffentlichen Dienst. Tarifpolitik der Gewerkschaften und Interessenpolitik der Beamtenverbände*, Frankfurt and New York.

Keller, B. (1989) 'Co-operation and conflict in public sector labour relations: the Federal Republic of Germany', in A. Gladstone, Lansbury, R., Stieber, J., Treu, T. and Weiss, M. (eds) *Current Issues in Labour Relations: An International Perspective*, Berlin and New York.

Keller, B. (1993) *Arbeitspolitik des öffentlichen Sektors*, Baden-Baden.

Keller, B. (1997a) 'Public sector labour markets and labour relations in Norway: the exception from the European rule', in J. Dolvik and A. Steen (eds) *Making Solidarity Work? The Norwegian Labour Market Model in Transition*, Oslo and Stockholm.

Keller, B. (1997b) *Einführung in die Arbeitspolitik. Arbeitsbeziehungen und Arbeitsmarkt in sozialwissenschaftlicher Perspektive*, fifth edition, Munich and Vienna.

Keller, B. and Henneberger, F. (1998) 'Privatwirtschaft und öffentlicher Dienst. Parallelen und Differenzen in den Arbeitspolitiken', in W. Müller-Jentsch (ed.) *Konfliktpartnerschaft. Akteure und Institutionen der industriellen Beziehungen*, third edition, Munich and Mering.

Kißler, L., Bogumil, J. and Wiechmann, E. (eds) (1993) *Anders verwalten. Praxis und Perspektiven kommunaler Gestaltungsprojekte*, Marburg.

KGSt (1993) *Das neue Steuerungsmodell. Begründungen, Konturen, Umsetzungen*, Cologne.

Kohaut, S. and Bellmann, L. (1997) 'Betriebliche Determinanten der Tarifbindung. Eine empirische Analyse auf der Basis des IAB-Betriebspanels 1995', *Industrielle Beziehungen* 4: 317–34.

Lane, J-E. (1995) *The Public Sector: Concepts, Models and Approaches*, second edition, London.

Marsden, D. (1993) 'Reforming public sector pay', in OECD (ed.) *Pay Flexibility in the Public Sector*, Paris.

Martin, B. (1993) *In the Public Interest? Privatisation and Public Sector Reform*, London.

Merten, D. (1994) 'Das Recht des öffentlichen Dienstes in Deutschland', in S. Magiera and H. Siedentopf (eds) *Das Recht des öffentlichen Dienstes in den Mitgliedstaaten der Europäischen Gemeinschaft*, Berlin.

Mosley, H. and Schmid, G. (1992) 'Public services and competitiveness', Discussion Paper FS I 92–5, Berlin: Wissenschaftszentrum Berlin für Sozialforschung.

Naschold, F. and Arnkil, R. (1997) 'Modernization of the labour market organization: Scandinavian and Anglo-Saxon experiences in an international benchmarking perspective', in J. Dolvik and A. Steen (eds) *Making Solidarity Work? The Norwegian Labour Market Model in Transition*, Oslo and Stockholm.

Naschold, F. and Pröhl, M. (eds) (1994) *Produktivität öffentlicher Dienstleistungen 1. Dokumentation eines wissenschaftlichen Diskurses zum Produktivitätsbegriff*, Gütersloh.

Naschold, F. and Pröhl, M. (eds) (1995) *Produktivität öffentlicher Dienstleistungen 2. Dokumentation zum Symposium*, Gütersloh.

Naschold, F., Oppen, M. and Wegener, A. (eds) (1997) *Innovative Kommunen. Internationale Trends und deutsche Erfahrungen*, Stuttgart.

OECD (1990) *Public Management Developments: Survey 1990*, Paris.

OECD (1993) *Public Management Developments: Survey 1993*, Paris.

OECD (1997) *Trends in Public Sector Pay in OECD Countries*, Paris.

Oppen, M. and Wegener, A. (1997) 'Restrukurierung der kommunalen Dienstleistungs-produktion. Innovationsfähigkeit deutscher Kommunen in internationaler Perspektive', in Wissenschaftszentrum Berlin *Jahrbuch 1997*, Berlin.

Oppen, M., Naschold, F. and Wegener, A. (1997) 'Personal und Arbeitsorganisation im Modernisierungsprozeß', in F. Naschold, M. Oppen and A. Wegener (eds) *Innovative Kommunen. Internationale Trends und deutsche Erfahrungen*, Stuttgart.

ÖTV (1997) *Das Neue Steuerungsmodell der Kommunalen Gemeinschaftsstelle. Position der Gewerkschaft ÖTV*, Stuttgart.

Reichert, J., Stöbe, S. and Wohlfahrt, N. (1995) *Leistungsanreizsysteme im öffentlichen Dienst. Stand und Perspektiven der Einführung von Motivations- und Leistungsanreizen in der Kommunalverwaltung*, Düsseldorf.

Rosdücher, J. (1994) 'Kommunale Arbeitgeberverbände in den neuen Bundesländern', *Zeitschrift für öffentliche und gemeinwirtschaftliche Unternehmen* 17: 414–29.

Rosdücher, J. (1995) 'Beschäftigungssicherung im öffentlichen Dienst der neuen Bundesländer. Tarifliche Öffnungsklauseln und ihre Folgen', *WSI-Mitteilungen* 48: 590–7.

Rosdücher, J. (1997) *Arbeitsplatzsicherheit durch Tarifvertrag. Strategien – Konzepte – Vereinbarungen*, Munich and Mering.

Rosenboom, J. (1996) 'Der Wandel der Arbeitsbeziehungen im Bereich der Deutschen Bundespost/DBP). Eine Analyse der Postreform I und II dargestellt anhand der DeutschenTelekom AG, Deutschen Post AG und Deutschen Postbank AG', Verwaltungswissenschaftliche Diplomarbeit, Konstanz.

Rossmann, B. (1997) 'Leistungsmessung und Erfolgsmaßstäbe im öffentlichen Sektor', *Wirtschaft und Gesellschaft* 23: 171–91.

Shalev, M. (1992) 'The resurgence of labour quiescence', in M. Regini (ed.) *The Future of Labour Movements*, London.

Siedentopf, H. (1997) 'Der öffentliche Dienst in Europa. Grundsätze und Gefährdungen', in R. Morsey, H. Quaritsch and H. Siedentopf (eds) *Staat, Politik, Verwaltung in Europa*, Berlin.

Silvia, S. (1993) ' "Holding the shop together": old and new challenges to the German system of industrial relations in the mid-1990s', Berliner Arbeitshefte und Berichte zur sozialwissenschaftlichen Forschung 83, Berlin.

Simon, N. (1998a) 'Die Initiative "Zukunft durch öffentliche Dienste" heute. Erfahrungen und Erfolge', in U.von. Alemann and J. Schmid (eds) *Die Gewerkschaft ÖTV. Reformen im Dickicht gewerkschaftlicher Organisationspolitik*, Baden-Baden.

Simon, N. (1998b) 'Zur Reform des öffentlichen Diensts aus Sicht der Gewerkschaft ÖTV', in W. Damkowski and C. Precht (eds) *Moderne Verwaltung in Deutschland. Public Management in der Praxis*, Stuttgart

Sperling, H. J. (1998) *Verwaltungsmodernisierung und Partizipation. Konzepte und Erfahrungen der Kommunalverwaltungen*, Trendreport Partizipation und Organisation III, Bochum.

Statistisches Bundesamt (1996) 'Fachserie 14. Finanzen und Steuern, Reihe 6. Personal des öffentlichen Dienstes', Stuttgart.

Streeck, W. and Visser, J. (1997) 'The rise of the conglomerate union', *European Journal of Industrial Relations* 3: 305–32.

Studienkommission für die Reform des öffentlichen Dieustrechts (ed.) (1973) *Bericht der Kommission und elf Anlagenbände*, Baden-Baden.

Tondorf, K. (1995a) *Leistungszulage als Reforminstrument? Neue Lohnpolitik zwischen Sparzwang und Modernisierung*, Berlin.

Tondorf, K. (1995b) 'Beschäftigungssicherung in ostdeutschen Kommunalverwaltungen. Probleme einer neuen Tarifpolitik im öffentlichen Dienst', *Industrielle Beziehungen* 2: 180–202.

Tondorf, K. (1996) 'Leistungszulagen im öffentlichen Dienst – ein Instrument gegen den Strukturkonservatismus', *WSI-Mitteilungen* 49: 182–9.

Tondorf, K. (1997a) *Leistung und Entgelt im öffentlichen Dienst. Rechtliche Grundlagen und Handlungsmöglichkeiten*, Cologne.

Tondorf, K. (1997b) 'Leistungspolitik und Leistungsbezahlung im öffentlichen Dienst', *WSI-Mitteilungen* 50: 241–7.

Traxler, F. (1996) 'Collective bargaining and industrial change: a case of disorganization? A comparative analysis of eighteen OECD countries', *European Sociological Review* 12: 271–87.

Traxler, F. (1997) '*The State in Industrial Relations: A Cross-national Analysis*', Ms, University of Vienna.

Treu, T. (ed.) (1987) *Public Service Labour Relations: Recent Trends and Future Prospects: A Comparative Study of Seven Industrialised Market Economy Countries*, Geneva.

Treu, T. (1997) 'Human resource policy and industrial relations: the Italian experience', in C. Heidack (ed.) *Arbeitsstrukturen im Umbruch. Festschrift für Prof. Dr Dr.h.c. Friedrich Fürstenberg*, second edition, Munich and Mering.

Weiss, M. (1995) *Labour Law and Industrial Relations in Germany*, second edition, Deventer and Boston MA.

Wendl, M. (1998) 'Konkurrenz erzwingt Absenkung. Die Erosion der Flächentarifverträge des öffentlichen Dienstes am Beispiel des Personennahverkehrs', in O. König, Stamm, S. and Wendl, M. (eds) *Erosion oder Erneuerung? Krise und Reform des Flächentarifvertrags*, Hamburg.

Wise, L. (1996) 'Internal labour markets', in H. Bekke, Perry, J. and Toonen, A. (eds) *Civil Service Systems in Comparative Perspective*, Bloomington IN.

Wulf-Mathies, M. (ed.) (1991–94) *Zukunft durch öffentliche Dienste*, seven vols, Cologne.

4 Italy

A case of co-ordinated decentralization[1]

Lorenzo Bordogna, Carlo Dell'Aringa and Giuseppe Della Rocca

As in several European countries, employment relations in the Italian public sector still exhibit distinctive characteristics in comparison with those of the private sector of the economy; for example, their greater degree of juridification, and their marked dependence on the administrative structure of the state. But these differences have been decreasing; since the end of the 1960s, there has been a gradual and partial shift towards greater similarity with the private sector. Employment relations are now regulated by a set of laws that were often described as the 'privatization' of public employment when they were approved in 1993, thus indicating the meaning and direction of the transformation that the parliament wanted to impose on employment and labour relations in the sector.[2]

As in other countries, the reasons for the differentiaton between the two sectors was originally connected with the activities traditionally attributed to the public administration; that is, internal order, defence of the external boundaries of the country, justice and taxation. These activities arose from a conception of the state as the representative of the general interests of the nation, including the interests of employees. This led to an idea of the relationship between employer and employees that ruled out any possibility of opposition between them, leading to the two essential features of employment and labour relations in the sector: first, the denial of collective bargaining rights, in favour of unilateral regulation of employment conditions through laws or administrative measures, and, second, in compensation for this deprivation, a special employment status, consisting of various substantive and procedural prerogatives (Rusciano, 1978). The most important concerned employment security, but other distinctive conditions focused on aspects of the internal labour market, especially recruitment, the job classification system, vertical and horizontal mobility, careers, and compensation schemes. Thus the boundaries between private and public sector employment were clearly demarcated, on the basis of special legislation and a distinctive employment status.

Since the end of the 1960s, this clear-cut differentiation between the system of public and private sector employment relations has been reduced. This arose partly because of the great increase in state activities and functions outside the original ones, especially in the education and health sectors. For example, the Ministry of Education work force (mainly schoolteachers) increased from 259,000 in 1950 to 377,000 in 1959 and 944,000 in 1975. After a partial recognition of collective bargaining rights sector by sector, starting in 1969 with the public hospitals' employees and spreading through the 1970s to other sectors, two steps were crucial in this process: the framework law on public employment (*legge quadro sul pubblico impiego* No. 93/1983), and, ten years later, the group of laws on the so-called 'privatization of public employment'.

The 1983 law extended collective bargaining to most of the public service sector, precisely defining the structure and scope of bargaining (including compensation, working-time, and the organization of work), and the bargaining agents and procedures. It still preserved the unilateral regulation of several aspects of the employment relationship, and required that agreements had to be converted into a decree of the President of the Republic in order to be effective and binding.[3] The extension of collective bargaining rights, however, occurred without abolishing the special status of public employment. Thus it was not a substitute for the special prerogatives linked to that status, but an addition to them, giving rise to what has been called a regime of 'double guarantee', or of 'pluralism without market', unique in Europe (Rusciano, 1990; Giugni, 1992; Bordogna, 1994). This regime inevitably led to serious problems; notably, uncontrolled wage claims and leapfrogging settlements, union fragmentation and frequent conflict, which soon became unacceptable for the entire industrial relations system (Cella, 1991), as well as for the needs of public expenditure control.

A more marked shift in employment relations towards private sector models was initiated by the second set of regulations, which, under the pressures of the 1992 financial crisis, and the need to meet the Maastricht criteria for European monetary union, sought a wider reform of the organizational principles of public administration as a whole. On one hand, the reforms did not follow the path of transferring *tout court* components of the administration from the private to the public sector, as in the British experience (Ferner, 1994; Winchester and Bach, 1995), and only very partially tried to open public services to forms of internal competition, mainly in the health sector. On the other hand, the reforms attempted to modify profoundly the system of constraints and opportunities, and incentives and controls that shape employment relations in the sector. They promoted a logic of behaviour on the part of the actors, and a type of governance of labour transactions, significantly closer to those prevailing in the private sector of the economy (Bordogna, 1996, 1998a).

Definition of the public service sector

As in other countries, the definition of the Italian public sector is not unequivocal in the literature, with variations according to the analytical point of view adopted. Economists and public policy scholars refer generally to comprehensive aggregates, including all the activities financed with public money or carried out by organizations managed by personnel appointed by central or local governments (Rose, 1985). In the Italian case, this would include the employees of the state-owned companies (*partecipazioni statali*, e.g. Iri, Eni; public utilities such as Enel and Telecom; and part of the banking system) and those of the municipal companies (*aziende municipalizzate*, e.g. local transport, garbage collection, and some local public utilities like water distribution, etc.).[4] Such an inclusive definition might be relevant for the analysis of industrial relations, since it concerns aspects able to influence the behaviour of the actors (i.e. the political nature of the employers and, in some cases, the weakness of budget constraints). It covers employees, however, which lack the special employment status of public employees.

The focus of the analysis in this chapter is narrower: it covers all employees of public administrations whose employment relationship is 'contractualized', that is determined through collective bargaining – as opposed to unilateral regulation on the part of the government or the parliament, through laws or administrative measures – according to the provisions of the 1993 law (l. 29/93). This definition includes all the public service employeees for whom Aran (*Agenzia per la rappresentanza negoziale delle pubbliche amministrazioni*) is the compulsory employers' side bargaining agent in all national negotiations.

This definition of the public services covered just under 3 million employees in the mid-1990s, distributed in the following sub-sectors or bargaining areas (*comparti*; see Table 4.1):

- central government (ministries);
- local authorities, that is, municipalities, provinces, regions, chambers of commerce, although for the five regions with special statutes (Valle d'Aosta, Trentino, Alto Adige, Friuli, Sardegna e Sicilia) and for the two provinces of Trento and Bolzano the representation by Aran is not compulsory, but they can and usually do utilize it;
- non-economic public bodies (*enti pubblici non economici*, or *parastato*) including social security (INPS and INAIL), and the Italian automobile club;
- the 'state autonomus firms' (*aziende autonome dello Stato*) including four entities: firemen, state monopolies such as tobacco, Cassa deposity e prestiti, Aima;
- the national health system;
- public schools;
- universities (excluding university teachers, as they are not 'contractualized');
- public institutes of research (e.g. the National Research Council).

Two other groups can be added to these sectors. The first includes the employees of some minor agencies or administrations – such as the National Olympic Committee, state television, the national firm of flight attendants (Anav), and a few others – whose employment relationship has been regulated through collective agreements since the November 1997 amendment of the law brought them under the direct jurisdiction of Aran. The second group consists of the categories explicitly excluded from the process of contractualization under the 1993 law, their employment relationship being regulated through special statutes. This group includes higher-level diplomats, about 10,000 judges, state lawyers, about 52,000 university teachers, and by far the largest group of 460,000 police corps and armed forces. It also included 600 (civilian) general directors of the state, until their employment relationship was 'contractualised' in 1997. Together these two

Table 4.1 Contractualized public sector employment,[a] December 1995

Service	No. of adm. units	Non-managerial employees	Managers	Total	%
Central government	23	286,684	5,758	292,442	10.2
State autonomous firms	4	43,531	245	43,776	1.5
Public bodies	185	65,102	3,978	69,080	2.4
Local government	8,408	651,667	12,758	664,425	23.2
National health service	340	557,992	127,088[b]	685,080	23.9
Education	1	1,031,122		1,031,122	36.0
University	69	58,745	116	58,861	2.1
Research institutions	52	12,179	5,460	17,639	0.6
Total		2,707,022	155,403	2,862,425	100.0

Source: Department of Public Function, *Repertorio delle organizzazioni sindacali operanti nel Pubblico impiego e della loro consistenza associativa*, Rome, 15 December 1997.

Notes
a Under Aran jurisdiction.
b Of which 105,568 are doctors or veterinary surgeons, who have a separate collective agreement from non-doctor managers.

groups comprise 0.6 million employees, which brings total employment in public services to about 3.5 million, as estimated by the National Accounts statistics.

Excluded from this definition of the public employment sector are the employees of the state railways and of the state postal service, once by far the largest of the autonomous firms of the state, with more than 200,000 employees each. They were 'privatized' in 1985 and 1994 respectively; that is, juridically transformed from *azienda autonoma dello Stato*, strictly integrated within and dependent on the ministries of transport and telecommunications, to that of *enti pubblici non economici*, and finally into joint stock companies, in which the state is so far the only shareholder. This change meant that their employees lost their public employment status – a precondition for the policy of downsizing and massive redundancies pursued after the privatization, especially in the railways – and consequently their bargaining activity does not fall under the jurisdiction of Aran (although labour relations still remain highly politicized).

Thus the analysis in this chapter will focus mainly on the sub-sectors of education, health, local authorities and central government, which account for more than 90 per cent of contractualized public employees as defined above.

Organizational structure, employment and wages

Organization of the main sectors

The first column of Table 4.1 shows the number of administrative units in each sub-sector, which gives a rough idea of the organizational and structural differences within the public services. In particular, the organization of the school sector should be noted; about one million employees, mostly schoolteachers, are

Table 4.2 Percentage of various categories of workers in employment, 1994

Sector	Managers[a]	Female workers	Fixed-term contracts	Part-time workers
Central government	2.0	43.2	2.2	–
State firms	0.6	n.a.	n.a.	n.a.
Public bodies	5.8	46.9	3.3	0.5
Local government	1.9	42.3	5.4	1.0
National health service	18.6	54.6	2.0	0.5
Education	–	72.1	6.5	–
Universities	0.2	38.8	4.6	0.5
Total	5.4	55.3	4.9	0.3

Note

a The percentages of managers refer to December 1995 and are computed on the data in Table 4.1. In the health sector doctors are included, since they are considered as managers.

employed by a single administration, the Ministry of Education, and have their employment relationship regulated in an absolutely uniform way all over the country. (This uniformity could decrease slightly in the future, as a consequence of some financial autonomy allowed to the individual schools under the provisions of the 1997 law.) At the opposite extreme is local government, where 650,000 employees are dispersed over more than 8,400 authorities, which vary greatly in size, and exercise some autonomy in financial matters and personnel policies.

Composition of employment

Employment in the public service increased steadily until a few years ago. The rate of growth was particularly high in the first half of the 1980s, when employment in central government (including education) grew by almost 2 per cent a year. In local government (including health) the rate of growth was only slightly lower. At the beginning of the 1990s employment fell throughout the whole economy, but in the public service it decreased even more, so that for the first time in many years the proportion of public sector employment in the labour force declined, to slightly less than 16 per cent. Restrictive fiscal policies and measures designed to reduce the public deficit led public service employers to reduce drastically the recruitment of new staff. Special measures were taken by the government to reduce labour turnover and only a few exceptions to this general rule were allowed.

The composition of the employed labour force is described in Tables 4.1 and 4.2. Education is by far the largest sector and covers more than a third of total public employment; local government and health come next, each accounting for over 20 per cent of the total. Female employment is very well represented in the public service, comprising 55 per cent of total employment. The proportion of women is very high in education (72 per cent) and health. Although two occupations, teachers and nurses, largely account for this strong 'feminization' of employment, women's share is very high in all parts of the public service, and much higher than in the private sector, where it is around 30 per cent.

In comparison with the private sector, there are proportionally more managers in the public services, although they are not evenly distributed throughout the various sub-sectors. Tables 4.1 and 4.2 report no managers in schools, for example, since head teachers until very recently were not appointed as managers; only since 1998 (effective the year 2000) have they been recognized as managers by the government. For the rest of the public service, the proportion of managers is very high in the non-economic public bodies (mainly social security) and in the health service (where doctors are classified as managers). The employment of too many managers has been accompanied by problems of accountability, and in the achievement of a strong identification with the general goals of the public service.

The presence of atypical workers is not very extensive in Italy, either in the private or in the public sector. In general the degree of labour market flexibility is rather low throughout the whole economy. In the public services there are additional factors which explain the very limited diffusion of this particular kind of employment relation. The hiring of temporary and fixed-term workers is often used by public service employers to avoid the stringent rules that regulate the normal recruitment process: that is, recruitment has to follow a public and open competition which is usually burdensome and difficult to complete. This is partly because of the very high number of people that usually apply for vacant posts in the public service and this makes the whole process of selection time-consuming and costly. Moreover, the number of full-time and regular positions is determined by regulations and it takes time to change them. Public service employers thus find it easier and more efficient to employ temporary workers for which a public competition is not required. But there is a limit imposed on this practice, as the number of atypical contracts cannot be increased at will: temporary workers can be hired only to occupy specific positions in the organization, and cannot exceed a limited proportion of those already in regular and full-time positions.

The public sector labour market

The rules governing the recruitment process are one of the few remaining examples of the differences between private and public sector employment. As noted elsewhere in this chapter, the new legislation and the collective agreements in the 1994–97 period have changed many aspects of employment relations in the public service and made them more similar to those in the private sector. This is the case, for example, with the procedures to be followed in the dismissal of individual workers and with other disciplinary measures to be taken when misconduct or inadequate performance is ascertained. The rules concerning paid holidays, and other paid or unpaid leave of absence, are also similar to those in the private sector. Some limitations and differences from the private sector, however, can be found in the areas of working-time and promotion.

Although working-time is regulated by negotiations between the two parties, it must provide sufficient flexibility to enable public service employers to organize work in a way that satisfies the needs of the citizens. In fact, there is a widespread criticism from citizens and the mass media that the working-time of public employees is organized to satisfy their own needs rather than those of the public in general! This view provides one possible explanation of the very limited diffusion of part-time working in the public services (see Table 4.2): in practice, working full-time leaves enough spare time to be devoted to other activities, such as domestic work for female teachers, for example. The organization of working-time in public services is one of the most important components of the process of 'privatizing' employment relations on which the improvement of labour productivity crucially depends.

Promotion and the careers of individual workers are regulated not by collective bargaining but by unilateral administrative decisions. Promotion to a higher grade of the occupational hierarchy must follow the same rules governing recruitment from the external labour market, that is, through open competition. This may change in the near future because the unions, as well as the employers, want to change the system to avoid the time-consuming, costly and bureaucratic procedures. At the moment, however, the law forbids promotion without open competition in the majority of cases.

The classification of employees in different occupations is closely related to the determination of their pay levels. The system of classification is similar in the public and the private sector. The general content of different groups of jobs and occupations is described in national collective agreements in such a way that each occupation can be assigned to a specific grade on the pay scale. The number of grades (or of job classification levels) is low: usually eight, although in some sub-sectors there are nine or ten. Moreover, the lower grades, that used to be the points of entry for new recruits, are no longer used because new job vacancies are for occupations classified in the higher grades. Thus the vast majority of public service employees are distributed among no more than five or six grades. There is no progression of basic pay apart from promotion to a higher grade. As opportunities for promotion are rare, many workers stay in their initial grade for many years and receive no increase in their basic wage, apart from the general increases determined at the general sectoral or macro-economic level.

Wages and salaries

Basic pay for different grades is fixed by national collective agreements for each of the sectors – health, education, central government, etc. Nationally defined wage rates represent about 80 per cent of total earnings on average, but up to 95 per cent in schools. The rest is determined through negotiations that take place at the level of the individual administrative unit. As noted above, the number of units where decentralized collective bargaining occurs can be as many as 8,000 – the number of municipalities in local government – or as few as the number of ministries in the civil service.

National rates include a component called *contingenza* that exists in both the private and the public sectors and which in the past used to be linked to the cost of living through an automatic system of indexation. In 1993 the system was abolished in both sectors, and the amount of *contingenza* at that time was frozen,

Table 4.3 Pay components (as percentage of total pay)

Sector	National agreements		Local agreements		
	National rates	Overtime	Performance-related pay	Allowances	Total
Central government	82.1	3.5	5.6	8.8	17.9
Public bodies	76.2	3.4	15.8	4.5	23.8
Local government	91.7	2.8	2.7	2.7	8.3
Education	95.2	–	0.8	4.0	4.8
Research institutions	79.8	2.6	14.2	3.4	20.2

and included as a fixed component within the pay of each employee. Since then, collective bargaining has been the main method of determining pay in the public service. Also, the automatic link between wages and length of service has been abolished in most recent collective agreements. It is still in place, in a modified form, in schools, where promotion to higher positions is even more rare than in other parts of the public service; in this context, length of service is the only factor that can guarantee some individual wage progression.

Under the existing legislation, the national agreements determine not only the basic pay for different grades, but also the maximum amount of money wage increases that can be added to basic pay by the negotiations taking place at the decentralized or local level. These additional wage increases occurring at local level are predetermined at national level, making the whole system of wage determination very centralized in the public service.[5] At the local level the parties bargain and agree on the distribution of these additional wage increases among different groups of employees. They can take several different forms: overtime pay, allowances, and performance-related pay, as shown in Table 4.3. The amount and the types of allowance depend very much on the work done and on the particular characteristics of the working conditions (e.g. the presence of risk, heavy and dirty work, shift patterns, etc.), which vary according to the sector.

Also the component of pay linked with productivity or performance varies significantly across sectors: it is high in the non-economic public bodies and in research institutes (which employ only a small minority of public sector employees), and it is almost absent in other larger sectors, such as education. In general, the existing schemes of pay for performance are organized on a collective basis; that is, they reward the performance of teams rather than individual workers. Even so there is evidence that the existing schemes are not used, in the majority of cases, in an effective way: there is a sort of 'inflation rating' in the application of the appraisal system, so that almost all the workers in the administrative unit receive the same bonus.

Recent agreements signed by the state agency Aran for the period 1994–97 have introduced a scheme relating the premium to individual performance and, in order to avoid the danger of 'inflation rating', a quota system has been introduced, limiting the percentage of potential beneficiaries. Although the quota system presents many drawbacks, it may still be useful in forcing managers to assume

Table 4.4 Wage dispersion by grade within each sector

Sector	1985	1995
Central government	10.40	18.56
Public bodies	13.67	14.25
Education	8.72	14.89
Universities	10.01	15.68
Research institutions	17.42	17.57
Private sector (engineering)	23.89	29.72

Note: Wage dispersion is measured by the coefficient of variation ($\times$ 100).

Table 4.5 Wage differentials across sectors

Sector	1985	1995
Local government	100	100
Central government	104	119
Public bodies	119	138
Education	103	112
Universities	111	177
Research institutions	131	169

their responsibility in discriminating between different levels of individual performance. To assess its effects on management practice, wider implementation of
the system throughout the public service will be necessary.

The overall system of wage determination is such that differentiation of wage
levels between individual workers is very difficult to introduce. In fact one of the
main features of the public service is that the dispersion of wages is much lower
than in the private sector. Although the statistics on wages are rather limited, the
few available data give an idea of the difference. In Table 4.4 the dispersion of
wages by grades within each sector is measured by the coefficient of variation,
which gives an idea of the differences existing in the average wage levels of groups
of employees with different qualifications and responsibilities. The variations
refer not to different characteristics of the workers, but to different features of the
positions they occupy. The coefficient of variation is much higher in the private
sector than in the public service, and wage differentials are particularly compressed in education, the civil service (central government) and in the universities
(excluding university teachers).

Since the mid-1980s, however, the wage policy that inspired national negotiations has changed significantly, and wage differentials have been raised and almost
restored to their pre-1970 levels. Higher remuneration of more qualified positions has had an effect also on the differences in average wage levels for different
sub-sectors of the public service. The different composition by level of qualification of the staff employed in different sectors explains to some extent the increase
in wage differentials which occurred in recent years, as shown in Table 4.5.

Average wages have increased most in sectors where the level of skill or qualification is on average higher (e.g. research institutes and the health service).

Finally, trends in the relative pay of public and private sector employees should be noted. The only regular and complete source of information is published in the National Accounts. The limits of these data are well known: they suffer from a high level of aggregation, and they are affected by the composition of employment that changes over time in an unpredicted way. Since 1993 a new survey of public sector wages has been conducted which is disaggregated by different components of pay and for different groups of employees (and disaggregated further by sector, grade and gender).

The evolution of public service pay over the last twenty-five years shows irregular movements; large pay increases have been followed by periods of stagnation. Very large increases were awarded in the early years of each of the last three decades and pay relativities declined over the following years. This ten-year cycle in wage movements is a feature of the public service; nothing similar has happened in the private sector, where wages show a more regular pattern along an increasing trend. Wage increases in the public service have been more affected by the prevailing political conditions and by the condition of the public finances. Real wages have been compressed in periods of fiscal restraint and they have increased only when the political climate was more favourable towards public service employees; that is, in pre-election periods, and when it was no longer possible to keep wages well below the general trend in the private sector.

Since the early 1970s the pay of public employees has always been higher, in absolute terms, than that in the private sector. To a great extent this is due to the different composition of the labour force employed in the two sectors; for example, the higher proportion of white-collar employees in the public service. Recent studies have tried to estimate the wage differential between the two sectors, using individual data and controlling for the characteristics of different workers and different jobs. They have found that the wage differential depends very much on the year chosen for analysis, but, controlling for this factor, a small differential in favour of the public service seems to be the common conclusion of the studies.

Employers and employers' associations

State policies

The policies of the state on public service regulation exhibited several legal and institutional innovations in the 1990s, some of them with direct implications for employment relations. These innovations did not take the form of the radical privatization drive which characterized some other European countries (especially Britain); there was no attempt to abolish the public nature of services or a significant move to private ownership. A policy of privatization in this sense was, however, pursued in the case of several state-owned companies and banks (e.g. Italian Telecom, and the state-owned banks Comit and Credit), though their employees did not have public employment status. A partial exception was the 'privatization' of the state railways and the postal service noted earlier. Although less radical than developments in other countries, the series of reforms, which started in the 1990s, often stimulated by the increasing financial difficulties of the state, were, however, important, effecting change in several traditional features of public administration. Some of the most significant steps in this reform programme can be summarized in the following way.

First, the adoption on the part of the government since 1992 of very tight budgetary policies, and the series of measures aimed at increasing the account-ability of all administrative units and implementing more effective financial con-trol over their activities. Second, the reform of local authorities (regions, provinces and municipalities), allowing them greater administrative autonomy within a context of tighter financial responsibilities. It included a partial increase of their powers in relation to tax issues and budget financing, partly in compensation for the reduction in financial transfers from central government initiated in 1990. Third, a reform of the national health system, introducing some element of internal competition and changes to strengthen managerial autonomy in 1992. Finally, as discussed earlier, the 1993 legislation and subsequent amendments that introduced a clear distinction between the powers of the political authorities and those of the bureaucracy in the management of public administration. These included the reform of public managers' prerogatives and responsibilities, the 'privatization' and 'contractualization' of public employees, and the creation of a 'technical' agency, Aran, responsible for national negotiations and public sector labour relations more generally.

Some of these lines of innovation were taken up again and deepened within the project of 'fiscal federalism' (or the administrative decentralization of the state), approved by the parliament in 1997, which included some measures aimed at increasing managerial autonomy and financial responsibility in the school sector. Not all these reforms directly affected public sector labour relations, but all of them affected the financial and organizational context of employment relations, and the characteristics of the state as employer. Among these features there was a very high degree of centralization until the end of the 1980s. This was due mainly to the organizational structure of the state, very similar to the French case, in which the main functions were organized within the ministries (Cassese, 1983). Combined with this, and peculiar to the Italian experience, was the pervasive role of political authority in the functioning of public administration in comparison with the weak position and competence of the bureaucracy. This role was not limited to the responsibility of the government and parliament – often with over-lapping of competences – in designing the main guidelines on the goals and activities of the public administration; it often involved a direct and deep involve-ment in the detailed management of human resources and employment relations, especially concerning wages and recruitment. Under the regime of the 1983 law on public employment, this situation often made personnel and labour relations policies a matter of political competition, not only between government and the parliamentary opposition, but also between different parties and ministries within the government itself, leading on many occasions to violations of the financial ceilings fixed in the budget law of the state. Given the variety of actors entitled to intervene in the internal life of public administration, and in the determination of employment conditions, it was difficult to establish clearly the responsibility of the employer, and to develop the effective management of personnel and labour relations issues.

The characteristics of public service employers

These reforms, which tried to define the role and the responsibility of public sector employers, have had somewhat different applications in the various public services. The variations depend on the legal status and financial and organizational constraints of the individual administrations and managerial roles. For the sake of convenience, the analysis can be focused on the three key sectors of public administration: the health system, local authorities and education.

The health services

In many respects, the health sector represents the most advanced example of reform, because of the decentralization of functions to the regional and local governments, the diffusion of professional management, and the introduction of some sort of financial and performance competition between local units. Since the formal institution of the national health service by the 1978 law which created 'local health units' (*unità sanitarie locali*) covering the whole country, there has been a decentralization of competence from the Ministry of Health to the regional authorities, within the framework of the national health plan. In the early 1990s, new legislation reorganized the 'local health units' and defined them as 'companies', *aziende sanitarie locali* (ASLs) with their own legal, accounting, organizational and financial autonomy. A similar status was given also to a number of hospitals, provided that they satisfied certain criteria in terms of the variety and importance of services supplied, and organizational complexity.

From a legal point of view, the health organizations – ASLs and hospital firms – can now autonomously manage their resources. Their autonomy, however, is limited; it excludes entrepreneurial initiatives in developing new markets or services. In practice, the main competence attributed to them by the reform is to manage, effectively and efficiently, the resources assigned by the regional government with the aim of improving the quality of service, but not to identify new services (e.g. plastic surgery) or to search for new markets. These latter activities are in principle left to the regional authorities in their capacity as the financing bodies of the local health units and hospitals, although they are rarely pursued in practice. The regions are entitled to certain financial transfers from the national health fund according to a series of parameters, and are obliged to guarantee health services according to uniform standards defined by the national health plan. But they may also provide additional services beyond the national standards, utilizing the narrow margins of financial autonomy which are available to them. Before 1992 the financial system was based on regional refunds of the costs sustained by each unit during the year. After the 1992 legislation, each unit and hospital with 'company' status is financed on the basis of the services actually supplied, thus introducing limited competition between the different organizations, with some variations, depending on regional legislation.

Another important innovation in the 1992 reform was the creation of the role of general manager, previously absent, at the head of the ASLs and the hospitals with 'company' status. This role replaces that of the former management committee, whose members were chosen by local authorities, often according to political rather than managerial or professional criteria. The general manager is appointed by the regional government, chosen from a national list of candidates meeting certain professional requirements. The general manager is employed on a five-year private contract and is subject to control on the basis of the qualitative and financial performance of the organization for which he or she has responsibility. The skills required for this role are managerial, and the responsibilities include the power to nominate both an accounting director and a health director.

In comparison with managers in the private sector, the ASL or hospital general managers have more limited powers: in fact they work within the constraints of budgets assigned by the regional authority, and although they have an incentive to rationalize and organize the activities of the hospital, they cannot hire personnel or make decisions on important investments. The prerogatives in relation to expenditure are subject to a preliminary control (mainly of legitimacy) by the auditors' committee of each unit or hospital with company status (chaired by a representative of the Ministry of Finance), while the national Court of State Auditors (*Corte dei Conti*) exercises annual control over the overall financial activity of each unit.

The school sector

The financial autonomy of each school unit has only recently been recognized under the 1997 law on administrative decentralization of the state to be implemented in 1999. Until now, the school sector has been characterized by the highest degree of centralization. Unlike hospitals, the different units still depend on the central government (Ministry of Education) and are controlled by a peripheral body of the same ministry (Provincial Education Office), rather than by regional or local governments. School policies and administrative directives are issued by the ministry, as are many issues inherent in the management and recruitment of teaching and auxiliary staff. The individual school units have little financial autonomy; it is restricted to the management of very limited bonus schemes covering the services of staff not connected with teaching duties, which are already defined by the school syllabus (e.g. serving on committees, special assignments, etc.). The role of the school Head (*preside*) is an administrative and didactic one, similar to that of the head teacher in Britain. The Head does not, however, have direct teaching duties, and is assisted by the teaching committee, which includes all the teachers in the school.

Within the 1997 legal framework, each individual school has some autonomy in establishing relations and agreements with outside organizations (e.g. suppliers, clients). Furthermore, it has some autonomy in relation to the formation of classes, teaching methods, the development of research programmes, the introduction of complementary new subjects, the recruitment of teachers on temporary contracts (within specified limits), and the weekly calendar of five or six days. The same reform also granted school Heads the status of manager, although it does not specify their functions, or their precise powers in financial matters. The government continues to act as the financing body and sets the main guidelines regarding educational policy and personnel management. In comparison with the health system, in spite of the legal recognition of the school's autonomy and of the school Head as a manager, schools remain a part of the administrative and highly centralized bureaucratic structure of the Ministry of Education.

The local authorities

The 1990 legislation grants the municipalities and the provinces a degree of autonomy in choosing the services to be provided to citizens, and in defining their organizational structures. In turn, for the first time, the law on public finance allows local administrations to raise local taxes to a limited extent. Also, following the provisions of legislation introduced in 1997, each local authority is partially released from the very tight external controls to which it was previously subject and, as in the health sector, is allowed to appoint a general manager under a private contract. The logic of the reforms is that of greater legal and managerial autonomy than in the past, although the possibility of acquiring resources through direct taxation makes the municipalities more self-sufficient than the schools. The direction of the reform does not differ much from that of the health system, even though the structure and administrative arrangements of these organizations are such as to limit their autonomy in resource management. Financial and budget autonomy, not yet fully implemented, remains an important strategic guideline to characterize both the role and the type of regulation of these two sectors, namely a movement away from administrative regulation.

The status and role of managers

An important aspect of change in the sectors dicussed above is the possibility of promoting effective and authoritative management, capable of rationalizing and allocating resources, and directly interested in the effective functioning of the administration process. The 'privatization' of public management outlined in the 1993 law introduces two significant aspects of innovation: the separation between political and bureaucratic responsibilities; and the redefinition of the role of managers by strengthening their prerogatives in ways found in the private sector. The separation of political responsibility from administration is facilitated by the definition of two distinct spheres of influence: the government is given responsibility for defining the general goals, the financial constraints and assessment measures;

management has the responsibility of organizing, managing and spending the allocated resources. In particular, in relation to the organization and management of the work force, managers are expected to operate with the 'same capacity and powers as those of the private employer' (Article 4, law No. 29/93). This may include the reorganization of functions, the definition of work loads, the organization of working hours, internal mobility, and the hiring of personnel on temporary employment contract (within limits), and any other decision geared towards improving productivity (D'Orta, 1995).

The reform thus defines the responsibility of public sector management as directed towards achieving measurable results in terms of efficiency and effectiveness, rather than just towards assuring the formal legitimacy of administrative acts, as was the case in the past. This transformation from a bureaucratic-administrative role to a managerial one implies the responsibility for resources, and the granting to managers of autonomous spending power, within the limits of the budget allocated to them. For the first time, therefore, managers can be held responsible for operational results, and are subject to the control of an internal auditing body, whose task is to verify that 'goals have been achieved and financial management of public resources has been correct', and which responds to the political authority. Also the legislative reform outlined specific sanctions to be applied if these responsibilities are ignored or if mismanagement occurs.

These characteristics of managerial responsibility are, however, fully evident only in the topmost ranks of public management, that is, the 600 or so general directors of the state, excluded from the 'contractualization' of their employment relationship until the end of 1997. In comparison with the goals envisaged by the reform, the current management structure has significant limits. These include the fragmentation of departments and functions, ineffective co-ordination and lack of flexibility (Della Rocca, 1996). The hierarchical organization does not facilitate the integration of functions and departments. In many cases there is no strategic senior management, and the procedures for co-ordinating and integrating the fragmented organization are limited and inadequate. Thus the public services still remain different from the private sector, where such problems of fragmentation are generally ameliorated by specialized structures, common economic goals, budgeting mechanisms and information systems.

In summary, the major problems lie first in creating a sense of management accountability for the results demanded by the reform, and then in the weakness of the procedures available for co-ordinating efforts. It is reasonable to doubt whether it is possible to exercise the right to manage if managerial tools are not available or not known. This is not just a minor problem, because it produces a very narrow management perspective. Managers are unable to conceptualize the whole; that is, all the activities, results and resources for which they should be accountable. This fragmentation is often a source of conflict. Tensions that are difficult to resolve emerge around the borders of each manager's domain and concern the allocation of resources, and the distribution of areas of competence and responsibility. In many cases conflicts are resolved by creating new managerial roles without any logic in terms of organizational efficiency. The processes of innovation, when not contained within a single function, face an insurmountable barrier when seeking to integrate the efforts of more than one function.

A second type of limitation arises from the exceedingly high number of managerial staff with low levels of qualification. According to some research, the attempt to create better prepared and qualified managerial roles has always been hindered by the lack of appropriate selection and recruitment procedures. While the government structure in France has been created around a small, highly qualified group of bureaucrats, in Italy there is a low managerial profile in public services, with little visibility from a professional point of view, and subject directly to the political authority. The rules of public and open competition (*concorsi pubblici*) are weak and sometimes evaded in the recruitment of managers, thereby undermining the sense of commitment to the state and to its institutions (Cassese, 1994).

Employers' associations

The reform of the employers' delegation in collective negotiations proved to be one of the most significant innovations introduced by the 1993 reforms and the subsequent 1997 amendments. The creation of an agency for compulsory representation of public administrations in collective negotiations at national level (Aran) replaced a multiplicity of parties that previously intervened in the bargaining process, and helped to insulate collective negotiations from the political and parliamentary arena – at least to a much greater degree than in the past. Aran has legal status and organizational autonomy. It is governed by an executive committee composed of five members nominated by a decree of the presidents of the Councils of Ministers, one of whom is designated by the Conference of Presidents of the Regions, and another by the association of Italian municipalities and provinces.

During the negotiation of new collective agreements since the 1993 reform, the depoliticization of the bargaining agent on the employer's side has proved to be effective; it has strengthened the degree of autonomy of the bargaining structure from external intervention, and it has increased the transparency of the bargaining process. Some new tensions have arisen, however, from the strong degree of centralization of employers' representation (and in the bargaining structure), which, although efficient from the point of view of control of public expenditure, has nevertheless given rise to problems. This is especially true of relations between Aran and the local authorities (regions and municipalities), where the need for differentiated and co-ordinated management of labour relations is most acutely felt.

These tensions are inherent in the particular nature of the agency, as originally defined in the 1993 reform, which makes it different from private sector employers' associations. Since its creation, it has been clear that Aran could not be considered as a typical interest association, representing the interests of its rank-and-file members (individual public administrations), but should rather be viewed as a 'technical' task force of labour relations professionals. Aran is strictly dependent on government directives with respect first to the total amount of resource available, in accordance with those fixed in the budget law of the state; and, secondly, the main guidelines for the negotiations. Aran also has to operate within a complex procedural process before it can sign agreements, implying formal government authorization and control of economic cost of the agreements by the Court of State Auditors (*Corte dei Conti*). In its original terms, the 1993 reform did not envisage a significant role, other than a consultative one, for the local authorities in national negotiations, with the partial exception of the Conference of the Presidents of the Regions in relation to the approval of the collective agreements affecting their budgets.

These drawbacks have been partially corrected by the new rules introduced in 1997, which, while maintaining Aran's role as compulsory bargaining agency for all public administrations in national collective negotiations, also gave the latter (and not only central government) more powers to influence the bargaining process. The various administrations are entitled to send (through their associations) specific guidelines to Aran before negotiations start, and must be continually informed during the negotiation process. Aran is also obliged to obtain their consent to the proposed agreement before final approval (the law refers to the 'favourable opinion', in place of the previous government 'authorization'). For central government and the school sector, these powers are exercised by the government itself; but for local authorities, hospitals and the other public administrations, they are exercised by specialized *sector committees* created for the purpose. These changes make Aran less a technical and operational agency strictly dependent on central government and more similar to an agency in the service of the represented administrations, by which it is also financed.

The trade unions

Legal framework

There are no legal restrictions on trade union organization and representation for most public sector employees in Italy, except for a few qualifications covering the armed forces and police.[6] The right to organize, embodied in the republican constitution of 1948, does not discriminate between public and private sector employees. In practice, the unionization of the public sector was achieved on a massive scale after the early 1950s (Romagnoli, 1980, 1987; Bordogna, 1987).

Trade union membership

Three features characterize public sector trade unions by comparison with the private sector: significantly higher union density; much greater organizational fragmentation, well beyond the traditional political and ideological divisions between the three main confederations (Cgil, Cisl and Uil);[7] and a generally weaker organizational presence at workplace level.

The higher union density has been a constant feature over the entire post-war period. At the end of 1996, total membership (or, more precisely, the *deleghe*, that

Table 4.6 Union membership and union density (all organizations), 1996

Sector	Subscriptions			Union density (%)		
	Employees	*Managers*	*Total*	*Employees*	*Managers*	*Total*
Central government	113,106	2,634	115,740	39.5	45.8	39.6
State firms	25,414	205	25,619	58.4	83.7	58.5
Public bodies	39,781	3,974	43,755	61.1	99.9	63.3
Local government	316,714	7,704	324,418	48.6	60.4	48.8
Health	267,201	86,720[a]	353,921	47.9	68.2	51.7
School	378,669		378,669	36.7		36.7
University	22,436	55	22,491	38.2	47.4	38.2
Research	5,797	2,735	8,532	47.6	50.1	48.4
Total	1,169,118	104,027[a]	1,273,145	43.2	66.9	44.5

Source: *Dipartimento Funzione Pubblica.*

Notes
These figures refer to actual subscriptions or *deleghe*, that is, written notifications undersigned by the employees to check off union dues from their monthly pay. The validity of this subscription lasts until the employee cancels it in writing.
a Of whom 72,811 are doctors or vets.

is, employees' notifications to their employer to deduct – or check off – their union dues) is about 1.3 million (see Table 4.6). This represents an overall 'contractualized' public sector union density of about 45 per cent, around 7 to 10 percentage points higher than in the entire economy. Trade union density is different in various parts of the public services. In the school sector (including the non-teaching staff of the ministry of education) it is around 35 per cent, while in half of the sub-sectors it is higher than 50 per cent, and in some cases it is 70 per cent. The reasons for this phenomenon, found in many countries, were explored by Clegg (1976), and seem to hold in the Italian case too, with some qualifications (Bordogna, 1987, 1994).

Trade union structure and fragmentation

The most significant difference from the private sector concerns the greater fragmentation of the structure of representation, which is particularly marked in some sub-sectors. This can be seen in the presence of the so-called *sindacalismo autonomo*, that is, organizations which are not affiliated to the three main confederations and, since the late 1980s, in the phenomenon of the *cobas* (*comitati di base*), or rank-and-file committees. This fragmentation is linked with the traditional political and ideological cleavages in the Italian trade union movement, and is exacerbated by the more direct role played by the political parties in public service labour relations. It is also caused by a plurality of organizational criteria, almost unknown in the private sector. Although the industry unions (*sindacati di categoria*) and the general, territorial organizations to which they are affiliated (union confederations) remain the most prevalent type of organization, as in the private sector, representation based on craft and occupational criteria is also very important.

Many of these organizations are not affiliated to the main confederations. Some were created in the 1950s and 1960s as professional associations to lobby the political authorities, but have subsequently become union organizations, in the sense that they directly engage in industrial action and collective bargaining. This happened frequently, for instance, in the area of doctors working in the national health system. The widespread presence of such organizations, and others resembling 'company unions' (*sindacati di ente*), based in just one administrative unit, is encouraged by the nature of a labour market with a great variety of highly qualified employees, who are very jealous of their professional status and conditions, and unwilling to see them ignored or lost in the embrace of large general unions. Fragmentation is also facilitated by the organizational structure of the public services, which is characterized by the diffusion of positions with very high disruptive power; that is, services which allow forms of industrial action which have a disproportionate effect on the users of services and the general public in comparison with the cost of the action itself (Accornero, 1985; Pipan, 1989; Franzosi, 1992). The radical utilization of such disruptive power was a common feature of all cases of union power dispersion that characterized the sector in the second half of the 1980s, with the rise of the *cobas* (see Baldissera, 1988; Bordogna, 1989, 1993).

Thus trade union representation is much more fragmented and complicated than in the private sector, with such a variety of organizations in some sub-sectors that it is hard to identify or quantify all of them. In education, health, local government and central government, there can be forty or fifty different organizations, some of which operate only in one sub-sector. Sometimes as few as two or three members will subscribe to the *delega sindacale* – that is, notify their employer to pay union dues to an organization on their behalf.[8] This fragmentation and union power dispersion reached its peak during the second half of the 1980s and was a reaction against the previous phase of highly centralized union organization and bargaining pursued by the three trade union confederations, especially in the public sector (Cella, 1991).

The extent of union fragmentation in the mid-1990s can be illustrated by the data shown in Table 4.7. As can be seen, organizations outside the three main confederations account for about 27 per cent of union membership among non-managerial employees, 65 per cent among managers and 85 per cent or more among doctors. The presence of these unions is often significant not only in their share of total union membership in their area of representation, but also in absolute terms; for instance, the Snals-Confsal, the second largest organization among schoolteachers, has more than 100,000 *deleghe*. Moreover, the strength of these organizations resides less in the number of their members than in the disruptive power they often employ, and in their capacity to mobilize conflict which may be socially devastating.

Finally, as far as relations between the three main confederations are concerned, the Cisl (*Confederazione italiana sindacati dei lavoratori*) is the largest, though

Table 4.7 Number of organizations[a] and percentage of subscriptions by sub-sector and type of personnel, 1996

Sub-sector	No. of unions[a]	Cgil	Cisl	Uil	Others	Total
Central government						
Non-managerial	36	19.0	29.2	16.8	35.1	100.0
Managerial	23	6.7	12.7	6.5	74.1	100.0
Autonomous state firms						
Non-managerial	14	37.0	35.5	11.6	15.9	100.0
Managerial	6	10.7	16.1	2.9	70.2	100.0
Non-economic public bodies						
Non-managerial	17	16.6	36.1	13.7	33.6	100.0
Managerial	12	5.9	19.8	5.4	68.9	100.0
Local government						
Non-managerial	46	34.4	31.0	14.8	19.7	100.0
Managerial	23	20.7	21.5	7.7	50.2	100.0
Health						
Non-managerial	55	28.5	33.1	15.8	22.7	100.0
Managerial	26	11.4	8.8	4.1	75.7	100.0
Doctors and vets	46	6.2	4.9	2.4	86.5	100.0
School	45	19.5	36.5	9.3	34.8	100.0
University						
Non-managerial	32	30.2	33.2	14.1	22.5	100.0
Managerial	6	21.8	18.2	9.1	50.9	100.0
Research						
Non-managerial	13	25.1	31.7	20.7	22.4	100.0
Managerial	12	31.3	25.1	10.2	33.4	100.0
Total						
Non-managerial	258	26.0	34.1	14.2	25.7	100.0
Managerial	108	14.3	15.7	5.9	64.3	100.0
Doctors and vets	46	6.2	4.9	2.4	86.5	100.0
Total	412	24.6	31.3	12.5	31.6	100.0

Sources: Dipartimento della Funzione Pubblica (1997) and Bordogna (1998b).

Note
a Organisations of second affiliation, that is federations and confederations.

not in all sub-sectors, followed by the Cgil (*Confederazione Generale Italiana del Lavoro*) and, at greater distance, by the Uil (*Unione Italiana del Lavoro*). These relative positions are different from those in the private sector, where the largest organization is the Cgil. The relative strength of the three main confederations in the public sector, and its variations over the post-war period, are the result of their different organizational strategies, especially up to the mid-1970s. In particular, during the 1950s and part of the 1960s, the Cisl took advantage of its links with the largest government party to present itself as a privileged partner of the employer in the management of the internal labour market. In contrast, in the context of the collective mobilization of the 1970s, the Cgil was able to turn its previous marginality into a sort of 'opposition premium', reaping the fruits of the conflicts in terms of rapidly rising membership (Romagnoli, 1980).

The problem of trade union representativeness

The problem of fragmented union structure is connected with the problem of union representativeness; that is, the criteria used to select which organizations are entitled to union rights (e.g. time off and periods of leave for union duties) and bargaining rights. There is a complex pattern of multi-union representation in the workers' delegation at the bargaining table at national and local levels because of the strong pressure exercised even by the small organizations to be admitted to the negotiations. This problem had been dealt with in 1983 by the law on public employment through the principle of 'nation-wide major representativeness' (*maggiore rappresentatività a livello nazionale*), borrowed from the 1970 Workers' Statute for the private sector, which accorded primacy to the organizations affiliated to the three main confederations (Cgil, Cisl and Uil). In practice, the selective capacity of this principle turned out to be quite weak, as a consequence of its loose application, according to some observers (Napoli, 1989). Confederations viewed as 'major representative' have multiplied since then.

The principle of representativeness was considered in the 1993 reforms, but the abolition of the article referring to such a principle after a national referendum in June 1995 again opened up a normative vacuum which was overcome by new regulations only at the end of 1997. This decree precisely defined what a representative organization is, and how to measure such representativeness, not leaving it to the interpretation of political authorities or tribunals. According to the new rules, the organizations admitted to sectoral negotiations at national level are those which have a representativeness of at least 5 per cent within the relevant sector (or bargaining area), computed as the average between an 'associative' and an 'electoral' criterion. The associative criterion is the percentage of *deleghe* (check-offs) collected by an organization out of the total number of *deleghe* subscriptions in the relevant sector (or bargaining area). The electoral criterion is the percentage of votes collected by an organization out of the total number of votes cast for the election of personnel representative bodies in the workplace (created by the same law). In addition, those confederations to which an organization is affiliated which is recognized as representative within that sector are also allowed to participate in sectoral negotiations at national level. These rules should bring about their intended selective effects, reducing the number of trade unions admitted to national negotiations. In most cases this should mean no more than four or five first level organizations, and an equivalent number of confederations in each bargaining area, and around eight organizations in some bargaining areas for managers and medical doctors (Bordogna, 1998b). A substantial simplification should also follow in workers' delegations at the bargaining table at local level.

Representation at workplace level

In 1994 agreements were reached between Aran and the trade union confederations to create personnel representation bodies in the public sector, on the same model as that defined by the July 1993 tripartite agreement covering the private sector. The diffusion of these representative bodies, although uneven from sector to sector, has been less widespread and more uncertain than in the private sector (Carrieri, 1995). This issue was the subject of a legislative decree in 1997 which provides for the election of personnel representatives (*rappresentanze unitarie del personale*) within each administrative unit with more than fifteen employees. Following the Italian tradition of the 'single channel', these bodies are entitled both to bargaining rights and to information, consultation and participation rights. The decree leaves to collective agreements at national level the definition of the composition of such bodies and of the electoral procedures, but specifies features such as the secret ballot, the proportionality criterion and the frequent turnover of their membership. As noted above, the result of the election to these representative bodies is one of the two criteria for granting representative status to trade unions. The first elections (with the exception of the school sector) were held at the end of 1998, with a high degree of employee participation.

Public sector labour relations

The structure of collective bargaining

At the outset of this chapter it was noted that labour relations and methods of employment regulation have experienced significant evolution since 1945: from the phase of unilateral regulation, through the first legitimation of collective bargaining at the end of the 1960s, to its partial generalization under the 1983 law on public employment, to the full recognition of collective bargaining, on a model similar to that of the private sector, in the 1993 legislative decree, as amended in 1997. This evolution has been influenced by changes in the characteristics of the administrative and financial structure of the state, as well as by employment legislation.

Limiting the analysis to the period since 1993, two main innovations may be highlighted with reference to the previous experience. On the one hand, as emphasized by labour law scholars, a process of de-juridification of the employment relationship, and the legal recognition of collective bargaining, have taken place (Maresca, 1996; Rusciano, 1996). The bargaining method has been extended – on a collective, and in principle also on an individual, basis – to almost all public employees, as well as to all the issues not explicitly reserved to legislative or administrative regulation. In particular, the determination of wages and salaries, which in the past was often subject to intervention on the part of the parliament or the administrative courts), is now almost entirely given to the exclusive competence of collective negotiations. On the other hand, this process has been accompanied by a strengthening of the unilateral prerogatives of the employer, and is embedded within a context in which collective negotiations, especially at decentralized level, are not compulsory, but take place only in accordance with the free will and the calculations of the actors. Under the 1983 regime, however, along with a series of issues reserved to the law, there was another group of items – especially work organization and human resource management within the administrative units – over which the employer was subject to a sort of obligation to bargain and to reach an agreement with trade unions (Treu, 1994; Russo, 1996).

In the context of this greater degree of voluntarism in collective negotiations, and the more limited possibility of interference from other criteria of regulation of the employment relationship (Cella, 1996), the structure of collective bargaining envisaged by the 1993 reforms and realized subsequently resembled in many respects a more centralized version of the model designed by the important July 1993 tripartite agreement for the private sector.[9] This comprises an essentially bipolar structure, with the main pillar of sectoral negotiations at national level and a second tier of decentralized negotiations which take place only within the constraints set by national agreements. In addition to these main levels, there can also be multi-sectoral negotiations to define or change the bargaining areas or sectors (*comparti*) or to deal with matters affecting two or more sectors.

At the end of 1993, it was agreed between Aran and the main trade union confederations that the whole public administration should be divided into eight *comparti* (sectors or branches) for national negotiations covering non-managerial employees, plus eight bargaining areas for managers (see Table 4.1). The law states that employment conditions for managers must be dealt with in separate bargaining areas from those of other employees, which is a change from the 1983 regime (with only the partial exception of doctors; Zoppoli, 1993). As long as the present agreement on *comparti* remains unchanged, there are sixteen bargaining units and the corresponding collective agreements at national level: eight for non-managerial employees, and eight for managers. Within the school sector there is just one collective agreement, since there are no managers, but in the health sector doctors have a separate agreement from that of the other managers. Following the 1997 legal amendments, the bargaining areas for managers (with the exception of doctors) can be grouped into wider units across different sectors.

In line with the provisions of the July 1993 tripartite agreement, Aran and the main trade union confederations have agreed that sectoral national collective agreements have a four-year duration with respect to normative issues, and a two-year duration for pay issues. The agreements share with the private sector other features, including a no-strike clause for a four-month period around the expiry date of agreements, and a special allowance in the event of a delay in contract renewal of more than three months. Despite these common features, the process of negotiation designed by the 1993 law – although simplified in comparison with the previous regime – was still more complicated than in the private sector. The reason is that the government, as the *Corte dei Conti* (the supreme auditing authority of the state), could impose significant delays between the initial draft agreement reached by Aran and trade unions and its final approval. These procedures have been simplified by a 1997 legislative decree which states that the period between the draft agreement and its final approval should not exceed forty days.

Decentralized bargaining, subject to the budget constraints of each administration, can occur only on issues, and within limits, set by national collective agreements, and following the procedures that have been defined at the higher level.

Thus it has an integrative character in relation to national sectoral bargaining. Decentralized negotiations typically cover internal and external mobility measures, plans and activities in vocational training and, above all, the definition and management of systems designed to encourage collective and individual productivity. The latter includes the definition of general criteria for merit pay, with the aim of linking pay with quality or productivity improvement programmes, consistent with the role envisaged for this level of bargaining by the July 1993 agreement (Napoli, 1996a; Santucci, 1996; Fiorillo, 1996).

The importance of decentralized (or integrative) bargaining varies from sector to sector, and according to the financial resources available to the individual administrations. Currently it is more widespread in the health and local government sectors, and less so in the school sector. Greater significance could be given to this level of bargaining by the slightly greater degree of financial autonomy of the individual administrations, possibly even in the school sector, once the process of administrative decentralization initiated by the 1997 legislation has been implemented more fully.

The actors entitled to participate in negotiations vary according to the level of bargaining (see Table 4.8). As a consequence of the new rules approved at the end of 1997, the situation has been simplified in comparison with the 1983 law on public employment and also in relation to the 1993 reform, especially on the employees' side. For sectoral nation-wide negotiations, trade union organizations participate if they are recognized as representative in the relevant sector, plus the confederations to which they are affiliated. For negotiations on the definitions of *comparti*, or on issues involving two or more sectors, the participants are the confederations to which, in at least two sectors, representative unions are affiliated. And finally, for decentralized negotiations, the composition of workers' delegations must include the new personnel representation bodies elected in the relevant administration, but is defined by the sectoral agreements to which the individual administration belongs, so that may vary from sector to sector. On the employers' side, Aran is the exclusive bargaining agent – although it follows the guidelines received by the sector committees – in any kind of negotiations except the decentralized ones, where the main agents are the representatives of the individual administrations, who may choose to request assistance from Aran.

Collective bargaining trends and outcomes

Two main features of the bargaining experience and outcomes in the four years since the 1993 reform should be underlined. The first one, in a macro-economic perspective, considers the coherence of the new system with the incomes policy framework designed by the July 1993 tripartite agreement. The second one, from a micro-level perspective, concerns the degree to which the differences between the management of employment relations in the public and in the private sectors have been reduced in accordance with the aims of the reforms.

On the first issue, over the two contract renewal periods since the reform (1994–95 and 1996–97), wage increases negotiated at national level have remained

Table 4.8 Bargaining agents, at various levels[a]

Level	Employers' delegation	Employees' delegation
National agreements to define bargaining sectors or areas (*comparti*)	Aran	Representative trade union confederations[b]
National agreements on issues common to two or more sectors or areas	Aran	Representative trade union confederations[b]
Sectoral agreement, at national level (every four years for the 'normative' part; every two years for pay and compensation issues)	Aran	Trade union organizations (*sindacati di categoria*) which are 'representative' within the sector or bargaining area[c] Confederations to which representative trade union organizations within the sector or bargaining area are affiliated
Decentralized, 'integrative' agreements (local and individual administrative unit level)	Head of the administrative unit (or its representatives), with possibility of Aran assistance	Unitary personnel representation bodies Other representatives, according to the provisions of national collective agreements (possibly, representatives of each territorial structure of union organizations that has signed the national collective agreement or *comparto*)

Source: Bordogna (1998a).

Notes
a According to the provisions of the d. lgs. 396/97 (see also section 4.4).
b Those trade union confederations to which in at least two sectors or bargaining areas 'representative' trade union organizations are affiliated.
c Trade union organizations with representation in their sector or bargaining area of not less than 5%, as an average between associative and electoral criteria. Note that, before signing national collective agreements, Aran must verify that the trade unions with which the agreement has been reached together represent at least 51% of employees in the sector or bargaining area, as an average of associative and electoral criteria, or else at least 60% of the electoral criteria.

within the planned inflation rates fixed by the budget laws of the state, without the excesses often witnessed in the 1980s, when such ceilings were often ignored, not least by the ministers responsible for the negotiations (Dell'Aringa, 1997; Ambrosiano, 1995; Santagata, 1995). The 'depoliticization' of the bargaining agent on the employer's side has proved to be quite effective for this purpose. The overall economic and political context of the two bargaining rounds, however, was also important; it was such as to encourage responsible behaviour from all the actors involved. The dramatic financial crisis of the state in 1992 was followed by a strong and sustained commitment that Italy should meet the Maastricht convergence criteria for first-wave membership of European Monetary Union.

Moreover, the unprecedented series of scandals in which many politicians and political parties were found to be deeply involved brought about a partial renewal of the political and government leadership.

Also, where decentralized bargaining took place, it did not lead to the problems encountered under the previous regime; that is, uncontrolled use of various kinds of allowances, or shifts of large groups of workers to higher levels in the job classification system that were not justified in terms of professional skills. In comparison with the turbulent trends of the past, the first four years of the new system generally produced greater regularity of wage increases (despite some delays in contract renewal) and, at the same time, agreements that were not incompatible with macro-economic plans (Dell'Aringa, 1997; De Luca and Rossi, 1997). It cannot be ruled out, however, that within a context of very low inflation which should characterize the first phase of European Monetary Union, the functioning of the new public service bargaining system could become more troublesome than in the private sector, where higher productivity increases allow greater degrees of flexibility, both at the national and at the decentralized level.

Less clear-cut outcomes are detectable in relation to the second issue, the management of employment relations in the workplace. Under the 1983 law, several surveys highlighted the significant differences in human resource management practices across different parts of the public service (Natullo, 1990; Ronchi, 1993). They also revealed some important common features related to constraints which make the internal labour market very rigid; for example, the recruitment process, the job classification system and promotions, internal mobility, incentive policies and individual merit pay. On all these issues, many of which are not subject to collective bargaining, the constraints are much more severe than in the private sector, and they cannot be easily removed or changed in the short run (Della Rocca, 1996; Cerase, 1990).

None the less, there have been some recent innovations concerning these issues, leading to greater flexibility in the management of human resources at local level on wage and incentive issues (Cecora, 1996). The rule included in all national agreements (with the exception of schoolteachers) provides at decentralized level a form of 'compulsory selectivity' (Treu, 1995) in the allocation of incentives to collective and individual productivity. In order to reward the quality of performance of the individual employee, managers have the discretion to allocate a bonus to a small percentage of employees (between 7 per cent and 15 per cent), within a collectively agreed set of rules, in a sort of tournament where only the best workers win (Dell'Aringa, 1997; De Luca and Rossi, 1997). Although the amount of such awards is limited to about 1.5 per cent of the total annual salary of an employee (in principle, it could be given twice a year), they represent a significant innovation in the management of human resources in the public sector. To some extent they are like the lump-sum bonuses often utilized in the private sector, allowing pay differentiation on an individual basis for the first time.[10]

The utilization of these new incentive systems, to the detriment of the generalized increases so common in the past (Della Rocca, 1997), along with other techniques to motivate human resources, implies a real exercise of managerial autonomy and responsibility at local level, in accordance with the incentives and controls designed by the 1993 reforms. Comprehensive evaluation of this part of the reform is not yet possible. Collective agreements for managers in 1996–97, as well as amendments of the 1993 reforms included in the 1998 legislation, however, contain some premises for developments that would bring into the public sector some rules typical of the private sector. Among them are the possibility of removing managers if they do not achieve their objectives, greater importance of payment by results, and bonuses for the quality of individual performance within a system of assessment that involves the entire structure of personnel from the top positions to the bottom. Generally, the modest degree of innovation in developing more flexible and differentiated personnel policies reflects the difficulties of making them compatible with expenditure control; clearly budgets could be threatened by greater autonomy at decentralized level over pay issues and job classification systems.

Relations outside collective bargaining

Collective negotiations are not the only form of relationship between the administration and employees and their representatives. Traditionally, the public sector has been characterized by particularly intense forms of employees' or union involvement in joint machinery of various kinds, with responsibility for the management of the administrations, or for more specific issues connected with personnel policies, such as disciplinary and recruitment committees (see Irsi, 1981). Before the 1980s, lacking formal recognition of collective bargaining rights, such institutional consultation and participation channels often allowed a system of informal and lobbying relationships, including forms of real co-management of the internal labour market (Romagnoli, 1987; ISAP, 1987). Some of these relationships have survived the 1983 law on public employment, thus strengthening the confusion of roles between union responsibilities and managers' responsibilities, encouraged by the model of the obligation to negotiate and to reach an agreement typical of the 1983 regime.

The 1993 reforms put an end to this situation, at least in principle. Along with the collective bargaining method, it strengthened employees' and trade union participation in work organization issues, but with no expectation of co-management, and within a clear-cut framework of the responsibilities of the actors involved. Thus the administrations and their representatives are subject to a general obligation to inform employees' representatives and trade unions on issues concerning the quality of the working environment, as well as personnel management; information which, at their request, can give rise within fifteen days to a joint examination of the same issues. When this procedure has been completed, however, the administrations and their managers are free unilaterally to take the decisions they wish, on the basis of their own evaluation. There is the chance, of course, to turn the joint examination into negotiations, but there is no obligation to do so. The procedure, therefore, guarantees information and consultation rights to employees' representatives, but gives managers an additional degree of freedom in comparison with the 1983 regime: namely, the availability of that crucial re-source which in bargaining theory is known as a 'better alternative to the negoti-ated agreement'. This changes in a substantial way the bargaining relationship between the actors (Bordogna, 1996). It implies a serious weakening of trade union power to co-manage issues such as the mobility criteria, work loads, work-ing-time schemes and others which, under the 1983 law, were among the most frequent subjects of bargaining (Treu, 1994; Ronchi, 1993). Reinforcing this redefinition of union power and responsibilities in the management of the public sector is also the abolition (under the 1993 reform) of the right of employee representatives to sit on the boards of the administrations and on the recruitment committees, as well as a significant cutback in paid time off for union activities. It is not clear whether all these changes, which imply a limitation of the traditional co-management power of trade unions in public administration, will reduce the high union density typical of the sector.

Labour conflicts and the regulation of strikes

Until 1990 no legal regulation on the right to strike recognized by the 1948 constitution had been enacted, but several tribunal decisions recognized the right as valid in principle for public employees, with few exceptions, such as the police, the armed forces and the judiciary (Treu, 1987). At the same time, however, there arose the problem of regulating the impact of strike action in those sectors which provide essential public services. In several decrees the Constitutional Court set a limit on the right to strike where it impaired functions or services with the character of 'pre-eminent, general interest recognized by the Constitution law', with special reference to the protection of the health and physical welfare of citizens. The sanctions specified for actions which breach these limits, however, have seldom been implemented.

The problem of regulating the right to strike became particularly urgent dur-ing the 1970s and even more so in the 1980s, with the increasing spread of radical forms of strike behaviour from the industrial sector to public administration and public services which changed significantly the logic and parameters of industrial conflict (see Table 4.9).[11] Public service conflict has a multilateral character. Inevit-ably it involves actors extraneous to the matter at issue, especially the consumers of public services and the general public, who suffer the main costs of the strike; and it makes highly disruptive power available to the strikers (Kochan, 1974; Accornero, 1985; Pipan, 1989; Franzosi, 1992). This power was intensified by the regime of 'double protection' enjoyed by public employees under the 1983 law. Thanks to such a regime, even large groups, such as teachers or doctors, could enjoy the protection from the negative consequences of their own actions which should be exclusively reserved to smaller groups – according to Olson's well known theory (1965, 1982) – and were able to obtain, under this institutional shelter, the same privilege of 'irresponsibility' usually granted only to small groups (Bordogna, 1993). In comparison with the private sector, the balance between the costs of strike action and the potential benefits was very different in the public

Table 4.9 Public sector strikes (five-year averages)

Period	Services			Public administration			Services + Pub. adm./ Engineering		
	a	*b*	*c*	*a*	*b*	*c*	*a*	*b*	*c*
1960–64	375	215	5,284	212	378	7,297	0.82	1.11	0.95
1965–69	411	242	7,608	156	394	8,582	0.82	0.97	1.76
1970–74	526	324	7,720	401	496	16,642	0.89	0.60	1.01
1975–79	285	475	9,366	261	955	19,062	0.86	0.64	1.10
1980–84	184	378	5,612	170	538	5,203	0.70	0.60	0.55
1985–89	180	190	3,621	145	207	1,776	0.89	0.77	1.24
1990–94	132	86	911	66	43	418	0.77	0.53	0.46
1995–96	108	37	669	89	45	468	3.78	1.35	0.72

Source: Istat, *Annuario Statistico Italiano*, Rome, various years.

Notes
a No. of strikes; *b* No. of strikers (000); *c* No. of hours lost (000).
Sectors in strike statistics do not coincide exactly with those in employment statistics. However, *Services* include mainly health and education, while central and local government are included under *Public administration*. For 1964–66 *Services* figures include strikes in *Public administration*.

services. The *cobas* and other special-interest, narrowly based unions were thus repeatedly able to take advantage of their 'privileged' position in the late 1980s in their attempts to gain recognition in the representation arena, despite the rules of self-regulation of strikes with which the 1983 law had hoped to keep the problem under control. This law, in fact, required trade unions, as a condition of admission to the bargaining table, to adopt a code of self-regulation in respect of the right to strike, which then had to be attached to the sectoral collective agreements. But the codes were not really binding, and even less so for the new organizations.

After the failure of the experience of self-regulation to constrain dissenting unions, a law was finally passed in 1990 regulating the exercise of the right to strike in essential public services. This law was actively sought by the main union confederations, which were among the main victims of the *cobas*. It covers the postal service, banks, transport and other sectors which are outside the public sector as defined in this chapter, but it also covers schools, the health service, and many activities of central and local government which comprise the largest part of the public sector. The law includes a series of rules covering early notification of strikes, the length and forms of work stoppages, and the identity of essential services which have to be maintained at all times. The purpose of the law was to raise the cost of resorting to conflict, to make conflict more predictable and therefore less injurious to the public. The law established a Guarantee Committee (*Commissione di Garanzia*), appointed by the presidents of the Senate and of the House of Representatives, whose task is to ensure that employers, workers and trade unions comply with the new rules, especially the measures necessary to provide indispensable services during strikes. This committee, however, has very weak powers to impose effective sanctions on those who breach the rules, and it has no conciliation or arbitration competence.

From the point of view of the behaviour of the protagonists, the law has to some extent changed the balance in the relationship between the cost of action, the potential harm and the expected benefits, reducing the margin of difference from the situation typical in the private sector. The evidence of the first half of the 1990s shows that it has been quite effective in the school and health sectors and in other parts of the public administration (see La Valle, 1996). It met with serious difficulties, however, in the transport sector, where the diffusion of numerous functions and services with a very high disruptive power is associated with, and encourages, a chronically fragmented system of trade union representation.

Conclusion

For a long time, employment relations in the Italian public sector were characterized by marked differences from those in the private sector. The differences were justified by the concept of the 'sovereign nature' of the employer, and therefore by the peculiar juridical status of the employment relationship, but they were also rooted in an objectively distinct economic context, namely the absence or weakness of market criteria that could provide a basis for regulation as in the private sector. This political and economic context delayed full recognition of the basic features of collective bargaining until fairly recently. In its place, the unilateral regulation of employment relations persisted, mediated by informal bargaining and some elements of co-management of the administration process in post-1945 Italy.

Since the late 1960s, alongside the growing importance of state intervention in the production and provision of services, the differences between public and private sector methods of employment regulation have been reduced significantly. A gradual recognition of the method of collective bargaining for the determination of pay and conditions of employment of public sector employees emerged over the last thirty years, long after the right to strike and to unionize had been granted in the 1948 constitution law. The recognition of collective bargaining under the provisions of the 1983 law on public employment, however, was not a substitute for the special prerogatives associated with public employment status, but in addition to them, giving rise to the regime of 'double guarantee', almost unique – and uniquely troublesome – among European countries. This model of 'pluralism without market' was untenable: it lacked any criteria for effective regulation, apart from the interests of the largest trade union confederations in containing excessive divergence from private sector standards; and it could not prevent the outbreak of strikes in the second half of the 1980s, which had damaging effects not only on the public finances but also on the internal cohesion of the trade union confederations.

The institutional reforms started in 1993, with the strong support of the trade union confederations, widened the coverage of collective bargaining and reduced the role of legislation in employment regulation. This shift in policy, however, was accompanied by the tighter application of private sector-style criteria in individual and collective relations, and within the framework of a general strengthening of the managerial prerogatives of public employers. Innovations in the main features of the previous organizational model of public administration, together with the allocation of negotiation functions to the 'technical' competence of Aran, helped to create the conditions for a clear-cut demarcation between the interests of the various actors. The reforms also promoted a logic of behaviour among the actors and in the governance of labour transactions which was closer to that of the private sector, although without genuine market criteria of regulation.

The partial convergence of public and private sector labour relations was also supported by the adoption of the same bargaining structure as defined by the July 1993 tripartite agreement. It could be seen also in the greater degree of autonomy and voluntarism of the system of collective negotiation, in the increasing responsibility of the participants, in the diminishing competition from other forms of regulation (law and co-management practices), and in the declining intervention of processes of administrative justice which had previously been quite intrusive (Cella, 1996). Moreover, the outcomes of collective bargaining after the 1993 reforms also turned out to be rather similar to those in the private sector, in sharp contrast to the often radically divergent results of the 1980s. This convergence can be seen in wage and salary movements, the dismantling of some typical public sector prerogatives, the strengthening of decentralized and variable components of pay, and of its degree of selectivity. With reference to other features of public employment, such as recruitment, mobility and career patterns, the adoption of private sector practices has been more uncertain. Also, the development of an articulated system of direct employee-management relations, alongside the system of collective relations, has been very limited in comparison with private sector practice.

A more detailed and comprehensive assessment of these post-1993 developments would require survey data that are not yet available. It can be argued, however, that a central ambiguity in public sector labour relations still exists. It was apparent under the regime of 1983, and was inherited by the 1993 reforms, because of the context of strict financial constraints under which it took shape. The ambiguity derives from two conflicting demands facing public sector labour relations. First, they play a crucial part in the government's macro-economic policies (especially control of public expenditure and the containment of inflation), and thus encourage a high degree of centralization, or a substantial limitation on the autonomy of the collective bargaining parties. Second, they are an indispensable means of developing more flexible and effective management of human resources at the workplace level, to meet the demand for increasingly differentiated and better-quality services, which requires a more decentralized system.

These conflicting demands cannot easily be reconciled in the Italian experience or elsewhere (Bach and Winchester, 1994). This tension may give rise to a growing diversification across sectors, depending on structural differences in the degree of openness to quasi-markets or internal competitive mechanisms, as well as on the variable capacity to promote the autonomous interest of managers in the performance of their administrative units. Such processes could not be developed quickly, as they require administrative and financial reforms of the state, altering the financial autonomy of the administrative units, and budget control procedures, and changes in the recruitment, training and career patterns of managers.

As a radical programme of privatization of public services is not on the political agenda at present, and given the difficulty of transferring by decree into the public administration the high-powered incentives typical of the market (Williamson, 1991), it may be concluded that a political element – to some extent irreducible – will continue to characterize public sector labour relations in Italy.

Notes

1 Although the result of joint work, the section on 'Organizational structure, employment and wages' has been written by C. Dell'Aringa, that on 'Employers and employers' associations' by G. Della Rocca, and the remaining sections by L. Borlogna.

2 Legislative decree of 3 February 1993, No. 29, and subsequent modifications. Labour law scholars underline that the term 'privatization' is not correct, since the reform does not aim to simply integrate the public and private employment relationships, but rather defines a new legal framework for the public employment itself (see, for instance, Carinci and Carinci, 1993; Napoli, 1996b, ch. 2). All observers, however, agree that the meaning of such 're-regulation' is to shorten the traditional distance between the two sectors. This distance has been reduced even more by legislative decrees No. 396/97 and No. 80/1998, which in some respects amended the 1993 law. In the Italian legal system, a legislative decree (d.lgs.) is a law which the parliament authorizes (*delega*) the government to implement, on the basis of some broad guidelines defined by the parliament itself. This legal instrument has been very frequently used by the government in the process of public sector reform in the 1990s.

3 This is the reason why labour law scholars underline that under law 93/83 the employment relationship was not actually fully 'contractualized'.

4 These firms are totally or partially owned by local authorities (municipalities, provinces), but their employees do not enjoy public employment status and their collective agreements, on the employers' side, are not negotiated by Aran (see below).

5 The process of pay determination could become somewhat more decentralized as a consequence of the new provisions of d.lgs. 396/97, which allow the individual administrations – within their budget constraints – slightly greater bargaining autonomy, although still on the matters, within the limits, between the agents and according to the procedures defined by the collective agreements at national level. Perhaps this could bring about also somewhat greater differentiation of public pay.

6 They are allowed to join representative organizations, but these cannot be affiliated to any trade union confederation.

7 Over the entire post World War II period the Cgil, Cisl and Uil have been the three largest trade union confederations, traditionally linked, respectively, with the Communist and Socialist Parties, to the Christian Democratic Party and to other parties on the centre-left of the political spectrum (social democratic and republican parties). Since the mid-1960s these links with the political parties have slightly weakened, while the unity of action among the confederations themselves has increased.

8 This fragmentation is much higher if we look at the organizations of first affiliation (and not the federations or confederations to which they are affiliated, as in the first column of Table 4.7), amounting as a whole to more than 700 unions (Bordogna, 1998b).

9 The July 1993 agreement between government and social partners represented a far-reaching reform of the entire industrial relations system. The most important sections of the agreement are those relating to incomes and employment policy, to the structure of collective bargaining and to workers' representation at company level. It was a relevant step towards greater institutionalization of the system (of collective bargaining), previously often conditioned by the changing power relationships between the social partners.

10 In the literature on performance-related pay it is often underlined, however, that these bonuses – if quantitatively limited, on the basis of subjective criteria and linked with predetermined ceilings – could have little effect as incentive systems, or could even have counterproductive effects in terms of loss of trust, lower morale, increasing grievances and conflicts, etc. (Marsden and Richardson, 1994; Marsden and Momigliano, 1996).

11 Notice, however, that the growing social importance of public service strikes hardly shows up in quantitative terms, since they are often very short or involve very few workers, and at times are just 'virtual strikes', being called off at the very last moment without losing their disruptive impact (indeed a form of struggle short of strike action). Their relevance is therefore only partially captured by aggregate strike statistics (Franzosi, 1992; Bordogna, 1994).

References

Accornero, A. (1985) 'La "terziarizzazione del conflitto e i suoi effetti', in G. Cella and M. Regini (eds) *Il conflitto industriale in Italia*, Bologna: Il Mulino, pp. 275–313.

Ambrosanio, M. F. (1995) 'Contenimento del disavanzo pubblico e controllo delle retribuzioni nel pubblico impiego', *Quaderni dell'Istituto di Economia e Finanza* 7, Milan: Università Cattolica.

Bach, S. and Winchester, D. (1994) 'Opting out of pay devolution? The prospects for local pay bargaining in UK public services', *British Journal of Industrial Relations*, 32,2: 263–82.

Baldissera, A. (1988) *La svolta dei quarantamila: dai quadri Fiat ai Cobas*, Milan: Edizioni Comunità.

Bordogna, L. (1987) 'La sindacalizzazione', in ISAP (ed.), *Le relazioni fra amministrazione e sindacati* I, pp. 91 197.

Bordogna, L. (1989) 'The Cobas: fragmentation of trade union representation and conflict', in R. Leonardi and P. Corbetta (eds), *Italian Politics*, London: Pinter, pp. 50–66.

Bordogna, L. (1993) 'Public sector labour relations between macro-economic constraints and union fragmentation: the Italian experience in comparative perspective', in IIRA (ed.) *Economic and Political Changes in Europe: Implications on Industrial Relations*, Bari: Cacucci, pp. 865–80.

Bordogna, L. (1994) *Pluralismo senza mercato: rappresentanza e conflitto nel settore pubblico*, Milan: Angeli.

Bordogna, L. (1996) 'Il sindacalismo nel pubblico impiego: l'impatto della privatizzazione', in M. Napoli (ed.), *Riforma del pubblico impiego ed efficienza della amministrazione*, Turin: Giappichelli, pp. 29–50.

Bordogna, L. (1998a) 'Le relazioni sindacali nel settore pubblico', in G. P. Cella and T. Treu (eds) *Le nuove relazioni industriali: l'esperienza italiana nella prospettiva europea*, Bologna: Il Mulino, pp. 297–330.

Bordogna, L. (1998b) 'La rappresentanza sindacale nel pubblico impiego alla metà degli anni '90: un'analisi quantitativa', in C. Dell'Aringa (ed.) *Rapporto Aran sulle retribuzioni, 1997*, Milan: Angeli, pp. 231–55.

Carinci, F. and Carinci, M. T. (1993) 'La "privatizzazione" del rapporto di lavoro', in supplement to *Diritto e pratica del lavoro*, 15/1993: iii–xx.

Carrieri, D. (1995) *L'incerta rappresentanza*, Bologna: Il Mulino.

Cassese, S. (1983) *Il sistema amministrativo italiano*, Bologna: Il Mulino.

Cassese, S. (1994) 'Il sistema amministrativo italiano, ovvero l'arte di arrangiarsi', in S. Cassese and C. Franchini (eds) *L'amministrazione pubblica italiana: un profilo*, Bologna: Il Mulino.

Cecora, G. (1996) 'La prima tornata di contrattazione collettiva dopo la riforma del 1993', *Rivista giuridica del lavoro e della prevideza sociale*, 3,4: 335–51.

Cecora, G. (ed.) (1990) *Pubblico impiego: struttura e retribuzioni*, Bologna: Il Mulino.

Cella, G. P. (1996) 'Quale modello di contrattazione nel pubblico impiego?', in M. Napoli (ed.), *Riforma del pubblico impiego ed efficienza della amministrazione*, Turin: Giappichelli, pp. 23–8.

Cella, G. P. (ed.) (1991) *Nuovi attori nelle relazioni industriali*, Milan: Angeli.

Cella, G. P. (ed.) (1992) *Il conflitto: la trasformazione, la prevenzione, il controllo*, Turin: Giappichelli.

Cerase, P. (1990) *Un'amministrazione bloccata*, Milan: Angeli.

Clegg, H. A. (1976) *Trade Unionism under Collective Bargaining*, Oxford: Blackwell.

De Luca, P. and Rossi, F. (1997) 'Livelli, dinamica e struttura delle retribuzioni: un confronto pubblico-privato', in C. Dell'Aringa (ed.) *Rapporto Aran sulle retribuzioni, 1996*, Milan: Angeli, pp. 61–124.

Dell'Aringa, C. (1997) 'La contrattazione e le retribuzioni pubbliche nel periodo 1994–97: una breve (e parziale) cronistoria', in C. Dell'Aringa (ed.) *Rapporto Aran sulle retribuzioni, 1996*, Milan: Angeli, pp. 9–33.

Dell'Aringa, C. (ed.) (1997) *Rapporto Aran sulle retribuzioni, 1996*, Milan: Angeli.

Dell'Aringa, C. and Cananzi, G. (1997) 'Le dinamiche retributive dei rinnovi contrattuali di pertinenza Aran, 1994–97', in C. Dell'Aringa (ed.) *Rapporto Aran sulle retribuzioni, 1996*, Milan: Angeli, pp. 34–60.

Della Rocca, G. (1996) *Lavoro pubblico, lavoro privato: imprese e amministrazioni nella regolazione sociale*, Messina: Rubbettino.

Della Rocca, G. (1997) 'La differenziazione retributiva nel pubblico impiego: il caso degli istituti della produttività e della indennità di funzione per dirigenti nel settore degli enti locali', in C. Dell'Aringa (ed.) *Rapporto Aran sulle retribuzioni, 1996*, Milan: Angeli, pp. 345–80.

D'Orta, C. (1995) 'Qualifiche e funzioni dirigenziali', in F. Carinci (ed.), *Il lavoro alle dipendenze delle amministrazioni pubbliche dal d. lgs. 29/1993 alla finanziaria 1995*, Milan: Giuffrè.

D'Orta, C. and Talamo, V. (1996) 'Italy', in D. Farnham, S. Horton, J. Barlow, and A. Hondeghem (eds) *New Public Managers in Europe*, London: Macmillan.

Ferner, A. (1994) 'The state as employer', in R. Hyman and A. Ferner (eds) *New Frontiers in European Industrial Relations*, Oxford: Blackwell, pp. 53–79.

Ferraresi, F., Romagnoli, U. and Treu, T. (1981) *Il sindacato nella pubblica amministrazione*, Rome: Edizioni Lavoro.

Fiorillo, L. (1996) 'La nuova struttura della retribuzione nel lavoro pubblico', *Giornale di diritto del lavoro e di relazioni industriali*, 71: 483–99.

Fiorillo, L. and Russo, C. (eds) (1995) *Lavoro pubblico: manuale di diritto del lavoro e relazioni industriali*, Rome: Edizioni Lavoro.

Franzosi, R. (1992) 'Toward a model of conflict in the service sector: some empirical evidence from the Italian case, 1986–87', in G. P. Cella (ed.), *Il conflitto*, Turin: Giappichelli, pp. 7–34.

Giugni, G. (1992) 'La privatizzazione del rapporto di lavoro nel settore pubblico', *Lavoro informazione*, 11: 5–8.

IRSI (ed.) (1981) *Il sindacato nello Stato*, Rome: Edizioni Lavoro.

ISAP (ed.) (1987) *Le relazioni fra amministrazione e sindacati*, Archivio nuova 4 (2 vols), Milan: Giuffrè.

Kochan, T. (1974) 'A theory of multilateral collective bargaining in city governments', *Industrial and Labour Relations Review*, 27,4: 325–42.

La Valle, D. (1996) 'Nuovi scenari sindacali: una valutazione econometrica degli effetti sulle relazioni industriali dell'accordo sul costo del lavoro del 1993 e della legge n. 146/90', *Polis*, 10, 3: 433–51.

Maresca, A. (1996) 'La trasformazione dei rapporti di lavoro pubblico ed il sistema delle fonti', in *Giornale di diritto del lavoro e di relazioni industriali*, 70: 1817–24.

Marsden, D. and Momigliano, S. (1996) 'L'utilizzo di sistemi di incentivazione individuale nel pubblico impiego: problemi e possibili soluzioni', *Lavoro e relazioni industriali*, 4: 35–70.

Marsden, D. and Richardson, R. (1994) 'Performing for pay? The effects of "merit pay" on motivation in a public service', *British Journal of Industrial Relations*, 32,2: 243–61.

Napoli, M. (1989) 'I sindacati maggiormente rappresentativi: rigorosità del modello legislativo e tendenze della prassi applicativa', *Quaderni di diritto del lavoro e delle relazioni industriali*, 5: 7–48.

Napoli, M. (1996a) *Questioni di diritto del lavoro*, Turin: Giappichelli.

Napoli, M. (ed.) (1996b) *Riforma del pubblico impiego ed efficienza della pubblica amministrazione: una riflessione a più voci*, Turin: Giappichelli.

Natullo, G. (1990) 'La contrattazione decentrata nel pubblico impiego', *Lavoro e diritto*, 1: 103–27.

Olson, M. (1965) *The Logic of Collective Action*, Cambridge MA: Harvard University Press.

Olson, M. (1982) *The Rise and Decline of Nations*, New Haven CT: Yale University Press.

Pipan, T. (1989) *Sciopero contro l'utente*, Turin: Bollati-Boringhieri.

Romagnoli, G. (1987) 'Introduzione', in ISAP (ed.), *Le relazioni fra amministrazione e sindacati*, I, Milan: Giuffrè, pp. 5–25 and 373–83.

Romagnoli, G. (ed.) (1980) *La sindacalizzazione tra ideologia e pratica*, Rome: Edizioni Lavoro.

Ronchi, R. (1993) 'Le relazioni sindacali nel pubblico impiego: una rilevazione quantitativa in Lombardia', *Ires Lombardia*, Collana 'Ricerche', 35.

Rose, R. (ed.) (1985) *Public Employment in Western Nations*, Cambridge: Cambridge University Press.

Rusciano, M. (1978) *L'impiego pubblico in Italia*, Bologna: Il Mulino.

Rusciano, M. (1990) 'Lavoro pubblico e privato: dalla "separatezza" all' "unificazione" normativa', in M. Baglioni *et al.*, *Stato sociale, servizi, pubblico impiego*, Naples: Jovene, pp. 7–32.

Rusciano, M. (1996) 'La riforma del lavoro pubblico: fonti della trasformazione e trasformazione delle fonti', *Giornale di diritto del lavoro e di relazioni industriali*, 70: 245–64.

Rusciano, M. and Zoppoli, L. (eds) (1995) *Lo 'spazio negoziale' nella disciplina del lavoro pubblico*, Bologna: Il Mulino.

Russo, C. (1996) *Poteri, responsabilità e partecipazione nel lavoro pubblico*, Turin: Giappichelli.

Santagata, W. (1995) *Economia, elezioni, interessi*, Bologna: Il Mulino.

Santucci, R. (1996) 'Le retribuzioni incentivanti nel pubblico impiego', *Giornale di diritto del lavoro e di relazioni industriali*, 71: 501–23.

Talamo, V. (1995) 'Contrattazione collettiva e diritti sindacali', in L. Fiorillo and C. Russo (eds), *Lavoro pubblico*, Rome: Edizioni Lavoro, pp. 157–284.

Treu, T. (ed.) (1987) *Public Sector Labor Relations*, Geneva: International Labour Organization.

Treu, T. (1994) 'La contrattazione collettiva nel pubblico impiego: ambiti e struttura', *Giornale di diritto del lavoro e di relazioni industriali*, 61: 1–52.

Treu, T. (1995) 'Rinnovi nel pubblico impiego', *Diritto e pratica del lavoro*, 10: 653–9.

Williamson, O. (1991) 'Comparative economic organization: the analysis of discrete structural alternatives', *Administrative Science Quarterly*, 36: 269–96.

Winchester, D. and Bach, S. (1995) 'The state: the public sector', in P. K. Edwards (ed.) *Industrial Relations: Theory and Practice in Britain*, Oxford: Blackwell, pp. 305–34.

Zoppoli, L. (1993) 'I comparti pubblici dopo la riforma del rapporto di lavoro', *Lavoro Informazione*, 10: 5–9.

5 France

The restructuring of employment relations in the public services

Phillippe Mossé and Robert Tchobanian

In the economic crisis which France like other European countries has been experiencing, productivity gains cannot be achieved in the public sector in the same manner as in the private sector. Civil servants have almost total job security and redundancies cannot be the adjustment mechanism. In order to achieve the fiscal objective of lowering levels of national debt, a primary adjustment mechanism has been to privatize former public sector enterprises. In the public service sector the aim has been to curb the growth of staff. A central dilemma for policy makers is that privatization, and other forms of modernization, could jeopardize the acquired rights of French citizens. In effect employment security, which is integral to public sector employment, is not simply a reflection of union influence and capacity to maintain civil service 'privileges'; it also provides the citizen with a guarantee that civil servants are independent and not subject to the moral hazards of the private sector. Job security also provides an incentive to acquire high levels of competence and to use this expertise in the collective interest rather than in the individual's own self-interest. Moreover, it must not be forgotten that the counterpart of job security is lower wages. Whilst gradually reducing the advantages traditionally associated with public sector employment, forms of privatization have eroded some of the independence associated with public sector workers and their willingness to gain further qualifications in a more uncertain context.

Definitions of public service sectors

As Table 5.1 shows, in 1994 public sector employment comprised approximately 6 million staff out of a total labour force of 25 million. In the post-war period there has been a substantial increase in employment. In 1947, the public sector employed more than 3 million people out of an active labour force of 20 million. So from 1947 to 1994, the share of public employment increased from approximately 15 per cent to 25 per cent (Rouban, 1995). There are three separate components: public enterprises, social security organizations and the public service sector.

First, public enterprises employ approximately 1.5 million workers. They were usually natural monopolies, wholly owned or substantially controlled by the state,

Table 5.1 Public sector employment in 1994 (000)

Public enterprises	1,500
Social security	220
Central government, local authorities and hospitals of which:	4,340
Central government	2,200
Local authorities	1,300
Public hospitals	840
Total	6,060

Source: Ministère de la fonction publique, 1995.

and provided services in the transport and energy sectors. There were three waves of nationalization: in 1936, at the end of World War II, and in 1982. Conversely, privatization policies were pursued vigorously during 1986–88 and in 1993. Privatization has fundamentally altered the landscape of the former nationalized industries. Thus, in 1983, more than 10 per cent of the total French work force was employed in this sub-sector, whose employment conditions can be characterized as lying somewhere between the private sector and the civil service. Since this period a large proportion of industrial firms, as well as banks and insurance companies, have been totally or partially privatized. For example, Renault has been partially privatized and the state owns no more than 47 per cent of the shares. None the less, the state remains the major shareholder, which explains the importance of state action in response to Renault's closure of the Vilvorde plant in Belgium during 1997. The movement towards privatization has been strong, gathering momentum since the late 1980s. It has resulted in diverse systems of corporate governance, with some limited liability companies (but with the state retaining some shares) whilst others more closely resemble private companies. The latter are usually concentrated in the rail and utilities industries.

Second, social security organizations, with 220,000 employees, are usually regulated by private law (*droit privé*). They have welfare and redistributive functions covering sickness insurance, pensions and unemployment benefits. These services are provided directly by central government in most countries, but in France they are managed as a partnership between trade unions and employers' associations under the regulation of the state.

Third, the public services comprise approximately 4.3 million employees. A substantial proportion of them are established civil servants (*fonctionnaires*), which has a more specific meaning than the generic term *fonction publique* and indicates that these civil servants are covered by a statute defined by administrative regulations and not by employment law. Although there are specific characteristics attached to each particular public service statute, the general principles are the same and derive from the general regulations of the public service, which until 1984 were not subdivided. Subject to precise rights and duties, civil servants' employment status differs from that of other workers, including the employees of public firms. This situation is the outcome of a long historical evolution which defines a unique place for individuals working for the state that makes them independent of political influence. It also reflects the centralization and uniformity which characterize the political economy of France.

As we discuss below, however, many public service employees who undertake civil service work are excluded from attaining *fonctionnaire* status. A continuous demand of trade unions has been for civil service status to be extended (termed 'titularization'), and this has happened at periodic intervals (Meurs, 1996). A countervailing trend is that the reformed postal and telecommunication services are categorized as public firms and are therefore no longer directly governed by the public service regulations. Despite these changes, most staff in these sectors have retained their civil service status, and in 1995 approximately 400,000 employees remained civil servants out of a total of 460,000. This threefold division of the public sector can be subdivided further. The public services comprise three separate components: central government, local government and hospitals. These provide the primary focus of this chapter and each component requires separate discussion. In addition, the education sector has its own specific features.

Organizational structure, employment and wages

Organization of the main sectors

Central government

Central government remains the most important part of the public service, even with the establishment of separate employment categories for health and local government since 1984. It includes the central functions of the state, including the military, the judiciary and the police, and many aspects of education and other services delivered at local level. All services that have not been delegated to local government or to public hospitals form part of the central government sector. It also covers some employees in the postal and telecommunication sector as well as teachers in private schools when financed by the government, but neither of these two cases will be considered here.

For the most part, civil servants work for the central state itself. This reflects the very highly centralized character of public administration and the weakness of local government structures, at least before the 1982 law on decentralization. Thus the role of civil servants, employed under the civil service statute, is not limited to central administrative activities. The central state provides many services at local level and it is estimated that only 4 per cent of central government civil servants are directly involved in the administration of central government. In comparison, 14 per cent work at the regional or department level and 81 per cent work in decentralized local services. Two levels of state services have to be distinguished. The central services comprise either central government (organized into different ministries) or functional and technical services with a national competence. The decentralized services operate at the local level, the most important of which are under the authority of a prefect (*préfet*) who is the direct representative of the state.

The relationship between central and local government has altered since the decentralization reforms of 1982. The department became an autonomous political entity, managed and governed by a local assembly (*conseil général*) electing its own president. But at the two other intermediary tiers, the regions and communes, central government employees still perform activities which might be expected to be undertaken by local government workers. The police are an illustrative case. Even if local police exist, they play a secondary role in the maintenance of law and order to the national police force. The boundaries between central government and local government activities are therefore not always precisely defined. Decentralization has changed the division of functions between central and local government to some extent, but the core public functions remain dominated by central government policy making and regulation.

Local government

Local authorities exercise considerable power in France despite the highly centralized structure of the state; the creation of departments was a legacy of the French revolution. Prior to the 1982 law employees were employed by communes under a variety of different employment conditions. This heterogeneity resulted in arbitrary recruitment and career decisions. Until 1972 a city employee had to be dismissed from a city to be re-employed by another: no direct transfer was possible. Alongside this picture can be added devolved central government (for example, the prefecture), which was well organized with a uniform status and a strong influence at local level. The overall situation was of a strong disjuncture between a weak local government and a powerful central government implementing its policies at local level. The need for more independent local government was evident.

March 1982 marked a symbolically decisive shift away from the unitary nature of the French state. The 1982 Act codified a three-tier local government structure with 36,500 communes, ninety-six districts and twenty-two regions (Mabileau, 1991, cited in Keraudren and Baka, 1998). Currently about a quarter of all public employees are employed by these separate employers. Their activities differ from those of central government and about half the departmental budget is allocated to health and social services. The reforms brought more formal independence and greater legitimacy to local government, with elected local councils. In addition the measures introduced by Le Pors, a Communist Party member and minister in the Mitterrand government, provided local government employees with the same kind of advantages as those working in central government. Decentralization, however, brought few new resources because many of the competences transferred to local authorities were already managed locally and therefore administrative disruption was limited (ibid., 1998). Despite these limitations the introduction of a specific local government employment statute in 1984, even though based on the general statute for central government, was a historic turning point because France, even prior to Napoleon, was a very centralized country.

National health service

The health services involve a heterogeneous and complex group of employees, although the medical profession remains dominant. The public hospital system contains regional university hospitals, which provide specialized services and undertake research and education, and more numerous local hospitals. The private hospital sector is very significant and the combination of the private for-profit and the private not-for-profit hospitals account for a third of total hospital capacity and patient admissions. The 190,000 full-time employees in private hospitals may be paid for by public funding (either directly or by means of the social security system, which finances the whole hospital sector) but, as their employment status is different from that of public employees, they will not be considered in this chapter.

Growth in hospital expenditure has been a continuing problem despite the introduction of an annual global budget for each hospital in the 1980s, designed to ensure tighter financial control. More recently the financing of public hospitals has been changed to include case-mix information in the global budgeting system. The aim has been to link the budget more effectively with the actual activity undertaken by hospitals. A new definition of a hospital unit and the creation of a patient-orientated information system have been the two main ways used to inject a new dynamism into the management of the hospital system. Since a major reform in April 1996, each hospital has to conclude a 'contract' with its local hospital agency, the latter being directed by a manager appointed by the Ministry of Health. These agencies are under the direct control of central government and the national health insurance agency. This 'contractualization' process is linked with the aim of decreasing the overall number of beds nationally by 50,000 over the next five years. Furthermore, an accreditation procedure is being implemented in hospitals on a voluntary basis in 1996–2001, otherwise the regional agency has the power to force each hospital to be assessed. Private management techniques are also being promoted, such as quality management, competition among units either vertically (between medical unit and support service department) or horizontally (between medical units). The problem is that these managerial reforms do not sufficiently take into account current changes in service delivery, especially hospital mergers.

In considering the health sector it has to be borne in mind that the medical profession is dominant in shaping health care provision, even though few medical staff are direct employees of the public sector. Of the approximately 170,000 French doctors, 45,000 are employed full-time by hospitals (either private or public) but none of them is categorized as a civil servant. Some medical staff are, however, civil servants, but they are not employed by hospitals or health centres, working instead for local government agencies. They comprise a very small proportion, about 8,000. The public hospitals, with over 800,000 staff, employ a very diverse range of occupational groups. The formal hospital statute was established only in the mid-1980s, but the hospital sector has been the object of much attention as governments have tried to reconcile lowering costs, with wages accounting for more than 60 per cent of expenditure, whilst maintaining quality and the active co-operation of staff.

Education

The education sector is dominated by the state and, in particular, by the Ministry of Education, which manages over a million personnel with civil service status. The education sector, however, is not a separate branch of public administration, because employees in this sector can be employed at different levels or in the private sector. The education sector comprises around 4 per cent of the work force, and in this chapter the focus will be the public sector even if in private schools most teachers are paid by the state.

The organization of the education system combines interventions from central and local government and the private sector. In practice the vast majority (1.1 million out of a total of 1.5 million) are employed by central government. Ninety per cent of teachers and 52 per cent of other staff groups are therefore civil servants, and teachers comprise a little under half of all state civil servants (800,000 out of 1.9 million). Education and teaching are largely under the control of the Ministry of Education, which despite the decentralization laws still retains control over the curriculum, training and all aspects of personnel management. For example, the Ministry of Education's control extends to every diploma awarded, except in the case of some agricultural qualifications. The decentralization laws did provide local authorities with some new competences in terms of building maintenance and investment but these were relatively minor innovations.

Universities are financially dependent on the state but they have a certain amount of autonomy in terms of both curriculum and management. The basis of the relationship with central government is a four-year contract signed with the ministry. Secondary and middle schools are public local establishments having a degree of management autonomy. In the same way as universities, they have internal administrative boards (*conseils d'administration*) with staff representatives. Primary schools and nurseries are directly managed by the communes, which also employ the non-teaching staff.

Composition of employment

As noted earlier, the public sector comprises three separate components. In 1947, there were 1,152,000 workers in the public enterprise sub-sector, which increased to 1,852,000 after the last period of nationalization in the early 1980s. By 1994 public firms' employment had shrunk to 1.5 million (approximately 8 per cent of the work force). This total has been boosted since 1991 by the inclusion of 430,000 employees working in the postal and telecommunication services who were formerly categorized as civil servants. The second component, social security organizations, employs 220,000 people.

Of the public services, central government is the most long-standing and numerous, comprising 2.2 million employees in 1994. Approximately 200,000

Table 5.2 Evolution of public service employment, 1969–89 (000)

Service	1969	1980	1985	1989
State civil service	1,635	2,260	2,401	2,392
Army	433	459	454	438
Local authorities	618	1,021	1,185	1,254
Hospitals	360	702	787	807
Total	3,046	4,442	4,827	4,891

Source: Quarré, 1992.

employees were not established civil servants (*non-titulaires*). In 1984, following the decentralization law of 1982, a separate local government statute was established. About 1.3 million people were employed in this sector in 1994, mainly in the smallest municipalities (*communes*), but also in the *départements* and *régions*, which are less numerous and cover a broader geographical area. Finally, there is a separate public statute for public hospital workers. The public hospital sector employs 840,000 workers, including acute and psychiatric hospitals and nursing homes.

Public education is not regulated by a separate public statute. Most teachers are employed under the central government, i.e. civil service, conditions of employment, whilst non-teaching staff in nursery and primary schools are classified as local government employees. Overall, 1.1 million employees work in the education sector, the majority of them – 813,000 – teachers. Private education is important because approximately 17 per cent of pupils are educated in the private sector. Most of the private sector is under the trusteeship of the state, which controls the quality of teaching and the curriculum. In 1995, 144,000 teachers employed in private schools were in fact state wage-earners. The education and hospital sectors are the only public services in which state regulation and funding are dominant, but with a substantial proportion of services undertaken by private providers.

In the post-war period the number of civil servants increased dramatically until the early 1990s. This growth varied between sub-sectors and occupational groups. It is difficult to be precise about developments, not least because the compilation of the data altered with the creation of separate statutes for health and local government in the early 1980s, and the definitions of the sectors have altered over time. Furthermore, the totals can differ according to whether non-permanent staff are included. As Table 5.2 shows, between 1945 and 1989, when the data were compiled consistently, the total work force increased from 2 million to 5 million (Quarré, 1992).

Not all the 4.3 million public service workers are civil servants, and other differences include gender and working hours (full-time and part-time). In the public sector as a whole, the percentage of women is very high. In 1995, one estimate suggests, the proportion of women was 57 per cent among civil servants (Audier, 1997). This amounts to 29 per cent of the total female work force. Women are very numerous in education, local government and health. The high

Table 5.3(a) Changes in part-time employment, 1969–89 (%)

Employer	1969	1980	1989
State civil servants	5	7.5	12.5
Army	0.5	0.3	1.9
Local authorities	32.7	27.9	28.9
Hospitals	11.6	9.5	16.8
Total	10.6	11.6	16.4

Sources: Quarré (1992), Walter (1997).

Table 5.3(b) Part-time employment in 1994 (%)

Employer	Part-time employees
State	11.4
Local authorities	30.3
Hospitals	14.2
Total	18.6

Source: Walter (1997).

percentage of women is partly explained by the growth of part-time jobs, which in general is a relatively recent innovation, although working part-time has been a long-standing feature of casual employment in small towns. Since 1970 a legal framework has been implemented and it was reformed in 1982. Several types of part-time job are available, and as Tables 5.3 (a) and (b) illustrate, the share of part-time employment has increased. By the end of 1994, 18.6 per cent of public service employees were working on a part-time basis, higher than the 15.2 per cent in the private sector (Walter, 1997).

The public sector labour market

The civil service

Civil servants are split between three categories – A, B and C. Table 5.4 illustrates the link between occupation and category which is based on the type of work, or administrative, technical or other tasks performed. Each category and each job corresponds to the entry level qualification required. University level qualifications are required for category A, *baccalauréat* for category B, and lower diploma or no diploma for category C. In 1994, 41 per cent of civil servants were classified as category A, 27 per cent as category B, and 32 per cent as category C. Central government staff have higher qualification levels than the other sub-sectors, mainly because of the high percentage of senior civil servants and the high proportion of teachers. Most teachers are in the A category, including primary school teachers, who were progressively upgraded from B to A in the 1990s.

Table 5.4 Examples of the three public service categories

Role	A (Management)	B (Application)	C (Execution)
Administrative	Senior civil servants	Middle-ranking civil servants	Administrative assistants
Technical	Public works engineers	Qualified laboratory staff	Skilled workers
Other	Teachers Tax inspectors	Police inspectors Nurses	Prison officers Nursing aides

The central government sector comprises 2.2 million employees, of whom 1.9 million are civil servants. Around 240,000 work in central and general administration, 210,000 in specialist functions, 200,000 in technical administration, 800,000 in education, 300,000 in the army, 115,000 in the police, and 35,000 in the judiciary. Excluding the army, women are more numerous than men (55 per cent). Feminization is strongest in professions such as teaching and nursing and, as noted earlier, feminization has contributed to the growth of part-time employment.

Not all central government employees have *fonctionnaire* status and as a result not all of them have job security. Those without titular status are either on probation or on short-term contracts. In 1994, 14 per cent of state employees were not permanent. The number of temporary workers is almost certainly an underestimate because the exact number of employees with precarious status (such as CES, see below) is not known.

Of the 1.3 million workers in *local government*, the major increase in employment occurred before the decentralization process. Between 1970 and 1983 the increase was around 4 per cent a year; since then it has been under 2 per cent. The vast majority are employed by the communes. Only 150,000 work for the departments and fewer than 7,000 are employed by the regions. In terms of occupational groups, the most numerous (600,000) are clerical and technical workers. Each level (commune, department, region) specializes in particular functions. When analysed by job classification, it appears that qualification levels are lower than in central government, but the position differs considerably according to local government tier. In 1993, the proportion of managers was 39 per cent at the national level, 10 per cent at the departmental and regional level, and only 4.4 per cent at city level, although the level of qualifications is increasing, with the lowest category (D) abolished and the proportion of category A increasing. The age profile is declining. In 1974 the average age of a manager was fifty-two, it is now around forty-five. By gender the tendency is towards the feminization of staff. The proportion of women was 56 per cent in 1982; it is now 59 per cent. There are some differences according to levels, with the percentage of women highest at the departmental level because of its health and social service responsibilities.

One main difference between local government status and the others concerns recruitment and mobility. In terms of career management, local government employees are mainly the responsibility of specific institutions. It is thus rather paradoxical that the main institution designed to harmonize human resource management across the country acts at national level. Named the *Centre national de la fonction publique territoriale* (CNFPT), this agency deals with important subjects, such as the recruitment of managers and training. At the local level the agency is represented in each department and even in some cities. A recent tendency (for instance, exemplified by the 27 December 1994 Act) is to give local management centres more responsibility and to reduce the power of the CNFPT. Recruitment at national or local level is mainly by competitive examination (*concours*). It is possible in some cases, however, to hire employees without setting formal examinations for category C workers. The decision, which is left to local employers (the city mayor or departmental president), has been criticized because it allows 'clientelism'. The 'Hoeffel law', introduced in December 1994, narrowed the autonomy of local government on this issue. Finally, in terms of dismissal procedures, formal dismissal is not possible, but in practice an employer can remove an employee. The procedure often results in the geographical mobility of the individual (Schrameck, 1995).

Public hospitals

In public hospitals, the increase in employment from 300,000 in the 1970s has not been uniform across occupational groups. Many former hospital activities have been externalized, such as the after-care of patients, some surgical operations, maintenance, cleaning, etc. This trend explains why the number of technicians employed in public hospitals decreased from 100,000 in 1987 to 92,000 in 1995. But at the same time, the number of medical staff, nurses and administrative staff has increased. With a substantial increase in hospital admissions and a reduced length of stay, the average productivity of each hospital employee has increased dramatically over the last decade.

Recruitment and mobility rules are defined in the January 1986 statute. One difference between the hospital employees' statute and the general civil servant statute concerns nationality. French law has prevented non-French citizens from working in the civil service, but hospital employment is an exception, as any EU member may be hired in public (and private) hospitals. As in the other parts of the public sector the *concours* is the main way to enter the hospital sector. Some exceptions to this general rule exist. For instance, non-permanent positions are excluded and staff on short-term contracts may in exceptional circumstances be recruited directly by a hospital director. After the *concours* a probation period is served, generally for a year, at the end of which the employee is usually put on a permanent basis.

Education

As Table 5.5 shows, in the late 1990s the number of teachers increased dramatically, by as much as 28 per cent in the universities, 7.4 per cent in secondary schools, but only 1.5 per cent in primary schools. Around 290,000 people work in

Table 5.5 State employment in education, 1996

Level	No. 1996	% change 1990–96	% of women	% of part time
Primary school teachers	314,560	1.5	76	5
Middle and high school teachers	399,000	7.4	56	11
University professors	61,947	27.7	30	2
Teachers in training	37,621	1.9	63	1
Non-teachers	296,415	−0.4	65	19
Total	1,109,540	3.9	63	11

Source: Ministère de l'éducation nationale.

an administrative or technical capacity within the education sector, and 63 per cent of the staff are women, employed particularly in non-teaching occupations. Among teachers the percentage of women differs according to the level, varying from 30 per cent at university level to 76 per cent in primary schools. Most teachers are drawn from category A, even among primary school teachers, who used to be category B. But among non-teaching staff half are drawn from category C, mainly blue-collar workers. Although the number of non-permanent staff is low among teachers it is 22 per cent among non-teaching staff.

Special job creation contracts (*contrats emploi solidarité*, CESs) have been introduced since 1989. In 1994, more than 715,000 people were working under this type of contract. It has been focused on the unemployed and poorly qualified young people, for a two-year period on a part-time basis. They are mostly subsidized by the state, and employers have to be either public or non-profit organizations. In public hospitals the measure has been very successful. To circumvent limits imposed by the Ministry of Health on civil servant recruitment, most hospitals have hired employees (especially in clerical departments) on such special contracts. Strong incentives for hospitals from the ministry also explain why the formula has been so widespread. In effect the Ministry of Health was willing to pay to integrate the unemployed because it viewed this goal as part of the hospital sector's social obligation. The ministry's social balance sheet (*bilan social*) shows that in 1994 more than 54,000 people were employed on such contracts in public hospitals, especially smaller local ones. Unfortunately the integration process has failed, and only 6 per cent of these employees have gained permanent employment. Moreover, apart from the social and psychological problems for the individual, precarious employment can jeopardize the whole hospital organization at a time when every employee is being asked for more commitment and participation.

Since 1996 an agreement signed between the government and the main unions has aimed to avoid the use of precarious jobs. The second goal of the agreement has been to offer permanent jobs to a significant percentage of persons hired on a short-term or part-time basis in recent years. In 1997, the government announced plans to create 350,000 jobs for young people in specific activities and sectors such as education and social welfare.

Table 5.6 Average wages by category and age, 1994 (francs)

Category	Up to 25	26–35	36–45	46–55	56–65
A	108,740	144,290	175,640	192,910	237,640
B	98,380	108,940	12,470	135,260	145,730
C	89,760	96,510	105,710	106,700	105,610

Source: INSEE, 1996.

Wages and salaries

The pay determination system for civil servants is highly centralized, with a single pay classification system. As noted earlier, there are three general categories (A, B and C) which define overall career boundaries and pay progression. However, each group of civil servants (*corps*) – of which there are more than 1,800 – has some specific terms of employment; for example, the number of years it takes to progress to the next level (Meurs, 1996). In practice, most civil servants belong to a small number of *corps* and the top civil servants belong to about ten élite *grand corps*. The government establishes a general index at national level for increases in the basic salaries of all civil servants. The whole structure of indexes defines the grid of possible outcomes. Each of the three categories has a minimum and maximum number of points, and pay negotiations focus on the value of the index point. Basic pay is therefore a combination of the employment category which is defined by qualification level, length of service, different social or geographical supplements (depending on family circumstances) and bonuses (*primes*) that differ between jobs. In 1995, the gross wage (before social contributions) was 164,000 francs, of which 15 per cent comprised basic wage supplements (see Table 5.6).

Generally, wage differentials are narrower in the public than in the private sector. The highest 10 per cent earn 2.4 times the wages earned by the lowest 10 per cent. In terms of wage trends between 1994 and 1995 the increase was 1.8 per cent, divided equally between a basic wage and career-related factors. Thus because of higher qualification levels, and the increasing average length of service, wages have increased automatically according to the formula termed GVT (*Glissement – Vieillissement – Technicité*). The method used to determine wage levels has a crucial bearing on overall public sector wage growth and has been a controversial issue, causing tension between the state and trade unions.

In a highly centralized system bonuses have been an important adjustment mechanism to reward individuals or particular groups without eliciting comparability claims from other groups. From 1990 a national agreement granted to some local government employees, like other civil servants and hospital employees, special premiums linked with specific and arduous working conditions. Entitled, *Nouvelle bonification indiciaire*, this procedure was welcomed by the unions, as it was considered a way of introducing equity into an otherwise rigid system. This measure cannot be seen as a step towards individualization, as it only concerns a minority of workers and a very small percentage of their wages. But it has to be

Table 5.7 'Bonuses' as a percentage of wages in the public services

Wage	1984	1990	1994
10% lowest	0.1	0.1	0.0
10% highest	18.1	22.8	24.8

Source: INSEE.

remembered that basic wages do not account for total remuneration. Before the local government statute was introduced, many allowances and bonuses were given on an arbitrary basis by local employers. Even if the control of such 'privileges' is tighter now than a decade ago, they remain as much a matter of political as of financial judgement. Bonus payments remain a controversial issue because bonuses are much higher as a proportion of wages for the highest earners. For the lowest 10 per cent of wage-earners across the public services bonus payments are negligible, but for the highest 10 per cent bonuses comprise up to a quarter of salary (see Table 5.7).

After the political and social unrest of the late 1960s, the government started to consult the trade unions more formally over pay determination. This process culminated in the law of 13 July 1983 which formalized the right of trade unions to negotiate with the government nationally over remuneration. The law was more than symbolic. The government was socialist and the Minister of the Public Function was a member of the Communist Party, so the reforms may have been as much guided by political motives as industrial relations considerations. Furthermore, the law addressed other subjects in addition to pay determination. It recognized for the first time the right of trade unions to negotiate over work organization and conditions.

These reforms do not undermine the ability of the government to set or freeze wage rates unilaterally in the public sector. First, the government decides whether or when pay negotiations should take place. For instance, taking into account the Maastricht fiscal criteria, no negotiations occurred between 1995 and 1998. Instead, the government decided unilaterally on a slight increase in nominal wages to maintain civil servants' purchasing power. In February 1997 the Juppé government awarded a 1 per cent pay award after a freeze in 1996. Second, the social partners negotiate within strict parameters. The negotiations focus on the value attached to the index point which underpins the wage structure and the number of points attributed to each given civil servant category. At the end of the negotiations an agreement, usually called the statement of conclusions (*relevé de conclusions*), or sometimes the *contrat* or *accord salarial*, is almost always signed by the social partners. This agreement has no legal status and is not needed to alter wages. But, because it is the outcome of a political compromise, all players, including the government, adhere to it. As a result, the statement of conclusions is always confirmed by parliament and implemented according to the negotiated schedule.

The most recent application of this procedure occurred during the winter of 1997–98. In the 'conclusions' of these negotiations (namely, a ten-page memo) most of the recommendations concerned recruitment, career progression and wages and, in particular, the position of the low-paid. From February 1998 to July 1999, the low paid will have gained a 2.5 per cent increase in the number of points and a general increase in the unit value of the point (about 3 per cent at the end of the two-year period). Other items concern issues not directly linked with wages. For instance, before implementing the thirty-five-hour week, a global assessment of the situation in the three public service sectors was conducted during 1998. The agreement also stated that new negotiations would start in 1999 to assess the effectiveness of the current agreement and to update the figures.

An assessment of the 1983 law is difficult. On the one hand, this law was a milestone in the convergence of private and public sector employment relations, as it tends to make public sector negotiations more like those in the private sector. On the other hand, it can be seen as no more than a political sop to the unions – recognizing their legitimacy but without giving them any substantial new power. The procedure is highly political and centralized, with the negotiated outcomes covering all civil servants despite the huge disparity in their employment situations. While trying to take into account specific problems among the lower categories, this is very difficult because of the centralized procedure adopted. Contrary to the increasing level of decentralization in the political field, the key financial issue, pay determination, is tackled only at national level. One compensatory benefit of the high degree of centralization and uniformity since 1983 is the opportunity for the unions to discuss wider topics than pay determination, such as employment levels, status and structure. This reformist strategy is mostly followed by the CFDT (*Confédération française démocratique du travail*), whilst the CGT (*Confédération générale du travail*) and FO (*Force ouvrière*) often do not engage with the conclusions and sometimes do not even take part in the negotiation process.

In a memo published in October 1997 by the public service ministry, it was suggested that, compared with other European countries, France has too many civil servants. According to this document, around 10 per cent of civil servants should not be replaced when they retire, to improve public sector efficiency and productivity. Furthermore, although their wages are lower than those in the private sector:

> In an economic context characterized by layoffs, low wages and the search for productivity by private firms, the public sector staff has quietly increased during the whole period: increasing by 500,000 from 1975 to 1980 . . . and by a further 112,000 from 1985 to 1990. In the meantime the purchasing power of public civil servants regularly improved. The tacit agreement that employment security was the counterpart of low salaries is no longer true. A study carried out in 1994 shows that categories B and C staff having the same responsibilities were better paid in the public sector than in the private sector. The range of differences was from 19.3 per cent to 23.6 per cent for the C category, and around 16 per cent for the B category.
>
> (Choussat, 1997)

As we saw in Table 5.6, although the average wage increases significantly with age, the qualification level obtained prior to recruitment and its category are the key factors. This is even more the case with the lowest category. At the end of their career category C civil servants earn less than a young category A civil servant. Age tends to widen the gap between the C and the A categories. At the beginning of their career the gap is around 20 per cent, at the end it is over 100 per cent.

In recent years, a new management approach has emerged based mainly on individual assessment. At its establishment in 1945, the civil service statute included the principle of individual scoring of each civil servant by their manager. Until recently the procedure has been symbolic, with each manager tending to score each civil servant as high as possible. This discredited the ratings as an effective human resource management tool. In 1998 the Ministry of Equipment decided to change this practice, introducing the individual interview as a precursor to the scoring process. To begin with, unions were opposed to the change; they were afraid that this new managerial power could jeopardize the main career rule, based on length of service. After some months most of them changed their minds. They acknowledged that an interview was a good opportunity for the employee to explain their own needs in terms of training, mobility and pay. The process is not formally implemented, however, and is still organized on a voluntary basis. The socialist government of Lionel Jospin decided to generalize such a procedure in the near future, but it is already predicted that it will be a difficult business.

Employers and employers' associations

State policies

The relative size and influence of the French state have scarcely any equivalent in Western Europe. This has not precluded debate about the modernization of the state, which has two key components. First, there has been consideration of the size and scope of state activities. For example, should the state be directly involved in the production of industrial goods or financial services? Second, what should be the balance between cost effectiveness and wider social goals? In the health sector these dilemmas have been felt acutely, with public hospitals weighing up the balance between cost effectiveness and equity considerations.

In terms of the size and scope of state activity there has been acceptance of a reduced role for the state in the direct production of goods and services where a market environment exists and since 1986 the state's role has shrunk. For more than a decade most banks and insurance companies have been privatized, and the nationalized sector has contracted. The process has been influenced by the financial health of each company, and some of them have been only partially privatized, owing to their financial problems. Public firms operating in the public sector are less involved in the process and their share of employment in this subsector increased to 58 per cent by 1994. Many public sector organizations are under pressure to compare their efficiency with that of private sector firms, as can be illustrated by developments in telecommunications. There was a shift from state ownership to public firm status in 1991 (France-Télécom), and in 1997, despite the electoral success of the socialists, partial privatization proceeded. Deregulation has ensured that at least one private company operates in this sector, opening the way to further competitors entering the market. Similar developments have occurred in broadcasting, following the creation of private channels and the privatization of the biggest public channel in the mid-1980s. Other former public services, such as water, are now largely provided by private companies.

In the public services, the debate about privatization has been less relevant and the main focus has concerned issues of service efficiency, quality and cost effectiveness. The proportion of central government expenditure and taxes spent on public services is among the highest in Europe. In 1995, the total amount was 44.5 per cent of GNP, about 25 per cent funded by taxation and 19 per cent by social contributions (managed by social security institutions). Despite this level of taxation, in a period when economic growth has been sluggish, expenditure has exceeded revenue. Between 1992 and 1995, levels of public debt were far in excess of the Maastricht convergence criteria. Efforts to limit public debt to ensure participation in the single currency area in 1999 led to pressure for more efficient use of public resources. It is in this difficult context that the debate about the modernization of the public services has occurred. Against such a background it is significant that, since June 1997, the ministry in charge of human resource management in the public sector has been renamed the *Ministère de la fonction publique, de la réforme de l'état et de la décentralisation*. Although the socialist government confirmed the importance of the public sector by halting the previous government's policy of reducing the number of civil servants, it recognizes that it is necessary to modernize the civil service.

The idea of modernizing the public sector has developed in an uneven way since 1986, not least because France experienced four changes of government, from left to right and from right to left. Between 1986 and 1988, the government started the privatization process in public firms and the modernization of public services. This modernization aimed to diffuse management techniques adopted in the private sector (e.g. quality circles) into the public sector. From 1988 to 1993, with the dominance of a socialist government, the privatization process was almost completely halted, but a new modernization policy, mainly in central government, was adopted. Based on the idea of the 'renewal of the public service', this initiative involved experiments with 'service projects' giving more autonomy to decentralized levels of public administration and more active human resource management. The policy had mixed results, for two reasons. First, economic recession reappeared after some years of growth, which stifled reform initiatives and, second, the right-wing parties were returned to government in 1993. Their focus was predominantly privatization rather than modernization. Massive social upheaval, however, occurred within public firms, demonstrating the limitations of such policies. New elections in 1997 returned the socialists to power and brought further policy changes, but the role of the state remained a controversial issue.

The characteristics of public service employers

In terms of personnel policies and labour relations, public employers at the local level have very little influence. Because the existing public service sub-sectors were inherited from the former single – and still strong – central government statute, the role of national rules and practices remains very important. Consequently, local employers have no interest in creating or entering any kind of employers' associations, mainly because such a lobby would not have any impact on decisions. However, the decentralization movement has had some effect in giving more autonomy to the local level, although its extent varies between different sub-sectors and services.

Education

The number of teachers is determined by national indices of need, with the level and number of staff depending primarily on pupil numbers and the socio-economic status of the community. Consequently, there is no freedom for any given school director to hire new teachers or staff. As each level of establishment in the educational system is linked with one of the three tiers of local government (nursery and primary schools being linked with communes, middle schools with departments and secondary schools with regions) even in the maintenance of their buildings directors have few decision-making powers. The school director has some limited autonomy in determining school priorities within the parameters set by the Ministry of Education. It is possible to define some specially adapted courses or academic needs for the students, hiring extra staff on a non-statutory basis to meet the objectives identified by school staff.

This rather limited freedom seems to be accepted. In effect the centralized tradition (alongside opposition to too much local autonomy) is one of the outcomes of the philosophy that the education provided for each citizen is the most efficient means of making France a united nation, grounded in republican values. A recent example of the strength of this ideology can be found in the case of mobility rules. If a teacher in a middle or secondary school wished to move from one school to another, the decision was taken nationally by the Ministry of Education, even if the move was to be made within the same department. As there are several thousand moves each year, the procedure was bureaucratic, lengthy and costly. In 1998 the ministry decided to change it and shift the level of decision making from national to local.

Despite union resistance to this reform decentralization had some impact. Even in an otherwise centralized educational system, one example can be given of the new autonomy. It concerns the global hours allocation (*dotation globale horaire*, DGH) and the flexibility within the formula. In every secondary school about 500 extra hours per annum are allocated and the director and teaching staff are free to use them as they see fit. Generally, the decision takes into account the establishment's educational plans, the needs of the pupils and the available resources. Grellier (1997) demonstrated that the differences between schools are quite significant.

Most hours are used to divide classrooms considered to be overcrowded, but often the DGH is used to develop a specific activity (social integration, health, etc.) linked with the school's social environment and the interests of the teachers. This example suggests that even if the scope to develop a specific local policy remains heavily circumscribed, the tendency of most public sector local 'employers' is to use the flexibility available to them more than in the past.

Differences from the private sector remain strong. Even in areas where competition exists, it is not on the same basis as in the private sector and questions about the survival of a public service do not arise. None the less, since the 1980s more and more public service managers have been adopting management methods that are similar to those in the private sector. The change is not due to financial and economic constraints *per se*; it is due to the liberalization movement that has developed alongside the crisis of the welfare state. Two illustrations can be provided of such developments, the first in local authorities and central government, the second in the hospital sector. In both cases it is clear that the way employers face the challenge of modernization consists in harmonizing, intentionally or not, their management policies. On the other hand, it appears that relations between local public employers and politicians, either at national or at local level, are decisive. These relations explain a large part of the current situation, which illustrates the balance that managers have to strike between the search for autonomy and the need for resources from central government.

Local authorities

France is one of the few European states where local authorities are organized around three different levels whilst being, at the same time, central government administratively defined areas and autonomous districts. As employers, each of the three levels has specific competences. The communes are the most important in terms of the number of employees. They are also the level where the employers, namely the mayors, have the most difficult role, particularly in small towns. In effect it is quite difficult to run a local territory mainly with volunteers or a small number of employees working a few hours a week, as is the case in many villages.

At the department level, employee numbers are disproportionately high in departments where the population is low because the scope of activities is so wide that few economies of scale are possible. In the communes the challenge is the same but resources are more scarce, reflecting the fact that 25,000 out of 36,000 French communes have fewer than 700 inhabitants and 80 per cent have fewer than 1,000 inhabitants. Formally, they all have the same functions and responsibilities but it is difficult to obtain and pay the minimum number of civil servants required to carry out the main responsibilities of each commune (police, road maintenance, etc.). A budgetary system implemented at the national level tends to establish a kind of equilibrium, if not equity, by transferring some resources from poorer communes to richer ones, but this practice is mainly limited to big towns. In most communes the only way to cope with the problem is to find other communes to co-operate with and to share resources in a rational way. Of course, this is made more difficult by the political game, in which politicians have to demonstrate that they are doing a better job than their neighbours.

Pragmatism is stronger than ideology, and for more than two decades city mayors have co-operated, encouraged by central government. The result has been a new division of labour between communes, departments and conurbations. Two main types of group exist. The first (*syndicat*) generally have no fiscal autonomy and cities delegate only a few functions to them; they are often seen as pilots for more integrated policies in terms of local development and human resource management. The second type (*groupes de communes*) are allowed to define their own fiscal policy, which can differentiate between each commune in the group. These groups are often organized around a big regional capital, with its suburbs and sometimes medium-size towns. Under the name of *communauté*, this more widespread approach was established in 1992. These diverse arrangements have grouped as many as 15,000 communes employing 100,000 people. Compared with the 6,700 employed by the regions, these coalitions have become a strong intermediate level built on local and personal agreement rather than national and geographical divisions.

At the departmental level the tendency is also to harmonize management but the approach is less organized, as no formal contract exists between departments. The harmonization process mainly comprises a national association with membership drawn from the presidents of the almost 100 departmental level councils (*conseils généraux*). The main purpose of the association is not to co-ordinate policies but to act as a lobbying organization to defend the department level against proposals to reduce its role and to give more responsibilities to the regions. Despite the absence of formal co-ordination, department policies are converging in terms of personnel and expenditure. In 1983, the government set up an agency to co-ordinate and control the activities of locally elected politicians. This national service helps advise the departments, regions and communes which have greater responsibilities than previously. Its most important tasks concern occupational training, statistical information and the evaluation of local policies.

The relationship between local civil servants and politicians is clear from a formal and legal point of view. The former are supposed to implement policies decided by the latter. However, because of the physical proximity and the often strong geographical and professional links, the actual relations are less clear-cut. Local politicians, such as the mayors of big cities or the presidents of departments, rely on civil servants to implement policies, especially social policy, some aspects of public health policy, local security and road maintenance – responsibilities devolved since 1982. Local politicians have to take into account the specific knowledge and qualifications of the civil servants they employ but have to apply national laws and until recently were judged in a mechanistic way against adherence to national policies. This rather mechanical approach has been changed and has become more complex.

To gain more autonomy and ensure tighter control over local activities, most politicians, particularly at regional and departmental level, have created a personal private office, staffed by political appointees. These advisers are often specialists in the same fields as civil servants. The job can be difficult, as the private office members act as a buffer between the political level and the executive level. It might be assumed that the existence of a private office would reduce the power of officials and transfer it to elected politicians, not only in the decision-making process but also during the evaluation phase. But the arrangement has certain advantages for employees (Schrameck, 1995). In effect, the existence of a private office entails a separation between political and executive decisions. Less power is the price to be paid for the benefit of being distanced from political decisions one may not agree with. In an era when corruption is increasing, politicians are some-times tempted to ask their employees to act in an inappropriate manner, and consequently the existence of a barrier between executive and political decisions means that employees are protected.

Public hospitals

In the hospital sector the tendency is towards specialization and mergers. This restructuring process has encouraged hospitals to share their resources with other private or public health care providers. The main goal is to increase hospital productivity through economies of scale. These developments have been made possible by the unification of the hospital directors' profession. Until recently, hospital directors were current or former employees of the hospital and therefore were susceptible to local medical power. Hospital directors had little legitimacy in either managerial or administrative terms to counterbalance medical expertise and clinical autonomy. Now there is greater recognition of the profession of hospital director. The main reason is the creation of a national school where all future directors are trained, with the focus on management, making hospital managers closer to higher civil servants. Since its foundation, it has trained a specific *corps* of hospital directors and managers.

For career development purposes, each manager has to work for a number of years in different types of hospital and in different geographical locations. Mobility is high and ensures that similar managerial policies are adopted across the public hospital sector because, faced with common problems, managers adopt similar approaches. For example, a recent trend has been to outsource peripheral activ-ities (laundry, catering, cleaning, some maintenance functions and even some laboratory tests). At the same time more rationalized management tools have been based on private sector practice. Some of these changes have been initiated by central government, but managers themselves have found a new legitimacy and influence in developing these policies.

The relationship between hospital directors and central government used to be a direct one. Until recently, a 'good' director was able to go to Paris and negotiate directly with the Ministry of Health to obtain more resources, in excess of the annual inflation rate decided at national level. This situation prevailed until the end of the 1980s and was particularly true of teaching hospitals. The local polit-ical level's key role was to lobby for resources to gain a prestigious new hospital. Rivalry, rather than competition, was the key word in the hospital sector. This was one of the reasons why the hospital sector expanded so rapidly during the post-war period despite the national containment control policies implemented from the early 1960s. Since the 1996 hospital reforms the only actor the hospital director has to deal with is the director of his Regional Agency for Hospitals (RAH). The main responsibility of this civil servant, who has strong powers, is to allocate resources between private and public hospitals, on the basis of a collectively defined plan and the public health needs of the region.

The twenty-six regional directors were nominated directly by the Ministry of Health and their salaries are much higher than is usual in such jobs. This is justified by the tough objectives they have to achieve in a short time scale: modernizing and rationalizing hospital management, reducing expenditure – mainly by a reduction in the number of beds – while maintaining quality care. Despite the arrival of this new and powerful player, hospital directors still have to contend with local politicians. Hospitals are often the main employer in a town and, as such, they are under pressure to maintain a certain level of activity and employment. This pressure has been formalized through the position of the mayor, who used to be, by law, the head of the hospital board. Since the 1996 Juppé reforms it is no longer mandatory, but in practice is usually the case. Paradoxically, this change, whether effective or not, is a sign that the power of the mayors is considered excessive, but at the same time it is difficult to reduce their influence.

Trade unions

The conflictual events of December 1995 revealed the magnitude of the problem of employment relations in the public sector. Conflict was more prominent in public enterprises than in the public service sector. The protests were illustrative of developments in the public sector unions, which cannot be separated from the experience of private sector unions, because they belong, in almost all cases, to the same confederations. However, the means are very different, first because collective bargaining was not formally recognized until 1984 and, second, because the representation of employees is more developed in the public sector. For instance, on the joint administrative boards (*commissions administratives paritaires*), unions, through their elected representatives, play an important role in the management of civil service careers. Union co-operation in these aspects of personnel management explains why union involvement is stronger among public service workers than among other employees. Thus national unions with both public and private employees in their membership obtain more than half the votes during elections and aim to confine representation on these bodies to union members. It has been the case for instance in 1994, when the CGT, CFDT, FO, *Confédération général des cadres* (CGC) and *Confédération française des travailleurs chrétiens* (CFTC) obtained more than half the votes. But public service unionism has specific characteristics, especially professional concerns, which explains why the most important unions operate with a professional orientation. It is, for example, the case in the school sector, where union membership remains very high. This situation also relates to the history of the French union movement.

Table 5.8 Administrative council election results in the civil service, 1976 and 1994 (%)

Union	1976	1994
CFDT	14	17.1
CGT	28	16.6
FO	19.6	16.2
FEN[a]	20.6	13.5
FSU	–	13.5
FGAF[a]	6.2	6.1
CFTC	3.9	3.1
CGC	2.1	2.9
Other	5.5	10.9

Source: Rouban (1995).

Note
a Both part of UNSA since 1994.

In 1947 the CGT split, with the majority (pro-communist) grouping staying in the CGT and the minority creating a new union, FO. Several federations, particularly in the public sector, rejected this schism and stayed united and autonomous. This was the case with the influential *Fédération de l'éducation nationale* (FEN). Until 1992 it remained the dominant union in the educational sector, with more than half of all teachers. In 1992, FEN split into two separate unions; one remained as FEN, the other established the *Fédération syndicale unitaire* (FSU), which has become dominant today. In 1993, FEN and other autonomous civil servant federations (such as the *Fédération autonome des fonctionnaires*, popular among policemen) created the national federation of autonomous unions (UNSA), becoming the sixth largest French union confederation.

One way to assess union influence is to examine the representativeness criteria. Recognition as a representative union enables the union to present a list of candidates for election to joint administrative boards. Since 1996 representativeness has been defined to take into account the whole public sector. As a result the five traditional national unions (CGT, CFDT, FO, CFTC and CGC) plus UNSA are the only representative unions. Other smaller unions have to show that they are representative of the sub-sector in which they want to field candidates. This applies to FSU, which is not representative except in the educational sector. It also applies to some autonomous unions in membership of the *Union syndicale groupe des dix* (Group of ten). In the public services it concerns autonomous unions, for example in customs, and some unions which are largely part of SUD (United and Democratic Unionism). The latter was the outcome of a split within the CFDT. Collective bargaining in the public sector is highly centralized and therefore the results of professional or sectoral elections (such as elections to administrative boards) provide a more precise picture of union influence. In central government the results for 1976 and 1994 are shown in Table 5.8 whilst Table 5.9 shows the result for category A workers, covering the most qualified workers, including teachers.

Table 5.9 Votes for each union in the public services among category A employees

Union	State (1994–95)	Local authorities (1995)	Hospitals (1992)
CFDT	16.6	30.9	32.1
FO	11.3	21.6	21.5
CGT	6.4	13.7	16.3
CGC	2.7	4.8	2.0
CFTC	1.9	4.5	4.4
UNSA (with FEN)	14.6	9.5	4.0
FSU	32.9	–	–
Other	13.9	14.9	19.9

Source: UCC-CFDT.

These results demonstrate that unionism in the public sector is even more divided than in the private sector. This arises from the extreme professional diversity of the public sector, according to sub-sector and skill level. It is not surprising that such diversity can be found among organizations which extend beyond ideological differences (Rouban, 1995). As for French unionism as a whole, this balkanization is the result of recent as well as old divisions.

It is difficult to estimate trade union density among civil servants. All attempts to assess overall union density conclude that it is low, especially in the private sector. Under 10 per cent is the usual estimate (Labbé, 1996). As contributions paid by individuals to unions are tax-deductible, it is theoretically possible to measure the number of unionists, using inland revenue sources. In 1991, for the whole economy, it was estimated to be as low as 6.5 per cent. However, this rate is conservative and the actual rate is closer to 8 per cent. France has witnessed a sharp decline, but the public sector has been regarded as immune from this crisis. Today the three unions which are the most representative in the private sector (CGT, CFDT, FO) also represent a large proportion of public sector workers.

Trade unions which are active only in the public sector (such as FEN and FSU) enjoy high levels of union density. Despite a steep decrease since the end of the 1970s, the rate of unionization in the public sector is much higher than in the rest of the economy and remains high among groups such as postal workers. In education, the relative strength of the unions corresponds to their participation in career management, but change is occurring and the decreases are significant. Many traditional unions have had difficulty adjusting to the modernization of the public services since the mid-1980s. The splits which have appeared within FEN/FSU and CFDT/SUD are mainly the result of a division between 'reformers' and 'radicals'. The latter, who support the *status quo*, have increased their support because of the threat that many civil servants perceive from the reforms. CFDT and FEN have both experienced difficulties because they were willing to negotiate on the modernization plans. But the reaction of public service workers to the reforms shows that what is perceived to be in jeopardy is not only the model of public service *à la française* but also the kind of human resource management linked with it (mobility rules, welfare state benefits, pensions, etc.). The 1995 social movement demonstrated how strong these feelings were and developments in health and education illustrate many of the same phenomena.

In the health sector, although doctors are not civil servants, their policies have a dominant influence on other professionals' strategies. Doctors' unions are numerous and divided along professional lines, with some organizations dominated by specialists while others are confined to general practitioners. These organizations have about 15,000 members among approximately 170,000 medical staff. The largest is the *Confédération syndicale des médecins de France* (CSMF) with 6,000 members drawn from across the profession. Furthermore, there are a myriad of medical societies acting as lobbies to promote their own, sometimes narrow, specialisms. The day-to-day settlement of conflicts between a patient and their doctor or between doctors is controlled by the medical professional body (*conseil de l'ordre*), organized on a regional and national basis, within which neither the state nor the citizen may interfere.

Under the socialist government of the 1980s, the dominant idea was to suppress the 'professional orders', not only in medicine but also in architecture and law, etc. But nothing has actually happened. On the contrary, in the 1990s the tendency has been to create new professional orders, and some nurses' organizations are now demanding them as well. This dynamic is the ideal vehicle for the pursuit of professional interests and strategies. It is then not surprising that in the 1990s the trade unions have had to compromise with a new type of independent worker organization based on the interests of specific occupations (*co-ordinations*). Competing with traditional unions and confederations, with a more professional than union orientation, this type of grouping appeared in 1988 when hospital nurses took industrial action and formed *co-ordinations* to obtain more social and economic recognition relative to other professions. It was the first time that women had organized on such a scale to lead a movement which defended their own interests and succeeded in gaining important concessions from the government on pay and working conditions.

Since then, and over the next four years in particular, the larger trade unions defending more traditional interests have lost out in terms of share of employee votes in the public hospital sector. In representative elections, their share was 90 per cent in 1988, falling to 82.4 per cent in 1992 and recovering slightly to 85 per cent in 1996. This trend is also evidence of the tension in reconciling narrow professional interests with broader collective interests. In the education sector, elections that took place in 1996 in middle and secondary schools (excluding universities) gave a large majority to the FSU. It obtained more than twice the number of votes in comparison with FEN. This totally new result marks a very significant departure from the previous situation, where, before the split, FEN had a dominant position, especially taking into account the professional categories that it represented (Geay, 1997). The tendency for the more militant unions to grow seems to be confirmed. It is also a sanction against the reformist unions' attitude towards both the 'Juppé plan', which aimed to alter radically the regulation of the social security system, and changes to the management rules within education. It reflects also the evolution of unionism in this sector, which has unique characteristics. Labbé (1996) estimated that union density was approximately 70 per cent in 1978 and declined to approximately 40 per cent in 1991, which remains a very high level for France. The majority of members were within FEN, which had 52 per cent of employees in 1978, but the figure had fallen to 29 per cent in 1991. Prior to the 1993 split FEN was dominant in the school system. This hegemony can be related to FEN's refusal to be drawn into the split between the CGT and FO in 1947 and it established an organization unconnected with any confederation. In effect, it remained a loose federation of autonomous unions with numerous rival factions. CDFT is the only union confederation which is also representative at national level in education, but less than 5 per cent of employees are members.

Unionism in education reflected the school structure. FEN was organized along lines defined by the different professions (primary schoolteachers, middle and secondary school teachers, university lecturers, clerical staff, etc.). Primary school teachers used to play the dominant role; they were more numerous because of the large number of pupils in that type of school. Behind its formal unity, FEN contained several factions. In the primary school sector the *Syndicat national des instituteurs* (SNI) was the most important and pursued policies close to those of the Socialist Party. In middle and secondary schools, the *Syndicat des enseignants du secondaire* (SNES) was closer to the French Communist Party. Thus many different ideologies coexisted within an organization structure based on occupational divisions.

The outcome of this complex structure was to increase FEN's dominance in the whole sector and warranted its strong participation on a variety of personnel management committees. In turn, this position increased the incentive for any given employee to be a FEN member. In addition, a whole set of professional associations were established, most of them linked with the management of mandatory social insurance, but also with other voluntary activities such as private insurance. These 'mutual' organizations contributed strongly to the homogeneity of the teaching profession, of which the high level of unionization was a key feature (Girault, 1996). Even if it was not mandatory to be a member of FEN to belong to these related associations, it bolstered the position of FEN, which was seen as offering practical services. Professional concerns, service provision and the ideology of public education made for strong unionism.

The arrival of FSU did not immediately alter this picture. FEN and FSU together achieved more than 60 per cent of the votes to joint administrative boards in 1996 (excluding universities) and FSU replicated the same type of professional divisions that already existed in FEN. Over time, however, FEN has experienced relative decline. First, secondary school teachers are now more numerous than primary school teachers, FEN's traditonal bedrock of support. Moreover, primary school teachers, who belonged to the B category, are gradually being replaced by schoolteachers belonging to category A with higher academic qualifications. The traditional type of primary school teacher, and FEN member, is in decline. Finally, the decline of FEN is also a sign that teachers are reluctant to accept the implementation of new management tools within the public services.

FEN was willing to negotiate on modernization; FSU's strategy aimed to defend public service values and maintain traditional criteria as far as mobility and career planning were concerned.

Public sector labour relations

Collective employment relations are organized in two main ways; collective bargaining, and joint consultative committees (*instances paritaires consultatives*). The latter play a very important role in monitoring the personnel management process in the absence of traditional collective bargaining and its uncertain legal status. This situation is changing, however, and the gradual development of collective bargaining is bringing the public sector closer to the model prevailing in the private sector.

Historical evolution and civil service status account for the importance of social dialogue between the social partners in shaping collective employment relationships. Civil servants are not managed through an ordinary employment contract as employees are in the private sector (i.e. the labour law), but rather by regulations deriving from administrative law. Thus employment relations are largely organized around respect for rights and duties, at an individual as well as at a collective level. Among employees, union influence is generally measured by elections to joint administrative boards, and the results are influenced by the type of control these committees exercise over administrative decisions in respect of personnel planning. As noted earlier, collective bargaining is centralized and focuses on wages, training, etc. In the context of modernization, there is scope for bargaining in the public sector to be broadened, though such a reform would reveal differences between the unions.

Collective bargaining

The 13 July 1983 law altered the civil service statute across the public sector. It gave representative unions the right to negotiate with the government before it decides on wage increases and allowed developments in work organization to be incorporated into the discussions. Before this law, collective bargaining did not have a legal existence in the public sector, whilst in the private sector – and in the small part of the public sector covered by labour law (*droit du travail*) – the first law on collective bargaining had been established in 1919. The 1983 law is an illustration of the process of partial convergence in the regulation of public and private sector employment. Collective employee rights, such as the right to join a union, the right to strike, collective bargaining rights, were established from the 1880s onwards, depending on the rights in question. But for a long time the position of a civil servant was unclear. Union rights were not formally recognized before 1946, even if earlier regulations provided a form of recognition. The right to strike, mentioned in the post-World War II constitution, was officially written in for the first time into the 1983 civil servant statute. It may still be limited for some categories. For instance, civil servants have to announce the intention to strike, giving a strike notice (*préavis de grève*) some days in advance, whereas no such constraint exists for private sector employees and unions because the right to strike is an individual constitutional right.

The 1983 law clarifies the role of collective bargaining. As in the private sector, wages have to be negotiated with representative unions. The Ministry of the Public Function, State Reform and Decentralization negotiates centrally with representative civil servant unions covering the three public service sub-sectors. If the negotiations fail the state can decide unilaterally the amount of civil servants' wage increases. The ministry is also in charge of the regulation of the whole public sector, with the monetary value of the 'point' which underpins the wage structure being negotiated. Agreements may include more specific measures involving, for instance, the minimum level of wages. If the agreement is signed, the government releases under a legal framework the decisions taken. Centralized negotiations extend to the wage scales. Each profession within the public service is defined as belonging to a *corps* having its own specific wage scale. The whole set of *corps* is divided into several categories according to the level of qualifications required. If a specific demand is addressed to a particular ministry (e.g. the Ministry of Health in the case of the 1988 nurses' dispute) it can be costly and difficult to respond to because the negotiations have to take into account the implications of specific demands for the consistency of the whole public service wage system.

In 1990, in order to allow diversity and flexibility in the wage and job classification system, an important agreement was signed by the government and most unions (except the CGT). Termed the 'Durafour agreement' (after the Minister of the Public Function at the time), its aim was to bring more coherence to the job classification system. It tried to reduce the inequalities between groups of employees which arose from the discrepancy between a fossilized wage structure and the skills involved in the work undertaken. For example, nurses felt especially aggrieved that their wages had not kept pace with the increasingly technical content of their work. Most of those involved in the public services agreed that, along with age, new variables upon which a civil servant career ought to be built had to be introduced. Increased specialization and qualifications, the appearance of new jobs and activities (computer skills, client relations, greater individual responsibility, etc.) called for the modernization of the criteria upon which the wage structure was based.

The agreement has been successful because most of the social partners were involved in its implementation and substantive changes were agreed. These include increasing the number of steps in any given category and improving and reorganizing professional mobility. The lowest D category has been phased out in the local government sector and is shrinking rapidly in other sub-sectors. Overall, the percentage of employees in the D category fell from 18 per cent in 1990 to 2 per cent in 1997. Other changes include the creation of a new bonus scheme (*Nouvelle bonification indiciaire*, NBI). It consists in defining the bonus which is awarded to some activities or professions. A certain number of 'points' (varying from ten to fifty) have been assigned to many professional categories. The rationale of such selective increases was to provide bonuses for jobs with specific skills and technical demands. Following this framework agreement, the list of professions or categories included has been established by negotiation within each ministry on a periodic basis. In local government, bonuses have been given to professions considered at risk. For example, around thirty points have been given to social workers whose job is to deal with severely socially disadvantaged people in the inner cities. In hospitals with more than 500 beds, forty-five extra points (an 8 per cent increase) have been allocated to chief nurses to reflect their responsibilities. Similarly, forty-one extra points were to be awarded to skilled nurses working in operating theatres.

In October 1997, a first assessment of the Durafour agreement was carried out. As a whole, wage increases arising out of the agreement, without taking into account the future increase in pensions, is as high as 9.3 billion francs for central government, 5.7 billion francs for hospitals and 7.1 billion francs for local government. As a result of the Durafour agreement the gap between wages and the true level of responsibility has been narrowed, and career opportunities for public employees have been enhanced. These measures, implemented during the 1990s, have contributed to greater efficiency and the modernization of the public sector, but have been focused on 'insiders', leading a trade union official to comment, 'Without doubt one can conclude that the agreement will have strong effects long after the end of its formal application. Furthermore, this agreement has now to be applied to non-statutory agents' (anon., September 1997). Looking ahead to the end of the century, the main problem is not so much wage levels or the remuneration system, but the capacity of the public sector to recruit and retain staff.

Other topics can be dealt with at the Ministry of Public Function level. For instance, during the years 1996–98, agreements have been signed on several topics, including organizing occupational training, decreasing the number of short-term contracts, and implementing a new early retirement scheme to create jobs for younger people. These framework agreements are then applied and adapted to each individual sub-sector according to its specific requirements. Negotiations on diverse topics can occur in one ministry or can involve several. Most unions, except the CGT, usually sign these non-wage agreements. Agreements involving wages, however, are not always agreed by the unions, and all governments have been inclined to decide wage increases unilaterally, to enforce a tough wage policy which forms part of their broader economic policy. Thus collective bargaining in the public services is a relatively recent innovation and supports rather than replaces the legal regulation of employment, in which the state remains pre-eminent.

Joint regulation

One of the reasons why collective bargaining was slow to evolve in the public services is the role that staff representatives play within personnel management. This representation exists in the private sector through works committees (*comités d'entreprise*), but in the public sector it has two specific features. First, employee representation occurs only in committees in which employer representatives are also present. These are joint institutions in which employees and the employers have equal representation. Second, even though these institutions are 'consultative' only because employers make the decisions, their impact on the individual or collective future of public service employees is very significant. These committees define general, well publicized rules limiting managerial prerogatives and, as such, play a co-determination role within a dense network of institutions.

At national level the *Conseil supérieur de la fonction publique de l'Etat* deals with all general issues involving administration, being under the direct authority of the state. Joint technical boards (*comités techniques paritaires*, CTPs) address topics such as work organization and related issues for staff across the public services. But the main forum of co-management lies in the joint administrative boards (*commissions administratives paritaires*, CAPs) which underpin union influence in the public services. Each professional *corps* has its own CAP. Employee representatives in the CAPs are elected from union lists, which is why such elections provide an effective means of gauging the relative influence of different unions. CAPs are consulted on many issues linked with human resource management: promotion, mobility, training, recruitment and selection and discipline. Each important decision regarding any individual civil servant is examined by the CAP to which he or she belongs. Proposals from the CAP are only consultative, but employers very rarely use their power to overrule them. The result is that the CAP system leads to the standardization of staff management rules, making them more transparent for employees, and limiting management autonomy. Over and above decisions about individuals, its influence arises from the establishment of a collective definition of management rules which are applied virtually automatically in all cases. The strength of the CAP is increased further by the role it plays in the selection and promotion process of the main civil servant *corps*, which, for the most qualified jobs, is by competitive examination. The composition of the juries and the date of the examination process, which is widely publicized, are defined in conjunction with staff representatives. Although the assessment of civil servants is mainly conducted by the employer, public rules have to be followed which are shaped by the CAP institutions. Through their intervention in the CAPs, unions and their representatives appear to influence decisions directly effecting civil servants. As a result, the influence of unions is much stronger than in the private sector, where such a role does not exist, except perhaps in an informal way. This explains the peculiar place of consultation relative to collective bargaining, which is different from the private sector and explains why unionization is greater in the public than the private sector.

In local government, collective bargaining institutions are similar to those in central government, but the management institution (*centre de gestion*) is unique to this sub-sector. From a formal point of view the major institution is the *conseil supérieur de la fonction publique territoriale*. Based on partnership, it comprises members of representative unions and employers (mainly city mayors, *conseils généraux* or regional committee presidents). The union representatives are selected by the unions at national level without a formal election, while the employers' representatives are elected from a nominated list of candidates. As a result the legitimacy of the whole institution is rather weak, and its financial and other powers are not very great.

As is the case in the central government sector other specific committees exist whose aims are diverse (e.g. health and safety, discipline, etc.). The functioning of these numerous committees differs from one department or city to another, but their influence is more technical than political. For instance, each local community with more than fifty employees has to have a joint technical board which must be consulted in the event of redundancies. Boards may also express their views about the economic and social management of the local community (city, department or region), but they have no influence either on strategic decisions or on the employees' status, which can be modified only by the national (*conseil supérieur*) level.

Education

The education sector is almost completely under the jurisdiction of central government. Even if local authorities have a more important role than before in budgetary terms, they do not have any influence on the hiring or career management of teachers. With the exception of universities, which have a degree of autonomy in terms of hiring and mobility, a teacher's career is not decided at the establishment level. The CAPs mainly deal with these issues. They rely on the skills and competence assessment undertaken by specific inspectors employed by central government. Teachers are separated into several *corps* according to their own skill level and the level of the establishment and school. In each *corps*, a CAP operates which is the major place for collective regulation. In this CAP unions which are powerful in the school system have found their niche and it provides the best opportunity to be visible to employees.

There is an ongoing dispute between the Ministry of Education and the dominant union (FSU) about the appropriate level at which secondary school teacher careers ought to be managed. The ministry wants to partly delegate the mobility process while FSU is opposed to this change. In practice, more than half of transfer requests involve internal moves at the local (i.e. regional) level, but it is still at national level that such decisions are taken. The ministry's proposals are to establish a two-tier transfer process, national and locally based, with the recruitment process remaining exclusively at national level. FSU objects to these proposals on the grounds of employees' interests and service quality. It suggests that a national recruitment and mobility process is a guarantee of equity and quality; it increases teachers' choices and enables a geographical distribution of teachers based on their skills and tailored to local needs. This rhetoric disguises more fundamental issues than the geographical mobility of teachers. The ministry wants to improve personnel management to fit jobs more closely to candidate profiles. FSU wants to keep the current procedure, where the whole process can be controlled through the CAP, where FSU is the dominant union. This case is illustrative of the difficulties faced by reformers. Modernization is perceived by at least some civil servants as a means to undermine a highly regulated system and to decrease union influence within it.

The same difficulties have arisen with other proposed reforms. In the early 1990s a reform of education was negotiated (the Jospin plan). The state proposed to increase resources for the school system (for example, improving teachers' careers) and, as a counterpart, the plan sought the modernization of the whole school system. In the course of the negotiations FEN, still united, was ready to accept some of the ministry's proposals. A minority, mainly represented by the union of middle and secondary school teachers, demanded more resources, but without accepting changes in management practices. Eventually the measures adopted, such as the creation of more highly qualified and better paid primary school teachers, did not change the system much. After the schism within FEN and the creation of FSU, elections to the CAP showed that the majority of teachers approved the strategy of blocking these changes.

Hospitals

Within the hospital sector the traditional decision-making and consultation institutions have been the *commission médicale consultative* (a powerful medical staff committee) and the hospital board (*conseil d'administration*) whose president was the mayor of the city in which the hospital is located (until the legislation of 1996). Formerly, these institutions were seen as very irresponsible and undemocratic. They encouraged profligate expenditure (e.g. prestigious and costly medical equipment) and they allowed medical staff to exercise absolute authority over decisions. These institutions were tolerated during the growth period of the 1960s but are ill adapted to the harsher fiscal climate of the 1990s. It is against this economic background that a reform of hospital organization has been developing since 1991. Its purpose is the implementation of institutions of direct participation within public hospitals. Two sets of measures provide the foundation of future hospital organization and employee relations. The first is the duty of every hospital to elaborate on a collective basis a business plan combining the objectives and interests of the different groups (doctors, managers, nurses, etc.). At the same time, the business plan has to take account of regional or local objectives in terms of level and quality of facilities (high-tech medicine, accident and emergency facilities, number of hospital beds by medical specialism, etc.). Established for a four-year period, this business plan is potentially an opportunity for dialogue and consensus to be reached about the future of each hospital. But its development, which starts with the medical staff and gradually integrates other perspectives, is still limited by professional divisions. There is no real collective plan but rather a succession of separate ones; the evolution is always piecemeal and a strategic approach is missing.

These professional differences are relevant to the rules about the right to strike. In effect, as the continuity of service has to be guaranteed at hospital level, the director has the right to demand a skeleton service. It is not a cumbersome regulation, as the hospital director may decide alone without asking for a special decree. This disposition gives the director strong powers. But the law forbids the so-called circulating strike (*grève tournante*) in which different occupations or departments go on strike in turn, except in cases when the strike does not impact on continuity of service (Clément, 1990).

The second set of measures is a list of new internal institutions designed to allow a voice and participation to each occupational group within each hospital and hospital department. This development has to occur without compromising the high level of expertise and skill of each professional, so the major challenge is to reconcile employee participation and medical responsibility. As Clément (1990: 161) observes about the hospital division of labour, 'Sooner or later a solution will have to be found to the contradiction between a medical science which asks for more participation from everyone and an organization which places authority in the hands of a single person.'

Some of the institutions of social dialogue are long-standing (e.g. health and safety committees) although the 1991 hospital reforms provided them with new areas of discussion (Guégan, 1995). Among the new committees, the departmental council (*conseil de service*) has a special place. In effect it is the first attempt to organize social dialogue at sub-hospital level in relation to topics such as working conditions and the functioning of departments. If there are fewer than thirty-two staff in a department all employees may participate. At the hospital level a new nursing committee (*commission de service de soins infirmiers*) has been implemented whose function is to address problems faced by nurses, whether from a practice, training or career point of view.

The objective of these reforms is to counterbalance the power otherwise monopolized by managers and medical staff. Taking into account that the changes were pushed forward by trade unions, one might conclude that something is changing in the social relations within hospitals. In practice the reforms have not been a complete success, and traditional sources of legitimacy remain strong. Effective for routine matters and when traditional topics are aired (working-time, shift patterns, etc.), these internal structures are not flexible enough to tackle issues such as work organization, technical changes, etc. Furthermore, these institutions, which are mainly focused on internal goals and conflicts, do not fit easily with the increasing co-operation between hospitals. Of course, national level institutions exist in the hospital field as in other parts of the public sector.

Conclusion

The two debates about privatization and modernization should not be confused but they are linked. Does more competition have to be established in sectors such as railways or airlines, in telecommunications or in energy delivery? In this context comparisons with other countries show that in France the state's role remains strong. European integration is forcing the French public sector to change dramatically, jeopardizing the 'French exceptionalism' of the public service. It is this kind of worry that explains the very large social movement France witnessed in December 1995. Even if the public services were only partially involved in the conflict, the protests highlighted the difficulty, at least for some public sector workers, of accepting new management principles within the public sector.

There has been much discussion of modernization and numerous government reforms, but the results remain extremely modest. The most important initiatives have been attempts to modify the centralized nature of the public services by decentralization measures in local government and policies to strengthen local discretion in health and education. Overall, however, there are a number of barriers to modernization. The historical legacy of a centralized state with influential élite civil servants and a strong tradition of unilateral state intervention has stifled modernization and there has been no obvious constituency supporting reform. For all governments the inability to reform the public services easily has at least been partially compensated for by the centralized determination of pay and employment levels. This has ensured that the government retains a strong hold over the public sector paybill. Trade unions through their institutionalized position at national and workplace level have been influential in shaping the evolution of public services and are suspicious of reforms which challenge deeply held convictions about the importance of retaining public service workers' 'acquired rights'. Moreover, this distrust of modernization, perceived as changing the conception of the public service, explains the variable influence of different trade unions during this period, with those opposed to reform benefiting the most.

Whether this situation will alter is an open question with the public sector at a crucial juncture. In the near future the main challenge facing the French public sector as a whole is competition. The most visible problem is the tension between state regulation and market co-ordination with increased emphasis on efficiency criteria. Internal competition between administrative levels, services and establishments is also on the horizon. Furthermore, new management tools implemented in the workplace may encourage competition between individuals. This will fundamentally alter not only the effectiveness of the public service but also its ethos, as every organization is ultimately reliant on the expertise and commitment of the work force to function effectively.

References

Audier, F. (1997) 'La fonction publique: un débouché majeur pour les jeunes diplomés', *Economie et statistique*, 303–5: 137–48.

Choussat, J. (1997) 'Brèves réflexions sur l'emploi public', note pour le Ministre de l'économie, Paris, 25 September.

Clément, J.-M. (1990) *Le Fonctionnaire hospitalier*, Paris: Dalloz.

Eenschooten, M. (1996) 'Les salaires des agents de l'Etat', *Insee résultats, emploi et revenus*, 106: 100–5.

Geay, B. (1997) *Le Syndicalisme enseignant*, Paris: La Découverte.

Girault, J. (1996) 'Syndicalisme enseignant, amicalisme et mutualisme: à propos de l'histoire de leurs rapports', *Revue de l'IRES*, 20: 111–33.

Grellier, Y. (1997) 'La répartition de la dotation globale', *Education et formation*, mars: 41–8.

Guégan, L. (1995) *Le Contractuel: un mogen ou une stratégie CFDT*, working paper, Paris: Confédération française démocratique du travail.

Keraudren, P. and Baka, A. (1998) 'France: a different approach to reform', in T. Verheijen and D. Coombes (eds) *Innovations in Public Management: Perspectives from East and West Europe*, Cheltenham: Edward Elgar.

Labbé, D. (1996) *Syndicats et syndiqués en France depuis 1945*, Paris: Harmattan.

Meurs, D. (1996) 'Employment and pay determination in the public sector: the French case', paper presented at the ARAN workshop on the restructuring of employment relations in public services in Western Europe, Rome, 25–8 January.

Quarré, D. (1992) 'Annales statistiques de la fonction publique, 1945, 1969, 1989', *INSEE Résultats, Emploi Revenu*, 28–9.

Rouban, L. (1995) *La Fonction publique*, Paris: La Découverte.

Schrameck, O. (1995) *La Fonction publique territoriale*, Paris: Dalloz.

Walter, J. (1997) 'Le travail à temps partiel', in *Avis et rapports du Conseil économique et social*, Paris: CES.

6 Spain

Public service employment relations since the transition to democracy

Pere Jódar, Jacint Jordana and Ramón Alós

Throughout the forty years of the Franco dictatorship, the public sector in Spain grew at a considerably slower pace than in most other Western European countries. The manner in which the pro-Franco élites traded government posts and other favours for political support, the lack of a democratic framework in which to put forward social demands, or simply the country's economic back-wardness, may go some way to explaining this situation. Spain in the 1960s was characterized by a stunted welfare state, a major shortfall in infrastructure, a strongly centralist administration and an extremely heterogeneous and costly set of state-owned companies.

With the transition to democracy, the elected governments began to address a large number of unsatisfied social aspirations, while at the same time implement-ing more realistic ways of managing the economy and measures to restructure the nationalized industries. The policies carried out by the centre-right governments (*Unión de Centro Democrático*, UCD) up to 1982, and then by the successive socialist governments (*Partido Socialista Obrero Español*, PSOE) up to 1996, were aimed largely at solving these problems and directing the economy and Spanish society as a whole towards greater growth and stability. As a result of the policies, state struc-tures underwent a profound transformation, including the emergence of a brand-new regional tier of government. In the course of this twenty-year period public sector employment increased substantially in both absolute and relative terms, comprising 23.6 per cent of all employees by 1995.

This large increase in the number of public sector employees was accompanied by a reduction in industrial public sector employment and took place amid huge changes in the relevant laws and regulations, including the modernization of the traditional forms of public service employment, without, however, managing to develop a sufficiently flexible overall framework. Thus, over the past two decades, Spanish public services have gone from a system in which employment relations were regulated almost entirely by legislative and administrative means to one in which, despite the predominant influence of civil servant status, employment relations shaped by consultation or negotiation have become increasingly import-ant. Over the same period, there was also considerable growth in the number of people hired to work in the public sector on ordinary employment contracts with similar terms to those prevalent in the private sector. All these changes have come about in a context of new social demands leading to policies of more flexible employment relations and increased efficiency and quality in public services.

Until the mid-1990s, one of the policy approaches common to all the governments of the democratic period was managing public service growth in a context of structural changes. Public expenditure increased substantially from 25 per cent of GDP in 1974 to 47.4 per cent in 1994. The scale of this growth can be judged by the fact that it is double the figure for the European Union between 1980 and the early 1990s. The expansion was based on normalizing taxation rates and the level of public borrowing and was directed mainly at basic welfare services and plugging some of the historical gaps in the infrastructure. All this happened at the same time as a fundamental and complex process of decentralization was proceeding, resulting from the creation of a new tier of government. In consequence, whereas in 1980 some 90 per cent of total public expenditure was in central government hands, by 1991 the figure had fallen to 66 per cent, while the autonomous governments controlled 21 per cent and local authorities 13 per cent. In 1996, with the advent of a minority conservative government (*Partido Popular*, PP), the autonomous communities' share increased further as this was the price paid for the support of the main nationalist parties in the Basque Country, Catalonia and the Canary Islands.

A second policy approach – reform and modernization of the public administration – was implemented particularly, although not very persistently, by the various socialist governments. Their achievements in this sphere have only been partially studied (Bañon, 1993; Subirats, 1990). However, their objectives are summarized in a document by the National Public Service Institute (Instituto *Nacional de Administración Pública* – INAP, 1996), the body in charge of civil service selection and training and which acts as a public services think tank. The main objective was to achieve 'better functioning public services at the service of citizens at the lowest possible cost' in a climate of budget austerity and economic internationalization and interdependence. This approach translated into modernizing policies aimed at redesigning organizational structures, transforming bureaucratic cultures, rationalizing work forces, flexibilizing management methods and making public services more receptive to society as a whole.

Finally, a third policy drive of the governments of the democratic period, which has been less successful than the previous two, was the attempt to develop a human resource policy for the public services. Having been dominated by the corps of top-ranking civil servants during the latter half of the Franco régime (Baena del Alcázar, 1984), by the 1990s it had begun to define certain elements of human resources management through a bargaining process with the major national trade unions, although there still remained huge gaps in the model to be implemented and numerous contradictions among different aspects of the system. Nevertheless, for many years into the democratic period, the failure to introduce personnel policies has led to tensions of a professional or corporate nature within the public services, and difficulties for the new political class in imposing its will on a sector which had grown used, under Franco, to protecting itself against the arbitrary actions of the dictatorship.

All these policy initiatives must be understood in the context of far-reaching economic and political trends. In Spain's case, there is a very specific factor which has to be borne in mind: the need to maintain the momentum of reform and economic growth for an extended period – from the late 1970s to the mid-1980s – in order to legitimate the new democratic system. This affected the public sector in two ways. On the one hand, it implied the consolidation of the entire range of social services (education, pensions, unemployment benefit and other types of social benefits) which had been kept at extremely low levels during the Franco era. On the other hand, it meant opening up the system, aided by the stimulus of Spain's joining the European Union in 1986, and involved a major effort to provide the country with the publicly financed infrastructure necessary to improve its economic competitiveness.

Nevertheless, it is important to recognise that in Spain the private sector continues to provide a large slice of public services such as education and health. This can be seen in the evolution of private spending on health care as a proportion of total health care expenditure (34.6 per cent in 1970, 18.9 per cent in 1985 and 21.8 per cent in 1995) and in the number of pupils attending private educational establishments. This figure declines sharply, however, towards the top of the educational system, falling from 35 per cent in primary and secondary education to 9.2 per cent of university students. Despite the fact that the welfare state model has tended towards universal provision policies over the past fifteen years (Subirats and Gomà, 1997), it has had to integrate many of the existing institutional arrangements and organizational forms which had emerged, with widely varying standards, in response to the absence of state intervention and provision under Franco.

As in other countries, the transformations of the 1990s have been accompanied by the privatization of a large number of state-owned enterprises and the elimination of legal monopolies in such areas as telecommunications, television, air transport and cigarettes. The state has ceased to carry out certain activities directly, for example, highway maintenance and the management of many social programmes, which are now contracted out to private companies in a process generically known as the 'private management of public services'. These practices include transferring activities from public service institutions to public corporations or publicly run companies which then adopt the management methods and financial criteria of private enterprise. This is reflected in the fact that those working for such companies lose their civil servant status and become ordinary employees. The health system is probably where this policy has had the greatest impact in Spain over the past few years.

This chapter presents an analysis of labour relations in the public sector in Spain, its recent evolution and the main challenges in this area. We examine the major groups comprising the public service system and the main employment trends. We explore the structure and role of the state as employer and assess public sector trade union representation, drawing out the differences from worker representation in the private sector. To conclude, we explain the principal negotiating and consultation mechanisms which have been set up, examine the dynamic they have created and assess the key problems in this domain. Our analysis is

Table 6.1 Public sector employees by type of administration (000)

Type of administration	1985	1990	1995	1996
Central government	571	555	570	587
Social security (incl. health service)	242	307	329	358
Autonomous governments	321	448	519	570
Local authorities	305	389	377	403
Total all governments	1,439	1,700	1,796	1,918
Nationalised industries and state-owned enterprises	396	417	332	324
Other	41	4	5	3
Total public sector	1,876	2,122	2,134	2,244

Source: Instituto Nacional de Estadística (1997).

Table 6.2 Public and private sector employees (000)

Type of employee	1980	1985	1990	1995	1996
Government (1)	n.a.	1,438.7	1,700.1	1,795.8	1,917.6
Public-sector (2)	1,565.4	1,875.6	2,121.7	2,133.8	2,244.4
Private-sector (3)	6,356.1	5,530.5	7,250.8	6,894.5	7,210.3
(1) as % of all employees	n.a.	19.4	18.1	19.9	20.3
(2) as % of all employees	19.8	25.3	22.6	23.6	23.7
(3) as % of all employees	80.2	74.7	77.4	76.4	76.3

Source: Instituto Nacional de Estadística (1997).

Note
Fourth quarter of each year, in thousands; *n.a.* no data available.

Table 6.3 shows the distribution of civil servants and hired personnel by type of administration. Caution is required in interpreting the table, because many of the data are incomplete, but three issues can be highlighted. First, a third of public employees are hired personnel, and this proportion has not altered markedly during the 1990s (although there are difficulties in comparing the rows in the table). Second, in terms of distribution, health and education services (including universities) employ civil servants almost exclusively (hired personnel are present only in exceptional cases). Third, there are differences by administrative tier, with central government employing few hired personnel but regional and local government, which grew rapidly during the 1980s, using a relatively high proportion of hired personnel (almost 50 per cent).

The creation of new, regional governments brought with it a major redistribution of employment between the different government levels. Thus, in the period under consideration, public employment dependent on central government fell from 39.7 per cent of the total in 1980 to 30.6 per cent in 1996, local authority employment remained virtually unchanged (21.2 per cent to 21.0 per cent) and social security employment (including the health service) went up slightly, from

Table 6.3 Civil servants and hired personnel (000)

Type of administration	1990		1997	
	Civ. ser.	*Hir. per.*	*Civ. ser.*	*Hir. per.*
Central government	422	147	401	122
Social security (incl. health service)[a]	285	–	337	–
Autonomous governments	115	83	148	116
Local authorities[b]	184	173	230	212
Education and universities[a]	406	–	369	92
Total all governments	1,412	404	1,484	543
Nationalised industries and state-owned enterprises[c]	–	360		61
Total public sector	1,412	765		

Sources: *Boletín Estadístico del Registro Central de Personal,* January 1991 and July 1997.

Notes

a Depending on its status each region has, social security, non-university employees are managed by the central government or by their autonomous government. University employees are managed by the autonomous governments (within this category, there is included a certain number of hired personal, but we are unable to separate the figures for 1990).

b Separate figures are not available.

c In 1997 state-owned enterprises are not included.

16.8 per cent to 18.6 per cent. Public employment dependent on the autonomous governments, on the other hand, rose sharply from 22.3 per cent to 29.7 per cent. The economic cycle also had an effect on the redistribution of employment. Whereas in the period between 1988 and 1992 employment rose across the public sector, between 1992 and 1995 it declined in central and local government, remained unchanged in social security and increased in the autonomous governments as a result of the continuing process of devolution and the consolidation of that tier of government. In summary, the most important feature is the maintenance of employment levels in the public sector during the periods of economic downturn, albeit at the cost of tensions in the distribution of personnel and budgetary resources between the different tiers and fields of government.

Table 6.1 shows that 21.7 per cent of public employees work for local administration, 30.8 per cent for regional administration, and 43.5 per cent for central – state wide – administration. Public universities' personnel account for 4 per cent of this total. The different proportions employed by central and regional administration as between regions depend on the degree of devolution within each autonomous government. For example, the proportion of public employees dependent on central government is relatively low in Catalonia, Galicia, the Basque Country and the Canarias and the reverse is true of regions such as Madrid and Castilla-León.

Several points need to be made regarding public sector employees. Perhaps the most important concerns gender distribution, with women workers accounting for an increasing share of the total. In 1980, 71 per cent of public sector employees were men, compared with 29 per cent women, but by 1996 the breakdown was

Table 6.4 Percentage of public and private sector employees by sex (%)

Year	Public sector		Private sector	
	Men	Women	Men	Women
1980	71	29	75	25
1985	69	31	73	27
1990	61	39	72	28
1995	57	43	70	30
1996	56	44	67	33

Source: Instituto Nacional de Estadística (1997).

Table 6.5 Public sector employees by professional category in 1996 (000)

Type of professional category	Men	Women	Both sexes
Top-ranking public services and enterprise managers	24.3	9.4	33.7
Professionals and qualified staff	344.7	421.8	766.5
Auxiliary professionals and qualified staff	123.7	97.1	220.8
Administrative officers	144.1	205.7	349.8
Skilled workers	446.6	145.1	591.7
Unskilled workers	142.8	103.7	246.5
Armed forces	57.6	0.4	58.0
Total	1,283.8	983.2	2,267.0

Source: Instituto Nacional de Estadística (1997).

56 per cent men and 44 per cent women (Table 6.4). By contrast, this trend was less pronounced in the private sector, where, in 1996, 66.8 per cent of the work force were male and 33.2 per cent female. Public sector employees overall also have a higher educational level than those in the private sector. In the public sector, 57.1 per cent of employees have a technical, professional or university qualification, as opposed to 26 per cent in the private sector. Between 1988 and 1996, a marked change in the age structure of public employees took place, with the upper (over-65) and lower (under-29) age groups declining while there was a major increase in the middle age range (thirty to forty-nine). The breakdown by professional categories in 1996 was as follows: 1.5 per cent were managers (mostly men), 43.5 per cent qualified personnel (the majority of them women), 15.4 per cent administrative staff (the majority of them women), 26.1 per cent skilled workers (the majority of them men), 10.9 per cent unskilled workers (equivalent numbers of men and women), and 2.6 per cent members of the armed forces (Table 6.5).

Another aspect requiring some comment is the ratio of permanent to temporary employment. Most employment in the public services is stable; in 1996, 67.5 per cent of public employees had been working in the sector for over six years (70.7 per cent among them men), as against only 12 per cent who had been in it for under a year. Temporary employment in the public sector rose very slightly

Table 6.6 Public and private sector employees by type of employment contract

Type of employment contract	1987	1990	1995	1996
Temporary contract, public sector	359.1	381.4	339.2	352.3
Indefinite contract, public sector	1,776	1,791	1,782.4	1,884
% temp. contracts, public sector	16.8	17.6	16.0	15.8
% temp. contracts, private sector	36.3	37.8	40.7	39.5

Source: Instituto Nacional de Estadística (1997).

until 1990, when it began a gentle decline. The proportion of temporary public sector workers has remained quite steady at around 16 per cent throughout the period for which statistics are available (16.8 per cent in 1987; 15.8 per cent in 1996) (Table 6.6). These figures stand in marked contrast to the 39.5 per cent of casual workers among those employed in the private sector at the end of 1996. Women account for a higher proportion of temporary workers than men in both the public and the private sectors. Similarly, in 1996, part-time working stood at 8.2 per cent in the private sector but only 3.9 per cent in the public sector, with the majority of workers in this category women in both sectors.

The public sector labour market

The defining feature of the public sector labour market derives from the constitution, which lays down that access to civil service employment is to be governed by equal opportunity, merit and qualifications. This applies not only to the selection and career paths of civil servants, but to all those working in the public services, including those on ordinary or temporary employment contracts. In addition, the law requires that all staff are hired according to objective, publicly known selection procedures guaranteeing compliance with such principles. However, the civil service reform legislation (LMRFP), enacted in 1984, two years after the socialist election victory, signified the emergence of a two-track system. In theory it laid down the rules and regulations designed for civil servants, but at the same time it opened up the possibility of a gradual move towards the predominant use of ordinary employment contracts in the public sector. Nevertheless, this possibility was closed off by a Constitutional Court ruling in 1987 which upheld the need to maintain civil service employment as the main form of employment in the public services. This partial move in the 1980s towards hiring workers on ordinary employment contracts was effected in a contradictory and to some extent hidden fashion, taking advantage of the legal loopholes left by the relative autonomy granted to the separate levels of government. This gives rise to two problems which may become worse in the future. First is the relative lack of legal protection for those not enjoying civil service status and whose contracts are often inappropriate. Second is the failure to address adequately the need for a specific personnel policy for this group, with its own recruitment, training procedures and career structures, differentiated from those of civil service staff.

Spanish law stipulates that public services must choose their staff, whether civil servants or hired personnel, by publicly advertising all job vacancies and then following a selection process involving competitive standardized general examinations, specific examinations or a combination of the two. The law lays down that the selection procedures must employ tests that are relevant to determining candidates' fitness to fill the particular post for which they are applying. In practice, however, this requirement is not always strictly observed, as the tests are often heavily weighted with questions on legal matters. These selection systems are supposedly different from each other, although certain ambiguities remain (Morey, 1989).

Another issue is the selection of temporary staff either to deal with urgent needs or to cover jobs for a specific period. The employment categories used here – temporary civil servant status and fixed-term ordinary contracts – involve less formal selection methods. Temporary civil servants are selected by means of tests and certain minimum qualification and aptitude requirements, depending on the type of job they will be doing, whereas other temporary workers are selected in accordance with the labour law concerning fixed-term contracts. In practice, this 'back door' entry into public employment is heavily used and in certain periods has tended to predominate. However, rather than representing a deliberate pattern, it is more the result of a multitude of initiatives taken by different public bodies, as it affords them greater flexibility and autonomy in staff selection. Once someone has been taken on in this manner, if their performance is judged to be satisfactory, the initial temporary selection becomes the first step towards a civil service career. This group, which is quite numerous in certain sectors (school-teachers, university lecturers, health care workers, etc.) is beset by problems similar to those described above for staff on ordinary employment contracts. In addition there is the problem of the group's sheer size. As the loopholes in the law are exploited to the full the number of people who have been working as temporary civil servants for longer than the legal maximum increases, as does the number of people on ordinary temporary employment contracts who are kept on by changing the type of contract they sign. The result is that in both cases their lack of protection and the precarious nature of their employment are prolonged.

In consequence, despite the declared aim of maintaining strict, objective selection procedures, the recruitment and selection process is fraught with ambiguities and contradictions. The Spanish public services still retain a set of formal rules and procedures for access to a professional civil service career which come close to the 'ideal type' of bureaucracy defined by Max Weber. However, as they exist side by side with new rules and informal procedures, some of their key premises are undermined. Criticism of the use of informal procedures is invariably directed at the public services even though similar practices are common in the private sector.

Over and above the debate about the advantages of public versus private sector personnel practices, there are several aspects of public service personnel policy which could undoubtedly be improved. One of the priorities for modernization is the introduction of new criteria for evaluating posts and objective criteria for allocating people to suitable posts. Although several studies and pilot schemes have been undertaken, a satisfactory outcome has yet to be achieved. To this impasse must be added the fact that the degree of autonomy granted to regional governments, and certain sectors of central government, is far greater than would appear from the letter of the law, so that the variety of situations and their complexity have tended to undermine the effectiveness of the measures taken so far.

The various public service organizations can select staff in one of two ways: either by making use of the civil service's traditional arrangements, or by analysing the particular post to be filled and adapting the selection procedures accordingly. Some experts have put forward the idea of a third possibility: combining public selection procedures with those prevailing in private enterprise. Within the civil service there is a distinction to be drawn between special corps and general corps. Special corps comprise individuals carrying out similar functions and activities which, as a rule, are associated with a particular profession. Entry into such corps requires the same knowledge and skills of all candidates and the duties performed are less administrative or bureaucratic than technical and professional. Once they have been selected, members' career prospects are based on principles of seniority and length of service, which, given similar starting points, are the chief indicators of experience and skill.

General corps, on the other hand, are made up of public employees performing administrative and management duties. The jobs undertaken by the members of such corps are quite heterogeneous, although they all involve certain common administrative activities. Given this heterogeneity, there is no clear definition of the education and training required for such posts or of how to determine the knowledge required in a selective examination. The selection procedure is based on tests covering general knowledge, which leads to a huge number of candidates coming forward and preliminary tests to narrow the field. Since the selection criteria are general, rather than geared to a particular job description, successful candidates require a period of training. Once civil servants have entered the public service, their career is based on the requirements of their post and their experience, although experience tends to be measured in terms of length of service or position in the hierarchy rather than by a real assessment of professional ability. Some élite groups of civil servants exist, with very rigorous selection procedures, which facilitates access to senior administrative positions. Most of them are within the category of special corps – for example, economists, accountants, diplomats or university professors (Parrado, 1996). Finally, the procedure for selecting directors and chief officers is slightly different in that appointments at this level can be made directly, which implies political decisions. To date, they have been limited to deputy director-general level, and other top management posts are based on more straightforward criteria of merit and qualifications.

Pay and salaries

The pay structure is currently determined by the 1984 reforms (LMRFP) and includes two major components, basic pay and supplementary pay. Basic pay is

Table 6.7 Groups and grades in the public services

Corps or scale group	Minimum level	Maximum level
A (full five-year degree)	20	30
B (three-year degree)	16	26
C (baccalaureate)	10	22
D (primary education qualification)	8	18
E (school leaving certificate)	6	14

determined by educational level and is the same for all public services for any occupational group according to their educational attainment. The LMRFP tackled the diversity of categories by assigning each of them to one of five qualification levels (Table 6.7). Basic pay consists of salary, which is fixed in the budget and governed by the general rule that the salary of group A should not be more than three times that of group E; automatic three-yearly length-of-service increments which are the same for each group; and two extra payments per year, each consisting of one month's salary and one month's length-of-service increments. Supplementary pay includes such items as a category enhancement according to the grade of the post held. Posts are divided into thirty grades.

A 'specific supplement' is linked with the characteristics of the job and is based on the special difficulties or responsibilities involved. Nobody may receive more than one such enhancement. The productivity supplement is designed to reward special performance, such as exceptional performance, commitment or initiative. The criteria of such enhancements and how to obtain them must be made public and known to all staff in the department or section and to the trade unions.

A study based on a job evaluation survey in the public services (Gutiérrez and Labrado, 1988) revealed the existence of a vast spectrum of different jobs. This can be seen in the huge differences in the complexity of the duties performed, ranging from low-skill posts (especially common in local government) to top management posts, of which there are more in regional and central government. Furthermore, as has already been mentioned, all posts held by civil servants have their own special category supplement according to the grade of the post held. The lack of clear rules on the allocation of these supplements has led to a minimum enhancement, defined by qualification level, being awarded to all civil servants not otherwise receiving a category supplement based on their job grade. However, several studies have shown that, given the absence of universal, objective criteria, there is a disjuncture between the importance of the duties performed and the category supplements allocated. There is a high degree of discretion in the awarding of category supplements, depending, among other things, on the tier of government involved, the group to which the civil servant belongs and the administrative unit in question. Gutiérrez and Labrado also found, in a comparison between fixed payments in public services and private enterprises, that public employees' pay was always lower and that the higher up the pay scale the greater was the difference. This means that senior posts in the public services are less well

Table 6.8 Comparison of inflation rate and pay increases (%)

Year	Inflation	Public services pay rises	Collective bargaining pay rises
1982	14.1	8.0	11.2
1983	12.2	9.0	11.7
1984	9.0	6.5	7.0
1985	8.1	6.5	7.8
1986	8.3	6.5	8.2
1987	4.6	5.0	6.3
1988	5.8	4.0	5.7
1989	6.9	4.0	7.3
1990	6.5	6.0	8.0
1991	5.5	7.2	7.8
1992	5.3	5.7	7.0
1993	4.9	1.9	5.5
1994	4.3	0	3.6
1995	4.3	3.5	3.9
1996	3.2	3.5	3.8
1997		0	n.a.

Sources: Inflation: Instituto Nacional de Estadística; public service workers (civil servants): central government budgets; collective bargaining: *Boletín de Estadísticas Laborales*.

paid than those of equivalent responsibility in the private sector. On the other hand, local government salaries emerged as slightly higher than those in regional or central government.

A comparison of average pay rises for civil servants since 1982 with those established by collective bargaining indicates that public sector pay has lost ground against the private sector. This can be seen in Table 6.8, which shows the evolution of inflation, civil service pay and wages negotiated by collective bargaining in the private sector. In the period between 1987 and 1994, wages fixed by collective bargaining agreements in the private sector stayed ahead of the retail price index, whereas this was seldom true in the case of civil servants and other public employees. However, the overall picture needs qualifying in light of the internal distribution of actual salary increases (taking into account special payments and certain relatively covert practices) among the different specialist groups in the public services which have their own specific negotiating procedures (although these are supposedly confined to other matters).

Employers and employers' associations

State policies

Following approval of the new constitution in 1978, a series of legal provisions, including the LMRFP law and several rulings by the Constitutional Court, have defined the framework for regulating labour relations in the public sector. In general, these laws and regulations provide that the Spanish government shall direct personnel policy and have executive and regulatory powers in regard to the public services dependent on central government, while, in accordance with the principles laid down in the constitution, each regional government shall have similar functions and supervise local government within its territory. Although there is still no basic Act of parliament, there are a number of different laws and regulations laying down the common rules with which all Spanish public services must comply (Sánchez Morón, 1996). The upper levels in each tier of government have the power to issue directives on personnel policy, including instructions to their representatives in negotiations with the trade unions; rules and guidelines for civil servants' pay; decisions on staff category structures, scale intervals between different posts and promotion criteria. In a word, they have the power to act as employers.

The INAP report (1996) provides a self-diagnosis of the public services' human resources policy and draws a number of rather pessimistic conclusions: personnel policy has been based on exercising control over employees chiefly through formal rules and procedures, direct supervision and hierarchical authority structures. This classical conception of organizational culture has not encouraged innovation, trust or dialogue and has similarly failed to promote real human resource management or expenditure control. Rigid, rule-based centralization of staff management has prevented senior management from implementing genuine human resource policies with the proliferation of different local situations based on *ad hoc* practices rather than explicit criteria. An attempt to overcome these problems has been the creation of separate agencies, as new public organizational forms, which bypass the public law and the hierarchical structures. During the 1990s, operating on the basis of commercial and civil law, several autonomous agencies were established with a more flexible statute. The postal services, public railways, airports, ports and tax collection were among the public services that changed their organizational status. In these services, new public management techniques were applied, including more active personnel policies (Parrado, 1996).

In the core public services, there are other features which characterise the state's role as employer. The state seeks to set an example, which has been especially important during recessions. Its championing of austerity policies has led it to impose stringent restrictions on public sector workers for many years. This has translated into public spending constraints affecting not only hiring and internal management policies (promotion, mobility, etc.) but also wages. Pay has either been frozen or linked with inflation forecasts, while the private sector has been more flexible in this regard. Performance incentives are rarely used and are frequently opposed by the unions. In any case, the total wage bill is kept under strict control by the Ministry of Finance. However, this centralization coexists with increasing moves towards decentralization, as seen in the appearance of different human resource policies between autonomous governments and local authorities on the one hand and central government on the other, and the decentralizing pressures within the realm of the various regional governments.

The characteristics of public service employers

With regard to central government, the most important body after the government is the Ministry of Public Services, set up in June 1986. This ministry is responsible for the general development, co-ordination and monitoring of government personnel policy. Within the ministry there is a Secretary of State for Public Services, whose job it is to take a lead in matters to do with the legal framework and inspection of the civil and public services, and a Director General of the Civil Service, who has power over all managerial and administrative measures that do not come under any other ministry or department. The Finance Ministry issues guidelines affecting staff costs and staffing levels through the central government budget. Most autonomous governments also have bodies of directorate-general rank with similar functions.

One of the most important co-ordinating bodies is the Higher Public Services Council which was set up by the LMRFP law. It is the peak level co-ordination and consultation body for the public services, bringing together central, autonomous and local government representatives on the one hand, and civil service staff representatives on the other, and is thus a most significant forum in labour relations terms. It comprises seventeen union representatives, in proportion to the number of elected delegates obtained by each of them, and equivalent numbers of local authority and autonomous government representatives. The Public Services Minister and three secretaries of state and the deputy secretaries of each ministry are also present. There exists also the Public Services Co-ordinating Committee, whose remit is to co-ordinate government personnel policy with a view to formulating a public employment plan and putting forward proposals on the measures required to implement the provisions in the civil servants' statutory regime. As it is not intended to involve staff, trade union representatives are excluded.

There is a certain amount of conflict within central government as a result of competition not only between various ministries, on the one hand, and the Ministry of Public Services and the Ministry of Finance on the other, but also between different public employee groupings (general corps versus special corps, conflicts among several *grand corps*, etc.). The remarkable increase in trade union influence within the public services during the 1990s may have contributed to these tensions (see below). In addition, Arenilla (1993) highlights that the autonomous governments with devolved powers are faced with fierce competition from central government within their own territories, which adds a further element of complexity to public service labour relations.

Finally, it is necessary to mention the public enterprise employers, although their number has decreased strongly during the last two years, because of privatization. Since the 1980s, these enterprises have joined the dominant private sector employers' association (*Confederación Española de Organizaciones Empresariales*, CEOE) and they have developed similar practices to private firms in these sectors. However, the political direction of public enterprises has always been in the hands of the government, and this has influenced their approach towards collective bargaining. For example, in the 1980s there were some attempts to influence the wage levels of some key economic sectors. There are no equivalent employers' associations for the public services.

The status and role of managers

Although defining the role of public services as employers and ascribing it to particular legal categories is a complex matter, work organization in the public sector is similar to the division of labour in the private sector. As the 1991 agreement between the government and unions states, work organization is the responsibility of the government, its directors and managers. This power extends over such items as the rationalization and improvement of operational processes, job evaluation, professionalization, promotion and performance assessment. It is the government which decides on the number, title and characteristics of posts and the requirements for filling them, classifying all posts throughout the public services in terms of common features.

Within the broad spectrum of public sector managers, several different types can be distinguished. Each managerial profile has its own special features, ranging from how such people are recruited to their relationship with, and degree of autonomy from, those in political power. For example, in some cases, particularly state-run enterprises and related organizations, a spoils system operates. Nevertheless, since there have not been many changes of government in the relatively young Spanish democratic system, it is still rather early to pick out clear trends as regards the stability, or otherwise, of public sector managers and their ties with political parties.

First, there is the 'political' manager, who came into being during the democratic transition period. This refers to the professional politicians, whose position and approach towards their job is strongly dependent on the party hierarchy. There is an important tendency towards professionalization and specialization among politicians, transforming themselves into political managers (especially at the local administration level), although styles vary considerably from one political party to another, not least in terms of their direct involvement in actual management decisions. Second, there is the administrative professional who is appointed by the government of the day. (This practice has recently been regulated so that a large number of top posts can be filled only by civil servants.) For the most part these are high-ranking civil servants in central and autonomous government holding management posts in the classical organizational structures regulated by public service administrative procedures. None the less it often happens that managerial offices with a markedly professional profile are in fact highly politicized, introducing instability in the management stance across the whole administration (Jiménez Asensio, 1998). They are not always dependent on party leadership structures, but are frequently a matter of personal acquaintance or friendship with the relevant political figure in the government. In line with this system of political patronage, members of the civil service élite still occupy the majority of such offices in the ministries from which they originally came, particularly in central government. Thus, for instance, almost all the directors-general and deputy directors-general in the Ministry of Foreign Affairs are career diplomats and a similar situation obtains in the Ministry of Finance with the financial inspectorate (Villoria and del Pino, 1997).

Third, there are professionals and specialists who have had no previous connection with the public service but are called in to work on a temporary basis on account of their political affiliation. They include managers and executives of state-controlled companies and related organizations who are mostly covered by private labour law and high-ranking officers, consultants and managers enjoying the political trust of the major departments – including education and health – who come under a recently passed special law (*Ley Orgánica 6/1997, de Organización y Funcionamiento de la Administración General del Estado*, LOFAGE) which lays down the managerial powers and staff of these political appointees in office. There has been considerable growth in the size and importance of the teams of high-ranking officials since the 1980s – an example of the increasing use made by the political parties of their ability to appoint people from outside the public service to politically sensitive posts.

This diversity of professional roles straddles political and technical responsibilities and the boundaries between the two spheres are imprecise, with important implications for the professionalization and decision-making capacity of the people involved. The existence of such diverse approaches to management has led to a permanent state of tension, mostly latent but occasionally rising to the surface, between the party decision-making channels and the politico-administrative channels present in each public service organization. Such dysfunctional arrangements may also have had something to do with professionals failing to exercise sufficient management responsibility and over-reliance on legal solutions. Legal regulations tend to take the place of decision-making structures and are one of the greatest obstacles to injecting more life into the decision-making processes of the public services. It seems quite clear that this is not the best context in which to develop new practices related to human resource management.

Trade unions

The legal framework

The legal framework governing trade union representation is based on periodic union, or workplace, elections with workers entitled to choose their representatives by voting for one of the slates put up by the different unions, professional associations or groups of independents. The total number of representatives obtained by each union in a particular sector or region is used to calculate how many representatives each organization is entitled to in the collective bargaining processes at the relevant sectoral or regional level. Designed for the private sector during the period of transition towards democracy, this basic worker representation model gave rise to a dual form of workplace representation: unitary representation, such as works committees and workplace delegates, on the one hand, and union representation, such as company branches or union delegates, on the other. The system was not introduced into the public services until several years later, and even then only with substantial modifications, although it was introduced rapidly for workers in the public services on ordinary employment contracts. Although there is a reference to unitary representative bodies for civil servants in the LOLS it has so far been underdeveloped. Unitary representative bodies or staff councils (*comités de empresa*) do exist, but their negotiating powers are severely limited. Trade union representation has been more fully regulated and developed, with the creation of joint bargaining councils at different levels, in which unions, fulfilling certain minimum representation requirements (see below), participate as the only staff-side representatives with negotiation rights. It is therefore important to focus on the role played by trade unions, as they are the leading actors in the representation and participation process for civil servants. This role can be understood only in the context of its consolidation during the transition towards democracy.

During the long period of Franco's rule civil servants were forbidden from joining trade unions, including the mandatory, official unions (*Organización Sindical Española*, OSE), and this forms a key element in explaining some of the problems besetting trade union representation in the civil service to this day. From 1976 onwards, the formation of civil service associations was permitted, but civil servants were still not allowed to join trade unions. However, under pressure from the unions, in 1977 the government agreed to allow trade union membership among civil servants. This did not prevent the proliferation of other forms of association, especially in the early years of the transition, which undermined trade union strength in dealing with central government (Arenilla, 1993). Similar caution was evident among the autonomous governments, which were pleased to assume responsibility for civil service functions and budgets but reluctant to set up their own negotiating arrangements.

Traditional forms of public employee representation include professional associations (termed 'colleges'), national associations and groups of civil servants belonging to the same branch. For a long time these associations were in direct competition with the unions in defending and promoting public service employees' interests. The existence of different corps (Beltrán, 1985) acting as informal support groups within the civil service, especially at the higher levels, represented an alternative to trade union representation and performed this role during the final years of the Franco regime. However, the reforms introduced by the LMRFP in 1984 did away with the representative or self-regulatory powers still held by the corps, and the following year the LOLS came down clearly in favour of a trade union model of representation, thereby aiding the large general class-based trade unions, which were already operating in the private sector, over the specialist professional associations (Suay, 1987).

Trade unions in the public services

The first union elections in the civil service were not held until 1987, ten years after they had been introduced into the private sector. These elections served as a springboard for trade union activity in the public services and enabled unions, which hitherto had a weak presence there, to increase their membership and bolster their organization. This delay was a clear indication of how far the steps necessary to define and co-ordinate staff-side representation lagged behind the government's power to centralize and organize labour relations in the public services.

The 1984 law, which is still the main point of reference on union representation, divides civil servants into three categories as regards trade union rights. The first category comprises civil servants who do not have trade union rights in the sense of being able to join a trade union, make collective demands or go on strike. This category mainly consists of members of the armed forces and other military-style institutions, including the civil guard and specific parts of the police, although semi-clandestine union organizations, such as the Unified Union of the Civil Guard (*Sindicato Unificado de la Guardia Civil*), have appeared in some of these organizations. The second category has the right to set up and join (corporate) associations to defend their professional interests, but not to belong to trade unions. This category is made up of members of state police forces of a non-military character, among whom the Unified Police Union (*Sindicato Unificado de la Policía*) has been created in the National Police Force (*Policía Nacional*). It also includes judges, stipendiary magistrates and public prosecutors, who are not permitted to join a union while they are in post. The third, and largest, category is comprised of all public employees enjoying broader trade union rights, including career civil servants, as the core group, plus those employed on a temporary or secondment basis.

The principal trade unions originated in the 1960s, still under the Franco regime, when several organizations linked with the major inter-sectoral confederations formed at that time began operating clandestinely. Such was the case of the FETE-UGT (*Comisiones Obreras de la Administración* and *Unión Sindical de Trabajadores de la Administración Pública*), which appeared together with the *Asociación Española de la Administración Pública*, founded in 1969. Throughout the transition their influence spread and their organization grew stronger. The *Comisiones Obreras* (CCOO) set up FSAP (*Federación Sindical de Administración Pública*), whereas the UGT, after a series of mergers between various sectoral organizations, eventually created the FSP (*Federación de Servicios Públicos*) in 1982, a macro-organization incorporating the Post Office and the health service. Although there is intense co-ordination of all public service sectors, these two branches have remained organizationally separate in CCOO. In general terms the major unions were faced with a much greater variety of trade unions and professional associations than in the private sector, as several independent organizations confined to a particular sector or profession emerged. One of the reasons for this was reluctance on the part of civil servants in certain grades to see themselves lumped together in the same trade union as other workers. Another factor was the enormous geographical and functional dispersion resulting from the extension and fragmentation of the public services, which made it difficult to formulate common objectives and so accentuated the spread of different demands and representative organizations.

So, for example, alongside the variety of class-based unions covering the whole of Spain, or a particular autonomous community, such as the nationalist trade unions in the Basque Country and Galicia, special mention should be made of the Independent Civil Servants' Union (*Confederación Sindical Independiente de Funcionarios*, CSIF). This organization, founded in the 1980s by a number of professional associations with a view to joining forces to present an alternative trade union approach to that of UGT and CCOO, has attracted widespread support. The picture is further complicated by the presence of a host of professional unions whose membership is confined to public employees, such as the *Unión Sindical Independiente de la Administración Local* and the *Federación Española de Asociaciones de Cuadros Superiores de la Administración Central*, and by the existence of a large number of civil service associations with a high degree of rivalry. Added to this, the trade union map in state education and health is also more varied than in the private sector, with powerful independent unions such as ANPE in education and CEMSATSE in the health service. Nevertheless, as we shall see, the 1990s witnessed an intense concentration of trade union representation and political influence around the axis of the CCOO and UGT as the dominant forces involved in negotiations.

Union membership

Trade union membership in the public services remained very low until the late 1980s, with just a few thousand members. This figure was extremely small, even taking into account the generally low level of trade union membership, and far below that among private sector workers at the time. Thus, for example, in 1983, the FSP accounted for 6.3 per cent of UGT's total membership, while data for the same year show that the FSAP (which did not include workers in the public health service or the Post Office) made up only 1.7 per cent of all CCOO members. However, following the trade union elections in 1987, membership began to rise substantially and eventually overtook the private sector in percentage terms. The opening up of negotiating opportunities, constantly rising employment and greater stability in the public sector all had an important bearing on this transformation. The figures speak for themselves. By 1993, FSAP membership had gone up to 9.1 per cent of the total for CCOO, while FSP accounted for as much as 18.7 per cent of all UGT members. To appreciate this increase properly, it is worth bearing in mind that between 1983 and 1993 the total number of dues-paying members of both CCOO and UGT doubled. It can therefore be said that this growth in the public services was one of the key factors strengthening trade unions in the late 1980s (Jordana, 1996). Union density in the public services (excluding health and education) in 1993 was estimated at around 30 per cent, as against an overall average for Spain of 16.4 per cent (including the unemployed in the calculations) (Jordana, 1996).

Morillo (1997) estimates union density at 27 per cent in the public services dependent on central government. The calculation takes account only of CCOO, UGT and CSIF, but excludes the smaller unions and the unemployed from the equation. A survey commissioned by UGT in 1994 highlighted the stability of its membership, as it found that less than 2 per cent leave the union. According to this survey the breakdown of union membership in the public sector was: UGT,

Table 6.9 Trade union membership in the public services, 1993 (000)

Service	CCOO		UGT		USO		Other		Total
	No.	%	No.	%	No.	%	No.	%	No.
Central government	71.6	27	123.8	48	5.8	2	58.4	22	259
Health	42.2	31	53.0	39	2.9	2	37.2	28	135
Education	43.8	28	53.5	34	7.3	5	50.9	33	155
Total (public and private)	740.6	37	850.0	43	62.4	3	341.7	17	1994

Source: Jordana (1995).

Note
Unemployed members included. Self-employed and retired members excluded.

Table 6.10 Union membership as a percentage of all employees, 1993

Service	CCOO	UGT	Total	Total
Central government	9.2	16.3	34.0	29.9
Health	7.7	9.7	24.8	21.8
Education	7.4	9.0	26.3	24.2
Total (public and private)	8.4	9.8	22.9	16.3

Source: Jordana (1995).

Note
Unemployed members included. Self-employed and retired members excluded.

38.5 per cent; CCOO, 31.1 per cent; CSIF, 7.4 per cent; and a multiplicity of other smaller unions organizing 16.4 per cent. Data from UGT and CCOO's internal accounts show that, between 1985 and 1995, union membership in the public services rose sharply and steadily, unlike overall membership, which also grew, but more slowly (see Tables 6.9 and 6.10).

Despite the lack of detailed figures for all organizations, there would appear to be a decline in the influence of the smaller unions in the public services in favour of UGT and, to a lesser extent, CSIF. Comparing trade union election results for the period 1987–95, we find that in 1986–87 UGT, CCOO and CSIF gained 79.6 per cent of the delegates, as against 20.4 per cent for all the other unions together, whereas in 1990 the percentage increases to 84.6 per cent. However, the trend was reversed in 1994–95 (82.1 per cent). The concentration of trade union representation, without actually eliminating all the smaller forces, is a fact. It has not prevented public service workers setting up specific structures within the major general unions for primary and secondary school teachers, police officers, prison warders, Post Office workers and university personnel, divided in turn into teaching staff and administrative staff. None the less, civil servants in central government, particularly in senior positions, seldom belong to any union.

Negotiating arrangements

In analysing consultation and negotiation arrangements a distinction needs to be drawn between civil servants and workers employed on ordinary contracts, even though in many respects the provisions are very similar. For workers on ordinary contracts, consultation and negotiation arrangements are governed by the same general labour relations legislation as in the private sector (albeit limited by certain formal budgetary controls), leading to numerous collective bargaining agreements at different territorial and sectoral levels. By contrast, the negotiating rights of civil servants are governed by a specific law, namely the Law on Bodies of Representation, Determination of Employment Conditions and Participation of Personnel in the Service of Public Administrations (*Ley 9/1987, de Órganos de Representación, Determinación de las Condiciones de Trabajo y Participación del Personal al Servicio de las Administraciones Públicas*, LORAP) as subsequently amended partially by law 7/1990 and law 18/1994. This legislation is a consequence of the application of the LOLS's recognition of the right to collective bargaining as a constituent element of trade union freedom (Mauri, 1995). One of the most important recent developments in labour relations within the public services is the change-over from a unilateral system of regulation to one in which civil servants negotiate their pay and conditions with their government employers. Nevertheless, this negotiating structure is different in many ways from collective bargaining arrangements in the private sector.

The first step in this direction was taken by LOLS, which required worker representation to be based on the unions' degree of representativeness. The LORAP then went on to define a fairly centralized negotiating model, with a general joint bargaining council for each territorial administration and several sectoral councils, while restricting the powers of the autonomous governments and local authorities. The law also made concrete provision for trade union participation, favouring what are known as the 'most representative' unions and coming down on the side of 'contractualizing', and stipulating that, where agreement was reached on matters falling within the powers of the body making the agreement, it would be known as a pact (*pacto*), and where the matters concerned were the responsibility of the Cabinet, autonomous community governments or full council meetings, it would be known as an agreement (*acuerdo*). At first, this legal framework severely constrained the autonomy of the bargaining process, as all agreements had to be ratified away from the negotiating table and so there was no certainty they would be fulfilled. Moreover, the fact that this still applies to matters with budget implications undermines trade union credibility (Morillo, 1997). More recently, new laws have regulated the frequency of negotiations, while the practice of almost automatically implementing the agreed items has become increasingly widespread, although controversy persists as to the legal status of the *acuerdos* and *pactos* (Mauri, 1995).

LORAP provided for different channels enabling public employees to have a say in deciding their employment conditions: negotiation, consultation and participation. The main items which could be the subject of bargaining, as laid down in the law, were pay, the preparation of job offers, job evaluation exercises, procedures for deciding entry into the service, staff requirements, promotion and other matters to do with conditions of service, and the relationship between civil servants and their trade union organizations, on the one hand, and the employers on the other. In the event of negotiations becoming bogged down, the law offered two ways out. The two sides could, by mutual agreement, appoint a mediator to help reach an *acuerdo* or *pacto*, or else the government could unilaterally fix employment terms and conditions.

The bargaining system is based on joint councils, or negotiating tables, at three levels. At the first level, there is a general council for central government, one for each autonomous community and one for each local authority. At the second level, there are sectoral joint councils, depending on the number of employees and the peculiarities of the sectors involved (Post Office, health, the legal system, schoolteachers, social security, etc.). The third level is far more decentralized and includes the possibility of *ad hoc* bargaining rounds wherever the employer and unions consider it appropriate. This bargaining structure is hierarchical and the matters which can be dealt with at each level are strictly defined. The general joint council deals with general employment conditions affecting all public employees dependent on central government and the employment conditions and trade union rights affecting all employees of the different administrations. Sectoral bargaining deals with the relevant sector's specific employment conditions as well as the application of agreements reached at the general council level. Before decentralized bargaining begins, agreement has to be reached on the criteria for setting up such specific negotiations. Usually it is a matter of units with specific problems, groups of employees with restricted internal mobility, a particular department or geographical area.

In line with these developments, subsequent agreements between government and unions in 1991 and 1994 took further steps to dismantle unilateral regulation by broadening the range of matters that could be tackled by the joint bargaining councils. This was the most important instrument for regulating public service labour relations in the 1990s in a context of new approaches to public management and stagnating employment growth (Villoria and del Pino, 1997). The agreements established a greater degree of co-ordination and decentralization of the different bargaining levels as well as setting up communication and arbitration bodies to resolve differences without recourse to industrial disputes. Efforts to take the bargaining process forward proceeded along three main lines: promoting collective bargaining as the chief means of participating in decisions affecting pay and conditions, co-ordinating the negotiating process to make it less cumbersome and more efficient, and setting up voluntary mechanisms for settling disputes between the two sides.

Representativeness and union elections

LOLS introduced the concept of the 'most representative' union into the public sector. In the case of national unions covering the whole of Spain, a 'most representative' union is defined as one which has obtained 10 per cent of the total number of delegates at this level. In the case of unions whose ambit is confined exclusively to a particular autonomous community, this notion is defined as one obtaining 15 per cent of all delegates, and a minimum of 1,500, within its particular territory. Applying the 'extension' principle, the law entitled the 'most representative' national unions to take part in all negotiations at every territorial and sectoral level. Likewise, unions operating only in a particular autonomous community could participate in all negotiations within that community and in all sectoral negotiations. 'Representative' unions, defined as those obtaining 10 per cent of all delegates in a particular territory or sector, were allowed to participate in their own sector, but the 'extension' principle did not apply.

Central government is divided into several large sectors, and both union elections and union representation, through the sectoral bargaining councils, are organized along these lines. The divisions are non-sectoral administration, education, universities, the health service, the Post Office and the courts and legal system. They are used for administrative purposes but not when totalling up the number of delegates in central government. The same rule applies to autonomous governments, where there are separate joint councils for non-sectoral staff, non-university education, universities and health.

Although the first union elections in the public services were held as early as 1978, they only involved workers on ordinary employment contracts and it was not until 1987 that the first union elections for civil servants took place. The turnout for these elections was 700,300 (72 per cent) out of a total electorate of 978,100. Ministry of Labour data show that union slates easily outnumbered independent groups of electors, with CCOO and UGT between them picking up almost 79 per cent of the delegates and the other unions obtaining 21 per cent. UGT obtained more delegates than the CCOO in local and regional government, with 49 per cent of the delegates. However, in public education the majority of delegates were not from the UGT and CCOO.

The 1990 elections confirmed some of these trends. The CCOO and UGT increased their dominance, gaining 85 per cent of all delegates in public administration and increased their proportion in education to 55 per cent. In addition to ELA, in Galicia CIG obtained 'most representative' status. The election results consolidated the dominance of the CCOO and UGT. The unions whose presence is confined to the public sector lost ground in certain areas. However, in the 1994–95 round of elections, although CCOO and UGT continued to dominate, some significant changes appeared. As Table 6.11 shows, UGT and CCOO combined gained only 68 per cent of delegates in public administration. (UGT experienced greater losses than CCOO.) In health, UGT and CCOO were defeated by sectoral unions, like CEMSATSE (representing doctors and health workers), the union with the most delegates in this sector. Other organizations which did well enough to gain representation on central government sectoral joint councils were SLCTCPA and in the Post Office (*Correos, Telégrafos y Caja Postal*) (see Table 6.12).

Apart from deciding the composition of the staff councils, the election results determine how many representatives each union has at the negotiating table,

Table 6.11 Trade union results in the public sector, 1995

Union	Central adm. Repres.	%	Education Repres.	%	Health Repres.	%
UGT	8,810	33.6	2,955	26.2	1,537	21.2
CCOO	9,021	34.4	2,721	24.1	2,340	32.2
CSI-CSIF	3,675	14.0				
ELA-STV	747	2.9	34	0.3	24	0.3
CIG	455	1.7	141	1.2	116	1.6
USO	498	1.9				
CEMSATSE	62	0.2				
OTROS	2,919	11.1	5,448	48.2	3,248	44.7
Total	26,187	100	11,299	100.0	7,265	100.0

or on joint councils. Staff-side representation on the joint councils is determined by the percentage of delegates obtained in the relevant administrative unit. This causes problems in representation in the civil service in some regions, because of the presence of the Galician and Basque trade unions. For example, although ELA-STV won only 3 per cent of the delegates elected in the whole of Spain, the fact that it achieved 'most representative' status in its own autonomous community entitles it to a place at all the state-wide negotiating tables, i.e. the general joint council and all the sectoral councils. CEMSATSE, on the other hand, with more delegates, failed to reach the threshold of 'most representative' status and so sits only on the corresponding sectoral joint council, not on the general one. (It is the same in the case of SLCTCPA in the Post Office and UCSTE in education.)

The composition of the staff side of the joint councils thus reinforces the consolidation of trade union representation among a few organizations (CCOO and UGT). CSIF's electoral setback illustrates the difficulties of establishing trade unionism confined to the public sector in the existing legal framework. However, this does not preclude certain organizations carving out a powerful negotiating role for themselves in specific sectors, which has happened in health, education and the Post Office. It should be noted that the draft public services statute could, if passed, lead to substantial modifications in trade union representation, providing more opportunities to achieve representation for the sectoral and professional unions.

Labour relations in the public sector

Throughout the 1990s there has been a steady increase in the role assigned to trade unions by the labour relations policies of public sector employers. The influence of trade unions is not the same in all sectors and regions, but, in general, it is considerable and, given the degree to which negotiations are centralized, the resulting *pactos* and *acuerdos* affect the vast majority of spheres at the different levels of state employment. This heavy centralization has not, however, prevented

Table 6.12 Types of bargaining council and trade union representation on them, 1990 (%)

Type of council	CCOO	CSI-CSIF	UGT	Other	Constituent unions (1990)
General; central, peripheral and institutional administration	31.83	34.52	21.68	11.98	CCOO, UGT, ELA-STV, CIG, CSI-CSIF
Sectoral, post office	31.58	15.26	33.55	SLCTCPA[a] 11.32 OTROS 8.29	CCOO, UGT, ELA-STV, CIG, CSI-CSIF, SLCTCPA
Sectoral, schoolteachers	25.17	16.46	16.66	ANPE 25.31 STES 15.10 OTROS 1.36	CCOO, UGT, ELA-STV, CIG, CSI-CSIF, ANPE Y STES
Sectoral, universities	34.07	27.21	27.21	10.84	CCOO, UGT, ELA-STV, CIG, CSI-CSIF
Sectoral, public health service	26.24	5.88	19.58	CEMSATSE 32.42 SAE 7.21 OTROS 8.67	CCOO, UGT, ELA-STV, CIG, CSI-CSIF, CEMSATSE
Sectoral, legal system	42.06	33.75	20.94	3.25	CCOO, UGT, ELA-STV, CIG, CSI-CSIF
Non-sectoral, autonomous governments	27.76	27.83	25.27	19.14	
Local government	27.01	18.01	38.06	16.92	

Sources: Arenilla (1993: 170); UGT (1994b).

Notes

a SLCTPA: Free Union of Postal, Telegraph and Post Office Bank Workers.

b It should be remembered that in each autonomous community there are further elections determining representation on the sectoral councils which, for reasons of space, cannot be included here.

numerous regional developments, with bargaining structures and significant agree-ments in most autonomous communities. These mainly affect the autonomous administrations concerned, but also exert some influence on local authorities in the area. Local authorities, for their part, have made full use of their autonomy to develop wide-ranging collective bargaining arrangements. As they have encoun-tered less resistance from political leaders, they have frequently gone much fur-ther than the more restricted approach to negotiations prevailing at higher levels of the state.

Since the early 1990s, with the implementation of the law on collective bar-gaining (LORAP) and the strengthening of the unions, there has been a major change in labour relations within the public services, with the consolidation of a new model based on reaching agreements with the unions. A unilateral and interventionist approach (laws and decrees introduced by parliament or the gov-ernment) was replaced gradually by a series of agreements between unions and the government. As a consequence, labour relations in the public services became more autonomous (see Table 6.13). This is the origin of law 7/1990 on collective bargaining and participation in determining the employment conditions of public employees, which was the result of a pact regarding collective bargaining for civil servants signed by the government and the unions (UGT and CCOO). The 1992 and 1994 plans for modernizing the public service, drawn up following the government-union agreements of November 1991 and September 1994, fit into the same framework. Both these agreements included a commitment to make certain improvements in employment conditions and to develop collective bar-gaining arrangements more fully.

Collective bargaining

In contrast to the collective bargaining agreements regularly negotiated between government and ordinary-contract public employees, those affecting civil ser-vants, who make up the majority of public service workers, have been of more limited, although, as we have seen, increasingly wide, scope. The break with unilateral regulation came in 1984 with the LMRFP, which formally, although not very precisely, recognised the collective bargaining principle within the public services while simultaneously granting the right to negotiate to the unions, leav-ing very little room for other representatives to take part. Nevertheless, this law imposed two important restrictions which still exist: the matters to be negotiated must be defined in advance and, in the event of negotiations being broken off, the government has the right to decide unilaterally on pay and conditions. This has meant that in comparison with the private sector, the scope of collective bargain-ing agreements is relatively limited, despite new areas – such as the moderniza-tion of the public service, the definition of employment plans and the conversion of ordinary contract workers into civil servants – having recently been included.

The powers of the respective general joint councils at each level of government have been defined in three ways. First, the councils can negotiate all matters affecting conditions of service (training, health and safety at work, etc.) and relations

Table 6.13 Main agreements between government and unions

Type and date	Government body signing	Union	Contents
Pact 1 June 1988	State Adm.	UGT, CSIF	On workplaces and permits for union functions
Agreement 15 March 1989	State Adm.	CSIF	Pay rise for civil servants of the State Administration for 1989
Agreement 28 June 1989	State Adm.	CSIF	Wage system of statutory personnel of the National Health Institute
Agreement 20 June 1989	State Adm.	CEMSATSE	Wage system of statutory personnel of the National Health Institute
Pact 18 August 1989	State Health Adm.	CEMSATSE, CCOO, CSIF	Permits and use of time off for union functions and INSALUD Health Institutions personnel representation
Agreement 14 March 1990	State Health Adm.	CEMSATSE, CCOO, CSIF, UGT	First aid teams
Pact 18 June 1990	State Adm.	CCOO, UGT	Collective bargaining of civil servants
Agreement 18 June 1990	State Adm.	CCOO, UGT	Compensation for imbalances between predicted retail price index and actual in 1989
Pact 8 September 1990	State Health Adm.	CCOO, CSIF	Statutory and professional career matters of statutory personnel of INSALUD
Agreement 16 November 1991[a]	State Adm.	CCOO, CSI-CSIF, ELA-STV, UGT and, during 1992, CIG[b]	Modernization of the Administration and improvement of work conditions
Agreement 15 September 1994	State Adm.	UGT, CCOO, CSI-CSIF, CIG	Conditions in the public services and civil service 1995–97

Sources: Arenilla (1993: 144–5); Roqueta (1996).

Notes

When agreement is reached on matters falling within the powers of the body making the agreement, it is known as a pact (*pacto*), and where the matters concerned are the responsibility of the Cabinet, autonomous community governments or full council meetings, it is known as an agreement (*acuerdo*).

[a] Agreement to last only until 1994, year of the new union elections.

[b] Constituting all the representatives at the core of the State Administration; CEMSATSE: Convergencia Estatal de Médicos y Ayudantes Técnicos Sanitarios; CIG: Convergencia Intersindical Galega.

between civil servants, their unions and the government. However, there are a number of restrictions limiting this apparently wide bargaining agenda. For example, the negotiators can determine, but not enforce, pay rates, and design, but not actually draw up, employment plans. Second, on a number of issues participation is confined to consultation. These include matters which can be decided only by laws or Acts of parliament, particularly budget-making laws (pay, job offers, entry into the service and promotion within it, etc.). Third, certain issues are excluded from the collective bargaining process, including the exercise of citizens' rights against civil servants and the government's freedom to organize the public services as it sees fit.

In conclusion, the negotiating arrangements have an ambiguous status compared with those in the private sector. There is little scope to influence items such as the application of agreed pay scales, job regrading and career structures, systems for entry into the service or offers of employment. Although there have been negotiations on such matters and agreements have been reached, there is no guarantee that the government will respect them, especially when they have budgetary implications or there is a change of government. Every government restricts the bargaining agenda in comparison with the private sector and so unions lack a 'guaranteed' negotiating framework. However, in some respects, especially job security and conditions, the public sector compares favourably with the private sector. There is a need for greater stability and guarantees regarding the matters open to collective bargaining, taking public service workers' special situation into account. It should be remembered, however, that the public sector context tends to favour workers against their employers because of the negative publicity for politicians arising from public sector disputes which may impair their electoral prospects. Under such circumstances, scope exists to raise demands and act on them via trade unions and other forms of lobbying, leading to extensive 'arm's length' bargaining, occasionally accompanied by strong mobilization in local authorities and sectors such as schools, health and the universities.

As noted earlier, a key feature of collective bargaining practice is the organizational strength and institutionalization of the 'most representative' unions. They dominate the staff side on the joint councils, while also participating in public organizations, including the National Institute of Employment, the National Social Security Institute, the Universities Council and the Economic and Social Council. This gives the unions, particularly the UGT and CCOO, access to a lot of information, a voice in many forums and the ability to monitor current developments. Although this model of 'government by agreement' has not been fully defined, the indications are that it will continue.

Disputes, mediation and arbitration

Strikes in the public sector, whether of civil servants or hired personnel, are legally permitted (they are forbidden only to the military and other special corps). However, the frequency of industrial disputes among public service employees is very low (see Table 6.14). In fact, the number of days lost to strikes rose appreciably

Table 6.14 Labour disputes: strikes and number of days lost

Service	Strikes				Days lost				No. of workers involved			
	1992	1993	1994	1995	1992	1993	1994	1995	1992	1993	1994	1995
Central government	51	29	19	16	660.221	21.790	19.046	4.561	1,112.731	80.574	16.416	7.810
Education	27	25	18	26	81.024	40.046	3.539	24.815	149.027	71.037	13.224	125.239
Health, veterinary and social services	47	28	29	37	80.930	31.461	49.851	171.853	173.402	49.872	37.949	154.321

Source: Instituto Nacional de Estadística, 'Estadística de huelgas y cierres patronales'.

Note
Excluding general strikes.

only in 1988 and 1992, years when there was a one-day general strike. Most disputes have been over loss of purchasing power as a result of government pay restraint policies in the 1980s and 1990s. Pay was also an element in the various general strikes, chiefly those of 1988, 1992 and 1994. Less frequently, disputes have arisen over workers being transferred from one level of government to another (usually from central government to one of the autonomous governments), staff freezes or cutbacks (local authorities, services, etc.), standards in education or the privatization of certain services.

The 1992 agreement between the government and the unions established a procedure for settling disputes over the interpretation and implementation of *acuerdos* or *pactos* through parity monitoring commissions set up in each collective bargaining sphere. The two sides were urged to submit their differences to the relevant commission before having recourse to any other administrative or legal channel. In addition, a means of preventing disputes arising out of collective bargaining procedures was put in place whereby unions undertook to notify the relevant body of such difficulties. Another possibility was for the two sides, by mutual agreement, to appoint a mediator to settle disputes deriving from the collective bargaining process. Traditionally, however, as happens in the private sector, the legal channel is still the main means of settling disputes. This can be put down to the persistence of certain cultural and social components in the way conflict is perceived, which, in the case of the civil service, often leads to administrative procedures being invoked (court cases brought against the state), since they are seen as the only effective way of resolving disputes.

Conclusion

Although labour relations in the private sector include some differences compared with those in other EU countries, they are by and large very similar. The Spanish constitution (1978), the Workers' Statute (1980), which provided for unitary workplace representation, the LOLS (1985), which laid down the system of trade union representation, and the Economic and Social Council (1993), are some of the legal and regulatory milestones along the road to normalization. Since 1986, employers' associations and trade unions have become more like their counterparts in the rest of the European Union. Although union membership remains near the lower end of the spectrum, Spain is no longer an exceptional case. Whereas the Spanish Employers' Confederation was immediately recognised as representing employers, there was a struggle among the unions to establish different models of trade unionism. This was reflected in the strong competition between the two major union organizations, the CCOO and UGT, which did not become fully independent of their respective ideologically similar political parties until the late 1980s. Their organizational consolidation took place later, but was nonetheless substantial. However, it is perhaps in regard to the rules governing collective bargaining and disputes that it is possible to speak of results illustrating the return to normality we have been talking about. Since there is such a close link between the subjects involved and labour relations dynamics, it is necessary to highlight the big increase in trade union membership at the end of the 1980s. Despite the very low starting point, membership levels have held up well, especially taking into account the recent experience in Europe as a whole.

When it comes to the public services the situation is appreciably different from the experience of the private sector. First, there is no overarching structure, such as would be provided by a public service workers' statute, so labour relations in the public sector do not have the type of overall framework which is found in the private sector. Second, without this basic element, the attempt to use the LOLS to set up a structure for trade union representation in the public services undermined the system's consistency. This can be seen in the improvised way the normalization of certain central aspects of labour relations in the public sector was tackled. Metaphorically speaking, a good case can be made out for saying that, while the constitution formed the foundations, work on the rest of the edifice started with the roof without waiting for the walls of the public service workers' statute to be erected. This lack of consistency arises from the problems bequeathed by years of dictatorship. Several of the vices and problems of the Franco period survived into the democratic era little changed, precisely because of the contradictory way labour relations in the public sector were regulated in the 1980s. The fact that there is still no public service workers' statute indicates some of the fears and obstacles blocking moves to draw one up at that time.

This chapter ends with three broad conclusions. The first is that, partly as a result of the problems described above, labour relations in the public sector are still at the consolidation stage and there has been a long delay in institutionalizing mechanisms of representation and structuring collective bargaining procedures, which would contribute to reducing conflict and fostering co-operation. One of the key elements explaining this situation is the fact that the first union elections in the public services were not held until 1987, ten years later than in the private sector, thereby favouring the emergence of a wide array of organizations. So, for example, it is noteworthy that even within the major, class-based, general trade unions there is a high degree of organizational dispersion, with the many different professions present among the public services each setting up their own structures. As a result, the activity of the public service workers' federations of the various unions, which are their basic operational units, is extremely fragmented.

The second conclusion is that, especially throughout the 1990s, the unions' capacity to intervene and negotiate – albeit without an adequate structure for controlling the negotiators – has grown to a considerable extent and this, together with a certain splitting up of the negotiating levels, has brought with it a real increase in worker representation in the various different areas and sectors.

The third conclusion highlights the process, from the early 1980s to the present time, which affects the civil service corps. Having lost their representative and self-regulating capacity to the unions favouring negotiated agreements with the employers, such corps have not disappeared or given way to selection criteria based on fitness for a particular job. Instead they have reorganized, divesting certain functions, but retaining their ability to select and assign specialist staff to the key posts in the political and administrative processes in the main public sector organizations.

References

Arenilla, M. (1993) *La negociación colectiva de los funcionarios públicos*, Madrid: La Ley.

Baena del Alcázar, M. (1984) *Estructura de la Función Pública y burocracia en España*, Oñaki: Instituto Vasco de Administración Pública.

Bañon, R. (1993) 'La modernización de la administración pública española: balance y perspectivas', *Política y Sociedad* 13: 9–20.

Beltrán, M. (1985) *Los funcionarios ante la reforma de la administración*, Madrid: Centro de Investigaciones Sociológicas.

Beltrán, M. (1991) *La productividad de la administración española: un análisis comparativo*, Madrid: Informes del Instituto de Estudios de Prospectiva, Ministerio de Economía y Hacienda.

Castells Arteche, M. (1987) *Proceso de construcción y desarrollo de la Función Pública Autonómica*, Madrid: INAP.

Collado Navarro, I. and Ramos Montañes, M. (1985) *Clasificación de puestos de trabajo en la Administración Pública*, Madrid: Instituto Nacional de Administración Pública.

Del Rey Guanter, S. (1986) *Estado, sindicatos y relaciones colectivas en la Función Pública*, Madrid: Instituto Nacional de Administración Pública.

Del Saz, S. (1995) *Contrato laboral y función pública*, Madrid: Marcial Pons.

Federación Sindical de Administración Pública CCOO (1995) 'Documentos del 6° Congreso', Madrid, CCOO.

Fernández Domínguez, J. J. and Rodríguez Escanciano, S. (1996) *La negociación colectiva de los funcionarios públicos*, Barcelona: Cedecs editorial.

Godino Reyes, M. (1996) *El contrato de trabajo en la Administración Pública*, Madrid: Civitas.

Gutiérrez Reñón, A. and Labrado Fernández, M. (1988) *La experiencia de la evaluación de puestos de trabajo en la Administración Pública*, Madrid: Instituto Nacional de Administración Pública.

INAP (1996) *La misión del INAP*, Madrid: Instituto Nacional de Administración Pública.

INE (1997) *Encuesta de población activa: principales resultados*, Madrid: Instituto Nacional de Estadística.

Jiménez Asensio, R. (1998) *Altos cargos y directivos públicos*, Oñati: Instituto Vasco de Administración Pública.

Jordana, J. (1994) 'Sindicatos y políticas en España: la influencia de las condiciones organizativas en las estrategias sindicales', *Revista Internacional de Sociología*, 8–9: 137–86.

Jordana, J. (1995) 'Trade Union Membership in Spain, 1977–94', *Labour Studies Working Paper* 2, Coventry: Centre for Comparative Labour Studies, University of Warwick.

Jordana, J. (1996) 'Reconsidering union membership in Spain, 1977–94: halting decline in a context of democratic consolidation', *Industrial Relations Journal*, 27, 3: 211–14.

López Camps, J. and Gadea Carrera, A. (1995) *Servir al ciudadano: gestión de la calidad en la Administración Pública*, Barcelona: Ediciones Gestión 2.000.

López-Nieto, F. (1989) *La administración pública en España*, Barcelona: Ariel.

MAP (1990) *Reflexiones para la modernización de la Administración del Estado*, Madrid: Ministerio para las Administraciones Públicas.

MAP (1993) *Acuerdo Administración-Sindicatos para modernizar la Administración y mejorar las condiciones de trabajo*, Madrid: Ministerio para las Administraciones Públicas.

Mauri, J. (1995) 'Problemas de la representación sindical y la negociación colectiva en la función pública: convergencias y divergencias con el empleo privado', *Documentación Administrativa*, 241–2: 127–272.

Montero, F. J. (1989) *Trabajar en la administración*, Madrid: Fundación Universidad-Empresa.

Morillo, R. (1997) 'La Administración Central: problemas y respuestas sindicales en Alemania, España, Italia y el Reino Unido', *Documentos de Gabinete Técnico Interfederal*, 3, Madrid: CCOO.

Morey Juan, A. (1989) *La selección del personal en la Administración Pública*, Valencia: Generalitat Valenciana.

Nieto, A. (1980) 'La noche oscura de la función pública', *Cuadernos Económicos del ICE*, 13: 9–18.

Parrado, S. (1996) 'Spain', in D. Farnham, S. Horton, J. Barlow and A. Hondeghem (eds), *New Public Managers in Europe*, London: Macmillan.

Ramió, C., Alcover, E. and Salvador, M. (1997) 'Mimetismo, clientelismo e innovación en las administraciones autonómicas', in Fundación Encuentro, *Informe Anual 1996*, Madrid.

Roqueta Buj, R. (1996) *La negociación colectiva en la función pública*, Valencia: Tirant lo Blanch/ Universitat de València.

Sánchez Morón, M. (1996) *Derecho de la función pública*, Madrid: Tecnos.

Suay Rincón, J. (1987) 'La reforma de la función pública: su impacto sobre la burocracia española', *Revista de Estudios Políticos XX*, 56: 511–28.

Subirats, J. (1990) 'Modernizing the Spanish public administration or reform in disguise', *ICPS Working Papers* 20, Barcelona: Institut de Ciències Politiques i Socials.

Subirats, J. and Gomà, R. (1997) 'Las políticas públicas', in M. Alcántara and A. Martínez (eds) *Politica y gobierno en España*, València: Tirant lo Blanc.

UGT (1994a) 'Afiliación y acción sindical en la Función Pública', *Boletín de información sociológica y sindical*, 3: 2–17.

UGT (1994b) 'Elecciones sindicales en la Función Pública', *Boletín de información sociológica y sindical*, 3: 38–76.

Vergés, J. (1997) 'Las privatizaciones de empresas públicas', en *Documentos de Trabajo* 6, Economía de la Empresa Pública, Universitat Autònoma de Barcelona.

Villoria, M. and del Pino, E. (1997) *Manual de gestión de recursos humanos en las administaciones públicas*, Madrid: Tecnos.

7 Denmark

Negotiating the restructuring of public service employment relations

Søren Kaj Andersen, Jesper Due and Jørgen Steen Madsen

In Denmark about one third of the labour force are employed in the public sector, which, by European standards, is a relatively large proportion of employment. Public sector activities can be placed in four socio-economic categories: *central administration*, covering state administration, the legal system, police, armed forces, diplomatic corps, etc.; *regional and local administration* of functions provided at these levels; *public services*, focusing mainly on education, health care and social security; and *public utilities*, covering areas such as public transport, postal services, telecommunications and water supply. It should be noted that Denmark's public sector has no 'fifth' segment, covering industrial production and financial services, although it has the relevant supervisory and regulatory bodies. An initial assessment of the four segments of Denmark's public sector can be focused on three overall trends which have been apparent for the past few decades: the devolution of responsibility for public services; citizens' participation; and market mechanisms, privatization and contracting-out.

Since the 1960s, which marked the commencement of the current process of development of Denmark's public sector, there have been gradual but significant changes in the forms of governance adopted for the sector. The concept of 'framework governance' was introduced in the 1960s, with the aim of releasing politicians from the burden of detailed governance, that is, from their accountability for the minutiae of public sector plans and budgets. But in the public sector a distinctly hierarchical governance philosophy still prevailed – a philosophy which was given a boost in the 1970s when the focus switched to planning. This led to the drawing up of what were referred to as 'perspective plans' for public sector developments.

During the 1980s, however, there was a shift in governance philosophy, mainly attributable to a growing awareness that neither hierarchical systems nor planning models were adequate. The solution was to adopt a new approach and new instruments, such as incentives based on economic rewards and sanctions. The pattern of development seen in the 1990s reveals a continuing determination to abandon centralized governance and planning; public sector functions have been devolved largely to the local level. The decision makers were made aware of the need to grant institutions and enterprises a certain freedom of action, including the opportunity to define precise goals for their range of activities. In the political sphere, the emphasis was to define and adopt overarching goals, frameworks and the rules of the game.

The municipal reform effected in the 1970s marks a turning point in decentralization of the allocation of functions in the public sector. Prior to the reform, Denmark had been divided into eighty-six 'market town' municipalities ('boroughs') and around 1,300 'parish' municipalities in twenty-five counties (*amter*). The boundaries were redrawn to create the 275 municipalities and fourteen counties which today constitute the politico-administrative entities at local and regional level. The municipal reform focused largely on reallocation of functions, whereby several administrative functions were delegated to the municipal level. This required the formation of entities with an adequate population to justify allocation of the relevant functions and big enough to justify the costs of maintaining a professional administration. But the reform also involved a reallocation of the financing of the various functions. Previously, the state had provided part-financing via refunds. The reform stipulated financing of municipal activities from three sources: a general state grant, economic equalization between the municipalities (whereby the richer municipalities transferred resources to the less well off) and municipal taxes. The goal was to achieve a more accurate balance between the competence delegated to the single municipality and its economic obligations. In 1992 one of the core functions of the public sector was transferred from state level to municipal level – primary and lower secondary school public education (the *folkeskole*). Prior to this transfer, teachers had been among those covered by collective agreements concluded between the state and the trade unions; they now became part of the municipal labour market.

In recent years a second central theme in the debate on public sector developments has been that of citizens' participation. The basic assumption is that the consumer/citizen, by entering into a direct dialogue with the management and employees of administrative bodies and institutions, can ensure the quality of public services. It is expected that consumer participation can engender – both in the consumer and in employees – a greater sense of responsibility and satisfaction in relation to specific public sector functions (Finansministeriet, 1993).

The existence of problems connected with this form of governance is evident in the Finance ministry's own publications. Devolved management, in its various forms, has been included as a basic requirement of the form of governance practised in the 1990s, that is, based on goals and frameworks adopted at central level. In its budget report for 1996, the Ministry of Finance emphasized that the focus has hitherto been on the framework, with less attention to the goals. The difficulties of measuring progress or performance, and the lack of interest in giving a higher profile to the delivery of public services, are identified as the villains of the piece. The budget report argued that the failure to focus on goals has created a 'governance vacuum' (Finansministeriet, 1996a).

The Ministry of Finance suggested three approaches to filling this vacuum. One would require closer involvement of the politicians at state, regional and local levels in the handling of individual cases, but previous experience shows that this approach is not ideal. The second approach would be to give consumers a more central role in the system, while introducing elements of market govern-ance. The necessarily limited experience of practising various forms of consumer participation suggests that a number of problems can arise: it is difficult for the consumer to exert much impact on employees and management in the public sector; consumer participation can result in the prioritization of narrow 'institu-tional interests' at the expense of broader socio-economic considerations; and the participation of so many actors in the governance processes can mean dilution of the sense of responsibility, so that nobody is accountable for the decisions taken. The third approach is to pursue a path of development featuring both centraliza-tion and consumer influence, achieved primarily via contract management of public services, in which there is a sharper distinction between the 'commissioner' (who finances and plans the function) and the direct 'provider'. If this third course is adopted, it represents a move from involvement of the citizens to considera-tions closely related to market mechanisms.

Analyses of developments in Denmark's public sector confirm that the devolu-tion of the provider function is one of the main features. Naschold (1996) includes this as one of the main trends, along with limited privatization, the introduction of market mechanisms and internal modernization. He adds that devolved man-agement places Denmark in the same development category as the Netherlands, rather than in the more obvious Nordic category. This viewpoint is supported by Lægreid and Pedersen (1994), who characterize the restructuring of Denmark's public sector as the expression of a south Nordic strategy, while emphasizing the same features as Naschold.

As used in this context, the term 'market mechanisms' refers to a number of initiatives concerning the identity of the parties which, respectively, *plan* public services, *produce* and *finance* them. The aim of separating these roles is to achieve a more direct focus on the supply and demand factors, so as to reinforce the competition incentive. The planning and production may be transferred to private suppliers via licence, authorization or contracting-out. Financing is linked with the scope of the relevant activities (applying the 'taxi-meter principle') or based on payment by consumers. Another element related to this development is con-tract management. These contracts are not strictly legally binding but represent a mutually binding agreement concluded between, for example, the central admin-istration and state agencies. They normally specify aims concerning efficiency and quality of services, etc.

With some notable exceptions, privatization in Denmark has been restricted to some large-scale public services – telecoms, postal services, Copenhagen airport and a shipping line belonging to Danish State Railways. In most cases the state enters the new enterprise structure as a majority shareholder, so that the process is often referred to as corporatization, as it fails to meet the more stringent criteria of 'classical' privatization (full transfer to private ownership). So far this form of privatization has produced encouraging results for the Danish state: income from the sale of shares, and dividends from enterprises in which it retains a shareholding (e.g. 500 million kroner in 1996 from TeleDanmark, in which it owned 51.7 per cent of the shares). In 1997 all state-owned shares in TeleDanmark were sold to an American company, however, and Danish State Railways (DSB) will become an independent limited liability company in 1999, cutting its formal ties with the state.

Contracting-out is another strategy adopted to introduce market elements in the provision of public services, although in recent years there has been only limited development in this area. This lack of enthusiasm among politicians at local and regional government level may be partly attributable to the adverse publicity surrounding some recent cases, most notably when the contracting-out of bus services led to disputes between trade unions and the new employers, with occasional eruptions of violence (Due *et al.*, 1996). In 1994 the percentage of operational functions in the state sub-sector performed by outside contractors was about 17 per cent, representing only a slight increase over previous years. In 1993 the corresponding figure for municipalities was 9 per cent, matching the level of previous years. At municipal level the main functions contracted out are technology-based, such as environmental and technical services and roads, although in recent years tenders have been invited for service functions such as cleaning and transport, and more specialized functions related to information technology (Finansministeriet/Indenrigsministeriet, 1995). In individual municipalities, selected social services – especially the care of the elderly – have been contracted out on a trial basis. Such pilot projects are likely to become more widespread, and to be adopted as permanent schemes. The social welfare legislation passed in early 1997 offers the recipients of home help greater freedom to choose between various options, thus paving the way for the setting up of new private suppliers of the relevant services. The pattern of development of public sector welfare services does not suggest any move to introduce large-scale privatization, resulting in a concomitant shrinking of the sector considered in its broadest sense. Rather, the tendency is towards a mix of privatized and public services, where the aim is to raise the level of efficiency by introducing market-type mechanisms.

Organizational structure, employment and wages

Organizational structure of the main sectors

Public services are provided at three levels in Denmark: state, regional and municipal. In addition there are 'subsidized institutions', which cover the private or independent organizations which have economic or other links with the state, regions or municipalities.[1] The regional authorities are the *amter* (usually translated as 'counties' or 'regions'), while at local level there is the single *kommune*, the local authority or municipality. The politico-administrative allocation of responsibilities plays a vital role in employment relations on Denmark's public-sector labour market, as it has a profound impact on structures and on the strategies adopted by trade unions and employers. Throughout the chapter, a distinction is drawn between employees working at state, regional and municipal levels, while occasionally referring to the special status of employees at the subsidized institutions.

Figure 7.1 shows the allocation of legal and administrative responsibilities among the state, counties and municipalities. It reveals a somewhat hierarchical pattern

---

Central government

- Central administration
- Defence
- Police
- Advanced studies and research
- Railways

Regional and local authorities[a]

14 counties	*275 municipalities*
• Administration	• Administration
• General hospitals	• Primary and lower secondary education
• Special care institutions	• Health and social services for children,
• Primary health care	elderly and disabled persons
(including general practitioners)	• Cultural affairs (libraries, etc.)
• Upper secondary education	

Note

a Although in terms of population there are large variations from county to county and from one
municipality to another, both entities are comparatively small by European standards. Most of the
counties have a population of 100,000–200,000, while the average municipality has about 20,000
inhabitants (*Statistical Yearbook* 1997).

Figure 7.1 The political-administrative structure and distribution of functions in Denmark

in the distribution, as the state maintains overall control of the activities conducted at the two lower levels, while in policy areas, such as the environment
and planning, the counties supervise the measures implemented at local level. In
general, however, the counties and municipalities are of roughly similar standing
vis-à-vis the state, which delegates certain responsibilities to both levels.

Public education is governed at three different levels: universities by the state,
upper secondary schools (*gymnasier*) by the counties, and primary and lower
secondary schools (the *folkeskole*) by the municipalities. The public health care
services are governed at two levels. Primary health care is provided by the counties
and the municipalities, and the counties are responsible for relations with general
practitioners and specialists (e.g. neurologists, psychiatrists). The municipalities
also play an important role in primary health care services for children, the
elderly and the disabled. The hospitals are governed by the counties, with the
exception of the metropolitan municipalities of Copenhagen and Frederiksberg
and the University Hospital in Copenhagen – a former state hospital – which are
operated by a joint authority referred to as HS. Thus the various public services
are provided at central and decentralized levels, and neither education nor health
care is delivered by a single entity.

The composition of public sector employment

The aggregate number of employees in Denmark's public sector increased by
3.3 per cent during the period 1980–95 (see Table 7.1), but the increase was not

Table 7.1 Employment in the public sector, 1980–95 (000)

Sub-sector	1980	1985	1990	1995
Central government	214	219	200	182
Municipalities	425	452	457	424
Counties	137	156	158	175
Subsidized institutions	112	123	128	136
Public sector total	888	947	944	917

Sources: Danmarks Statistik (1996: 193, 1997b).

Table 7.2 Male and female public sector employment in 1995 (000)

Sub-sector	Total	Male	Female Total	Full-time	Part-time
Total public sector	781	278	502	248	253
Central government	182	116	65	42	23
Regional and local authorities of which:	599	162	437	206	230
Education	127	46	82	44	38
Hospitals	102	20	82	46	36

Source: Danmarks Statistik (1997b).

evenly distributed. In the state sector, the number of employees declined from nearly 25 per cent to 20 per cent of the public sector work force, whilst there has been a slight increase in employment in the regional and municipal authorities, which together employ nearly two-thirds of public sector workers, and in the area designated 'subsidized institutions'. The decline in employment in the state sector during this period was mainly due to the transfer of a number of state services to independent enterprises, while the delegation of some functions to the counties and municipalities further reduced the number of state employees.

The growth in the number of county employees and the significant decline in the number of municipal employees between 1990 and 1995 is mainly attributable to the creation of a new entity – the Metropolitan Hospitals Authority (HS) – which covers the hospitals formerly operated by the metropolitan municipalities and the state-run University Hospital in Copenhagen. In official statistics, employees of HS are reckoned as county employees, somewhat curiously, as HS is controlled by the municipalities and the state and not by the counties.

Almost two out of three public sector employees are women. The figures of job distribution by gender in Table 7.2 reveal a difference between the state and counties/municipalities: two out of three state employees are men, whereas three out of four county and municipal employees are women. The imbalance is explained by the high number of typical 'women's jobs' in the three dominant areas in the non-state segment of the public sector: social security, health care and education.

Table 7.2 shows that more women work part-time than full-time in the public sector. The large groups of part-time women workers are employed mainly by the local authorities, especially in social and health care services. At local level there are also groups of part-time male employees, including more than 13,000 in teaching jobs. During the period 1983–93, there was an increase in the percentage of women managers on the Danish labour market – in both sectors – although particularly among senior executives in the counties and municipalities. The share of women senior managers in these two segments increased from around 1 per cent to more than 6 per cent during the period 1983–93, with a roughly similar increase in the state segment. During the same period there was also an increase in the share of women with middle management jobs—from around 10 per cent to more than 15 per cent in the counties and municipalities. There are comparatively fewer women managers in the private sector than in the public sector (Ligestillingsrådet, 1995).

During the period 1980–93, the increase of 40,000 in the aggregate number of jobs can be explained by the recruitment of women workers, as the number of male workers has remained stable at around 128,000. The distribution of male workers by job type (full-time/part-time) also remained stable, whereas a slightly higher number of women had full-time jobs at the end of the period. Most of the increase in employment can be attributed to the increased number of women in part-time jobs; during the 1980s it increased by more than 26 per cent, and subsequently declined slightly up to 1993.

A number of public sector organizations – such as kindergartens, nursing homes, care institutions and the postal services – make extensive use of casual workers and temporary staff. Although these temporary employees are not guaranteed fixed working hours or permanent employment, they are none the less covered by a collective agreement. The agreement guarantees temporary workers fixed hourly pay, supplementary amounts, holiday pay and working conditions similar to the conditions of permanent staff. The labour market parties do not perceive temporary employment of this type as a problem requiring special solutions. There is, however, another aspect of temporary employment which merits attention as an example of the approach adopted by the Danish model of collective agreements. The public sector has been given a special responsibility in the implementation of the active labour market policy, leading to the introduction of new forms of temporary employment for unemployed workers. Such jobs have two distinct features: they are regarded as a component of the 'activation' process, so the worker receives unemployment benefit, not pay; and the jobs are for a fixed term.

The public sector labour market

Slightly more than 20 per cent of public sector employees have civil servant status, which means that their terms of employment are covered by legislation rather than by collective agreement. The state sub-sector has by far the highest percentage of employees with civil servant status (almost 40 per cent), usually in senior positions, such as judges, police officers, the armed forces and certain

Table 7.3 Public sector employment, by terms of employment, 1995 (000)

Terms	Central government	Municipalities and counties	Total
Civil servants	69	95	165
Agreement-covered employees	95	420	515
Other employees	18	83	101
Total	182	599	781

Source: Danmarks Statistik (1997b).

groups in the State Railways. In Table 7.3 the category 'Other employees' covers staff with individual contracts – usually senior staff, whose remuneration takes the form of fees, and others employed in accordance with different sets of rules and regulations. Most of the employees in this category are considered as civil servants by the Ministry of Finance. The most important differences between the terms of employment of civil servants and others is that civil servants are not legally entitled to resort to industrial action (strikes). Also they are covered by a statutory pension scheme (in addition to the universal old age pension) and they are normally entitled to three years' pay if they are dismissed.

It is characteristic of the political system that politics and administration are, in principle, kept apart in the case of recruitment at all levels in the public sector. Senior positions are filled following the public announcement of vacancies, and appointments are made with the emphasis on explicit and checkable criteria – primarily educational qualifications and practical managerial experience. One of the inviolable rules is that, once appointed, managers are not replaced as a result of changes in the balance of political power, at state, regional or municipal level. It is a general principle for all categories of employees that they are recruited and promoted according to qualifications and professional experience. Vacant posts are advertised and filled according to a policy of 'open recruitment', so people already employed in the public sector are not preferred to external applicants.

Wages and salaries

The outcome of the collective bargaining round in 1997 signalled a decision to go ahead with the long-discussed proposal to reform Denmark's public sector pay system. The decision was reached primarily to meet employers' demands for a more flexible pay system. As far back as 1987 this pressure led to the first collective agreement on the issue; it was agreed that less than 1 per cent of the overall pay award could be allocated to 'pools' for distribution at a decentralized level. The local wage pools, despite the meagre allocation, proved to be unpopular among large groups of public sector employees. They were – and still are – referred to as 'the toady's supplement',[2] to be distributed by employers to workers who displayed high levels of zeal. This attitude prevailed, despite the fact that the local supplement could be distributed only following agreement between the

local parties. It has thus proved difficult to move closer to the goal of decentralized pay.

The result of the 1995 collective bargaining round was agreement to dismantle
the local pay scheme, but it was agreed to commence work at committee level,
with a view to introducing a comprehensive pay reform in 1997. The main goal
was to devise a public sector pay system in which aggregate pay would consist of
four separate components: first, a basic wage, fixed at central level; second, a
supplementary amount negotiated at either a decentralized or central level based
on job function (e.g. special areas of work, or responsibility); third, a qualifications
allowance (e.g. education, further training or experience) negotiated at either
decentralized or central level; and fourth, a component based on results or
performance (i.e. efficiency), to be agreed at decentralized level, and paid either
on an individual or a group basis.

Initially the aim was that the basic wage would account for 70 per cent of
aggregate pay, while the other three components would account for the other
30 per cent. Today the aims of the local level bargaining process have diminished
and it seems more likely that around 15–20 per cent of the total wage sum will be
determined at the local level. Considered as a whole, the reform can be perceived
as a showdown: a determined attempt to replace the automatic, seniority-based
pay increments with a system in which pay more accurately reflects the qualifications and performance of each employee, or group of employees.

The reform has had a different impact on various parts of the public sector. An
agreement was concluded in the state sub-sector on a voluntary three-year pilot
project commencing in January 1998, focusing on a new pay system. This pilot
project may determine the future of the new system. In the regional/municipal
sub-sector, the teachers have taken the lead in rejecting moves to fix pay at a
decentralized level, an attitude which is also reflected in the special negotiation
agreement with the employers. The agreement reached on the new forms of pay
covers only the managerial levels (Folkeskolen, 1997). This negative attitude is
not shared by the nurses' union, which has changed its position, and now sees an
advantage in the introduction of new pay structures. In this case the agreement
means that since April 1998 all nurses have been covered by a new basic pay
system, with three salary steps for ordinary nurses and just one for senior nurses.
This basic pay is topped up with the three pay components outlined above
(Sygeplejersken, 1997). It can be argued that the pay reform has been 'sold' to
employees by dangling the carrot of a general pay rise, as all nurses are to move
up by one to three salary steps upon the introduction of the new pay system. In
fact, its implementation has been impressive; it already covers more than half the
employees in the counties and more than 60 per cent in the municipalities. Some
difficulties have arisen, however, and the speed of implementation will probably
be slower than anticipated.

The old pay system by definition covered civil servants, but it was also applied
– whole or in part – to many employees covered by collective agreements. The
terms of employment for civil servants stipulate special obligations and rules
governing recruitment and dismissal, but there has been a general convergence

of pay levels and terms of employment for civil servants and agreement-covered employees. The old civil service pay system operates with fifty-five salary steps, forming the basis of forty-two pay grades which provide an overall framework for placing jobs when collective agreements are concluded. Employees automatically move up one salary step every other year until the final step in the specific pay grade has been reached, or until the employee leaves the service or is promoted to a new grade.

One of the important components of the public sector pay system is the pay adjustment mechanism whereby pay is adjusted in line with pay trends in the private sector. This guarantees that public sector employees are automatically awarded 80 per cent of the average pay increases agreed for the private sector labour market. The system incorporates a degree of geographical differentiation so that, for example, the pay for salary step 20 in the Copenhagen region is 6 per cent higher than for the same step in a sparsely populated district. Employees can qualify for various supplementary amounts: an availability (stand-by) allowance, an allowance for unsocial working hours, overtime, etc. (Finansministeriet, 1996b).

Employers and employers' associations

State policies

Almost inevitably, state policies in the public sector – the devolution of responsibility, citizens' participation, and the introduction of market mechanisms – have had an impact on the process of restructuring employment relations. In this process, the public sector trade unions have tended to change their stance, acting as partners rather than adversaries, although some groups of employees are still reluctant to accept some of the reforms. Another source of controversy has been the employers' policy of limiting the number of employees with civil servant status with a view to establishing agreement-based employment as the norm. This tactic was vigorously opposed by groups of employees with civil servant status, thus delaying implementation of the policy until recently.

Although restructuring plans have been initiated by the employers, the process has been conducted within the framework of the existing collective bargaining system. There has been no 'union-bashing'; employers' initiatives cannot be seen as an attack on public sector employees or on union rights enshrined in collective agreements. The employers accept a collective bargaining system for the public sector labour market, with a high rate of unionization. It can be argued that the constructive role played by the unions in the restructuring process is partly the result of the non-confrontational attitude adopted by the employers.

Pedersen (1996)[3] identifies three separate phases in his review of the response of unions to proposed reforms since the early 1980s: first, an ideological phase, in which the unions reacted passively or negatively; second, a technical implementation phase in which the debate was depoliticized and various concrete projects were set in motion; and third, an administrative policy phase, in which pay issues were increasingly woven into the fabric of central and local administrative policy goals. Pay is no longer considered in isolation, but as part of a broader spectrum of workplace issues.

This development logic has prompted the observation that the agenda for the modernization of the public sector is being drawn up – and defined in detail – with the active involvement of the labour market parties, in this case elected politicians and trade union federations. This can be interpreted as the outcome of the shift in the unions' position; that is, their fairly recent willingness to apply a broader socio-economic perspective when entering into dialogue with the employers, not only on pay issues but also on personnel and administrative policy issues. It can also be argued that this shift in policy has been influenced by a number of external factors, such as the devolution of the responsibility for public services, the employers' insistence on linking pay and personnel policy with administrative policy, and the reluctance of the politicians to define a tangible policy for the various areas covered by the public sector.

The involvement of the trade unions is closely related to their assessment of the potential benefits to be derived from the measures adopted in the public sector to promote 'developing work and employees' (*Det Udviklende Arbejde*) – a Danish or Nordic concept emphasizing that improvements in the efficiency and quality of public services are to be accompanied by improvements in working conditions, greater job satisfaction and the development of competences for workers. The term can be seen as a variant of 'new public management'. It also implies a tendency to move away from the traditional confrontational relationship between employers and unions. The emphasis is now on partnership and common interests.

These developments pose some problems for the relations between the parties in the public sector labour market. By becoming deeply involved in issues related to administrative policy, the trade unions have had to develop and maintain professional secretariats, capable of formulating new policies and conducting negotiations. This process can easily lead to a gulf between a union's officials and professional staff and its ordinary members. Furthermore, the unions have yet to adopt a common position in support of the steps taken to modernize the public sector and its pay system. One possible consequence could be a rift in the trade union movement. The question is thus whether the system of collective agreements is capable of encompassing and solving the complex problems which now appear on the agenda of negotiations.

Public sector employers

The fundamental reason for focusing on the state sub-sector is the insistence of the political system on retaining a measure of control of overall socio-economic development, especially control of the wide range of public functions performed at regional level and local level. Despite the extensive autonomy of the counties and municipalities – in particular the right to levy their own taxes – they are none the less subject to a considerable degree of state control over general economic policy, including the determination of pay and working conditions for employees.

The dominance of the state sub-sector in Denmark is made strikingly clear in the dual role played by the state employer party. The Ministry of Finance – with the minister very much to the fore – is both a prominent public sector employer and the agency responsible for overall economic policy, including the governance of regional and municipal economic policy. During the collective bargaining rounds, conducted at intervals of two years and commencing early in the year, the Minister of Finance plays an active role in trying to ensure state control and co-ordination of the overall pattern of public sector collective bargaining. With a single exception – during the 1989 bargaining round – the municipal employers have accepted this allocation of roles, despite the wish of both employers and unions to achieve greater independence.

One of the reasons for this stasis is that, a few months after the completion of negotiations on the collective agreements, the regional and municipal groupings have to meet the Minister of Finance for the annual review of the regional/municipal economy. If, in the opinion of the minister, the counties or the municipalities have 'behaved irresponsibly' during the recent bargaining round, it will inevitably have an impact on the general negotiations on the regional/local economies. The municipalities are reluctant to run the risk, and this helps to maintain state dominance in the collective bargaining system.

The municipal sub-sector is larger than either the state or the county/regional segment. The 273 municipalities (i.e. excluding the two metropolitan municipalities, Copenhagen and Frederiksberg) have formed a joint organization to promote their interests: the National Association of Local Authorities (KL). The organization represents both the municipalities' general political interests *vis-à-vis* the government (the *Folketing*) and the state administration and their employers' interests in relation to municipal employees and their trade unions.

Measured in relation to GDP, the aggregate primary municipal sector accounts for about half the public sector, or one-third of the aggregate GDP. The municipal segment is thus of major economic importance, and it is hardly surprising that the government – when conducting negotiations – attempts to ensure that it retains its influence on the economic development of the municipalities, and on their policies on salaries and related matters. The basic strategy of KL is to preserve municipal autonomy – including the right to levy local taxes – which is one of the main features of the public administration system. Denmark has developed '. . . a long tradition of local democracy and (local) provision of central welfare services . . .' (KL, 1997: 7).

If the municipalities are to succeed in maintaining this system, it is imperative to co-ordinate their wide-ranging interests, so that they can present a united front *vis-à-vis* the *Folketing*, the government, central administration, etc. Without this co-ordination, the municipalities would lose influence over the central governance of socio-economic policy, especially on the range of matters concentrated in the Ministry of Finance. Although KL is a democratic, political interest organization, with a leadership elected annually in relation to the number of seats won by the parties at the local elections, it is not an arena for open party political disputes. KL emerged in the wake of the municipal reforms of 1970, when the number of municipalities was reduced from 1,300 to 275. The formation of larger entities created new needs, and the three existing municipal groupings merged to form KL.

The Danish Federation of County Councils (ARF) is the special interest body formed by the fourteen counties. It represents their overarching political interests, and also functions as an employers' association. The ARF was formed in 1913 but its present form is the result of a restructuring of the old organization and the municipal reforms. The counties, which had previously covered only rural municipalities, were enlarged to include the urban municipalities. This restructuring meant the transfer of most hospitals to ARF's domain, along with the delegation of a number of other functions from state level to regional and local level. This conferred an entirely new status on the counties, which now became key actors in the public sector.

The counties assume overall responsibility for doctors working in the primary health care sector. In principle both general practitioners and specialists are operators of private business entities, but their fees are fixed in accordance with a collective agreement concluded with ARF's special Health Insurance Negotiating Committee. The health care sector is, however, at the same time subject to extensive state governance, via the National Health Board under the Ministry of Health. This is also an area which is closely monitored by the *Folketing* (for example, by ruling on allocations in relation to waiting lists for hospital treatment).

One of the inevitable effects of the introduction of governance by 'frameworks and goals', and the general process of decentralization, is that detailed state administration has been abandoned. This development has led to a situation in which many members of parliament are eager to seize upon 'individual cases', in an attempt to regain control of territory that has been formally ceded to regional and municipal levels. And one favourite, recurring theme is the alleged inefficiency of the county hospital services.

The status and role of public managers

A fundamental feature of the collective bargaining system is the centralized and simultaneous negotiations for all personnel groups. This means that, in principle, senior managers have their pay and working conditions fixed via the general negotiations between the Minister of Finance and the state employees' association (CFU), and the municipal employers' associations and their bargaining partner (KTO). The move towards greater flexibility and local influence in the determination of pay and conditions has, however, had a marked impact on public sector managerial pay levels. This trend was noted during the 1980s, with opportunities for employment under the terms of individual – and individually negotiated – contracts and fixed-term contracts. This solution paved the way to the payment of sizeable supplementary allowances in addition to the basic salary. Following the introduction of the first decentralized wage pools in 1987, later adjustments to the system made it possible to establish managerial-level wage pools, so that the opportunities for managers to qualify for supplementary performance-related allowances were negotiated outside the framework of the negotiations on pay and working conditions for other grades.

In principle, and in accordance with the terms of the collective agreement, however, trade unions continued to participate in the allocation of these supplementary allowances. In the state sub-sector a special senior managers' committee was set up to deal with pay and terms of employment for permanent under-secretaries and directors-general, with representatives from the Ministry of Finance and the relevant trade union federations. This trend – which was reinforced by the movement towards corporatization – has introduced a higher degree of flexibility into the previously rigid pay system for public managers, a system which had reflected the civil service ethos. In general, this has led to relatively large pay increases for managers during the past decade, although the rises have still failed to match those achieved by senior executives in the private sector.

There are single independent organizations for public managers, for example, the Municipal Executives (KC), but in general managers are members of the same trade unions as some of their employees. The choice of trade union is usually based on the manager's educational background. The result is that public managers usually find that their own pay and working conditions are negotiated by an organization to which many of their employees belong, and it is in respect of these same employees that the managers often will be delegated extended employer competence. This dual status – as manager and member of the employees' union – causes problems whenever an industrial dispute arises between the managers and workers belonging to the same trade union or federation. Despite the problem, the system is likely to survive, probably because relations between management and workers are consensual rather than adversarial.

The professional or *étatiste* ideology of the civil service system seems to have created a common identity which, in one important respect, seems to deviate from the traditional wage-earner ideology in the private sector, where it would be unthinkable for rank-and-file workers and managers to be members of the same trade union. In many areas a contributory – or even decisive – factor has been the professional or semi-professional character of the trade unions. Typically, groups such as teachers and nurses, backed by an education/training monopoly, seek to retain control of their area of employment to achieve better levels of pay and working conditions. And part of the strategy adopted to achieve this control is to ensure a representational monopoly embracing management.

Employers' associations

One of the significant steps in the centralization which took place in the state sub-sector in the 1970s was the transfer of the sole right of each ministry to negotiate its own pay and working conditions to the Ministry of Finance, which has subsequently acted as the employers' organization of the separate ministries and institutions. In the 1980s and 1990s, changes in the clauses of the collective agreements on working conditions and other factors restored decision-making competence to the local level, but it is explicitly stated that this competence – to conduct local negotiations on pay and working conditions – is to be exercised within a centrally adopted framework.

The Ministry of Finance has extensive powers in relation to the ministries with regard to budgets, and decisions on the size of the management teams in the institution. Within these limits, a single ministry and institution can decide how many staff it employs, but it is not empowered to determine the general rules for personnel covering pay, pensions, other terms of employment and working conditions. It is the Ministry of Finance, acting on behalf of the other ministries, which concludes the collective agreements (and in some cases prepares legislation) that sets these rules.

Since the early 1970s, the Ministry of Finance has developed into an independent employer party, with a modern organizational structure. 'The Ministry of Finance performs these tasks in co-operation with employers' associations in the private sector and the public sector (municipalities and counties), and increasingly closer co-operation with the European Union' (Finansministeriet, 1996b: 7). And, it can be added, in close co-operation with the Danish trade unions. Viewed in an international context, the choice of structure may appear odd: the ministry, rather than an independent agency or organization separated from the central administration. The Danish solution has been based on co-ordination of at least three interrelated policy areas: personnel, administration and budgets. The result is that the employer function is firmly anchored in what may be regarded as the most central component in the state's political and administrative apparatus.

There is thus a high degree of centralization, although it should be noted that a mechanism has been created whereby some decisions can be made at local level, within the framework adopted at central level. This is the phenomenon, closely resembling the structure adopted by the trade union side, which has been described as 'centralized decentralization'.

> What has occurred is a centralisation and professionalisation of, respectively, the employer function and the workers' organisations. At the same time competence has been delegated to, respectively, ministerial and workplace levels, on both the employer and the trade union sides.
> (Pedersen, 1996: 54; Due and Madsen, 1988: 292–4, 1996: 723–4)

KL is one of Denmark's largest employers' associations, accounting for 47 per cent of public sector employees. Among the largest groups of employees are clerical staff in administrative functions, teachers at the primary and lower secondary schools, teachers at child day-care institutions, personnel at geriatric day-care institutions, home helps, social and health care assistants, nurses in geriatric services, social workers and groups of graduates (e.g. law graduates, economists and engineers).

The collective agreements concluded by KL and the trade unions are binding on the municipalities, as they have delegated their negotiating rights to KL. The agreements do not come into force until they have been approved by the Municipal Salaries Board – a supervisory body – but its approval is a formality, as its municipal employers' representatives have a dominant position. KL's board draws up the general lines to be pursued during the negotiations, which are then delegated to the salaries committee. As the political representatives on KL's highest bodies are often mayors (and thus holders of many offices) their participation in the negotiating process is limited. Thus the administrative leadership of the salaries section plays a key role in conducting the actual negotiations. Usually the politicians participate only in negotiations on the general demands, and an important role is often played by the chair of the salaries committee, acting as a negotiator.

The changes in KL, like the changes in the Ministry of Finance, have merged more general issues related to overall economic policy with pay-specific policy. This linkage process has led to various internal clashes of interests between the two areas of policy. The core of the problem is that the interests at stake in reaching a settlement during the collective bargaining process can easily clash with the interests at stake in securing a satisfactory public sector economy. As a private, voluntary association KL resembles the employers' associations in the private sector. There is, however, a vital difference: KL's role is not restricted to that of municipal employer, as it also represents the municipalities in their capacity as democratic organizations exercising public authority. Its main function is to help to strike a balance between the exercise of authority at local and central levels. KL (along with ARF) has been described as a kind of 'second chamber' in the Danish political system, playing a dual role in the local and the regional areas.[4] In this respect KL and ARF are fundamentally different from the private employers' associations.

The ARF conducts negotiations and concludes binding collective agreements on behalf of the counties. It has attempted to promote the position of the counties and avoid relegation to 'junior partner' status in the overall regional and municipal collective bargaining system. It is, however, difficult to alter the existing balance, as the municipal area is more than twice as large, although ARF is the dominant partner in the hospital sector, where there has been intense activity in recent years, fuelled by the nurses' dissatisfaction with their pay levels.

As noted earlier, a new public employer in the regional/municipal economy was formed in the spring of 1994. The municipality of Copenhagen was experiencing economic difficulties, and to ease the pressures a new hospital body was created covering all the hospitals in the metropolitan area, under joint leadership: HS. The Minister of Finance was prepared to contribute a one-off sum of 1.0 billion kroner to relieve the pressure on the municipality of Copenhagen and to raise the level of efficiency of a major segment of the hospital services. Efficiency gains were limited, however, because the county of Copenhagen decided at the last minute not to join the new HS grouping.

On one level, the creation of HS could be viewed as a short cut to a modernization of Denmark's public sector; it has its own board and is relatively independent of the political system, and, without the county of Copenhagen, it has about 21,000 employees. It overcame a number of problems posed by the existing structure of three separate areas of authority at state, county and municipal level. It is hardly surprising that both KL and ARF opposed the formation of HS, which they hoped would be an isolated phenomenon. The two employers' associations are undoubtedly the key players in the co-operation between public sector employers. KL has been given a leading role, as the parties have agreed that the chair of its salaries committee should act as leader of the employers' political negotiations, while its salaries chief executive leads the protracted sequence of negotiations which are delegated to the executive staff by the elected representatives.

The trade unions

The legal framework

The statutory regulation of collective agreements for civil servants has played an important role in the development of labour market organizations. The amendments to the Civil Servants Act in 1969 ensured the status of the state civil servant area as the core of the collective bargaining system, despite the counter-indications in the pattern of public sector employment. After all, more and more agreement-covered employees were being recruited, and the growth was taking place in the regional/municipal sub-sector.

It can be argued that the collective bargaining system resulting from the amendments to the Civil Servants Act in 1969, and the municipal reform in 1970, were becoming obsolete even during the implementation process. The outcome was that the ensuing period has necessarily been one of adaptation, which has ensured a central place in the system for the new large groups of agreement-covered employees. The adjustments are reflected in the development of the trade union structure.

The current organizational structure can best be understood in relation to the framework created by the Civil Servants Act. But apart from this indirect influence on collective bargaining and organizational structures, the dominant factor in the representation of the interests of employees is the relevant collective agreement, as more and more employees are recruited with agreement-covered status. As will be indicated in the discussion of conciliation and the resolution of disputes, the regulation of relations for employees with civil servant status via legislation still plays an important role in the areas covered by collective agreements.

Trade union organization and structure

There are three important confederations or peak organizations in Denmark. The Confederation of Danish Trade Unions (LO)[5] organizes skilled and unskilled workers, but also many salaried employees, above and beyond these traditional groups. The other two federations are the Confederation of Salaried Employees and Civil Servants (FTF), which organizes medium-salary employees with middle-level educational qualifications, and the Danish Confederation of Professional Associations (AC), which organizes highly paid, highly educated personnel.

LO has around 1.2 million active members and is the dominant confederation. Almost 40 per cent of its members are public employees. LO is not empowered to engage in collective bargaining but has been able to exert influence in the private sector when the bargaining process is referred to the Public Conciliator. LO is extensively represented on public advisory bodies, and plays a major role in promoting the interests of its member organizations when dealing with high-level political issues at national and international level. The most important trade unions affiliated with LO are: the Union of Commercial and Clerical Employees in Denmark (HK), the General Workers' Union in Denmark (SiD), the Danish Trade Union of Public Employees (FOA), Dansk Metal – the National Union of Metalworkers and the National Union of Female Workers (KAD). Virtually the entire membership of FOA (over 200,000) is located in the regional and municipal sectors, in which FOA plays the key role. HK has 38,300 members in the state sector and 71,300 members in the county/municipal sectors.

FTF has 340,000 active members. This confederation, representing salaried employees and public/civil servants, was originally formed as a political alternative to LO. It adopted a neutral stance in terms of party politics, dissociating itself from LO's links with the Social Democratic Party. Nearly 75 per cent of its affiliates' members are public employees, so its member organizations play a vital role in the collective bargaining system. FTF is not empowered to conclude collective agreements but, like LO, it plays a major role in tackling political issues at national and international levels. The most important member unions are: the Danish Teachers' Union (DLF), the Danish Nurses' Organization (DSR), the Danish National Federation of Early Childhood and Youth Education (BUPL), the State Public Servants' Trade Union (CO II) and the Financial Services Union (FF). The first three of these unions all play a major role in the regional/municipal sector, while CO II operates in the state sub-sector.

The Danish Confederation of Professional Associations (AC) has a membership exceeding 125,000. Around 40 per cent of its members work in the private sector, and as a union for 'professionals', AC also covers self-employed members. It promotes its members' interests at the highest political level, and it is also represented on numerous public bodies. In contrast with LO and FTF, AC is directly empowered to conclude collective agreements, although solely for members in the public sector. Its most important unions are: the Danish Union of Engineers (IDA), the Danish Lawyers' and Economists' Association (DJØF), the Danish Medical Association (DADL), the Danish Association of Masters and Ph.D.s (DM) and the National Union of Danish Upper Secondary Teachers (GL).

The upper secondary school teachers in GL work in the county/regional segment, as do the doctors organized under DADL, while most of the graduates under DM are employed at state education/research institutions. Law graduates and economists are employed in all segments of the public sector. AC plays an important co-ordinating role for groups of graduates working in the public sector. But as in the case of LO and FTF it is a peak organization with affiliated unions/ federations which independently exercise a measure of influence.

The hitherto firmly entrenched position of public sector employees with civil servant status has inevitably led to major differences between the organizational structure of public and private sector unions. Even though the single public sector unions are closely linked with the main national union groupings (LO, FTF and AC) the hub of the organizational structure in the public sector is the cluster of union groupings for employees with civil servant status. It was not until 1988 that these groupings or federations admitted unions representing agreement-covered members, but, despite this change, there are marked differences in the organizational structures in the two main segments of Denmark's public sector labour market: the state and the counties and municipalities.

The state sub-sector

In 1988, the civil servants' joint bargaining committee (TFU) changed its name to the Danish Federation of State Employees (CFU), to signal that it had become a coalition representing both main public sector groups. The CFU coalition or cartel covers 225,000 members organized in four federations. The Association of Danish State Employee Organizations (StK), affiliated with LO, has forty-one unions with 136,000 members (clerks, skilled and unskilled workers, civil servants in the postal services and state railways). The State Public Servants' Trade Union (CO II), affiliated with FTF, has thirteen unions with 35,000 members (police, civil servants in the Inland Revenue). The Association of Danish Trade Unions for Public Servants and Agreement-covered Employees (TOK), mainly affiliated with FTF, has twenty-one unions in two central organizations (LC and OC) with 21,500 members (special groups of teachers, professional soldiers). The Danish Confederation of Professional Associations (AC) is both a negotiation cartel and main organization, with twenty-one unions and 33,000 members in the state sub-sector (lawyers and economists, engineers, university teachers). The coalition character of CFU is immediately apparent. It unites central organizations which together cover the pay system and the hierarchical system in the state sub-sector from top to bottom.

The county/municipal sector

In the county/municipal sector the workers are represented by the Association of Local Government Employees' Organizations (KTO). Although the bargaining is conducted by KTO, collective agreements are concluded (with the employers' side) by the constituent organizations. Viewed in strictly formal terms, KTO thus emerges as a loosely structured coalition. In practice, however, decision making is highly centralized, as a consequence of the procedures applied to determine the composition of KTO's steering committees and negotiations committee. The composition is determined on the basis of the component organizations' relationship with the main confederations: LO, FTF and AC. Each of the three component entities can veto any proposal. This centralization is underpinned by the formation in recent years by independent trade unions of cartel-like groupings on the basis of their affiliation with the main organizations: the Danish Confederation of Municipal Employees (DKK) in the LO area, FTF-K (municipal) and AC.

The following is a brief outline of the trade union organizational structure in the municipal and county sectors:

- KTO: the Association of Local Government Employees' Organizations (a cartel) (622,000 members).
- Fourteen LO affiliated unions with 390,000 members, including social and health care assistants, clerical staff, auxiliary staff at day care centres and skilled workers (DKK: the Danish Confederation of Municipal Employees).
- Twenty-seven FTF affiliated unions with 192,000 members, including teachers at the primary and lower secondary schools, nurses, staff at day-care institutions (FTF-K: the Confederation of Salaried Employees – Municipal).
- Eighteen AC-affiliated unions with 34,500 members, including lawyers and economists, engineers, upper secondary teachers, hospital doctors.
- Four unions with 5,500 members from LH (Organization of Managerial and Executive Staff in Denmark) or without any organizational affiliation.

In the municipal sector the LO groups have constantly accounted for such a large percentage of the aggregate number of employees that a representative from an LO trade union was more or less automatically entitled to serve as the chair of the trade unions' joint negotiations cartel, KTO.

In summary, three important features of trade union organization in Denmark can be emphasized. First, even though there is a plurality of confederations in the public sector, the relationship between the three dominant confederations is regulated (*inter alia*) through demarcation agreements, and it has thus proved possible to avoid damaging conflicts between the confederations. These three confederations constitute a coherent system. Despite some internal competition, they succeed in dividing the market between them, thus achieving a high rate of membership and organizational coverage impressively broad in scope. Their willingness to co-operate is reflected in the fact that all three organizations are affiliated with ETUC.

Second, the vast majority of public sector employees are unionized. The number of members represented by the two main bargaining cartels covering the state (225,000 workers) and county/municipal (622,000) segments shows that Denmark has a total of 847,000 unionized public sector workers. It is generally assumed that this figure represents a rate of unionization of about 95 per cent (see the total number of public sector employees – 917,000 – in Table 7.1). It is, however, impossible to calculate the rate of unionization in the various sub-sectors with the available statistical data.

Third, shop stewards play a pivotal role in workplace employee representation. Collective agreements have been extended by a set of special rules on shop stewards, who administer the collective agreement on a day-to-day basis with management, in both the public and the private sectors. Shop stewards are elected by a simple majority of votes cast by union members at each workplace. They work under an obligation to promote and maintain peaceful and satisfactory working conditions, and they enjoy special protection against dismissal. Shop stewards have been described as the focal point of the operation of the entire system of collective bargaining. The tendency towards decentralization of the level at which bargaining is conducted is expected to make their role even more important in the future. This is a development which has also influenced the role of shop stewards in the public sector and which is expected to be strengthened by the implementation of the pay reform. Shop stewards constitutes one part of the dual system of representation. The other channels of representation include the work councils (*samarbejdsudvalg*), and other structures of participation, which will be dealt with later.

Public sector employment relations

The collective bargaining system

The public sector collective bargaining system covers two distinct groups of employees: those with the status of civil servant, employed in accordance with legislation and the terms of the main agreements concluded between the labour market parties; and agreement-covered employees, employed in accordance with the terms of the main agreements between the parties. Both these groups conduct negotiations within the framework of a centralized collective bargaining system. Every two years, bargaining is simultaneously conducted on amendments of the collective agreement in the state and regional/municipal sectors. Up to 1995, renewal of the collective agreements was co-ordinated with the corresponding round of bargaining covering most parts of the private sector, a phenomenon which emphasized the highly centralized nature of the overall system.

Until the end of the 1960s, civil servants' pay and working conditions were formally regulated by 'unilateral governance'; that is, via circulars and notifications issued by the employers. The provisions of the 1919 Civil Servants Act had already established a *de facto* right to conclude collective agreements, however, so that changes in working conditions were negotiated in advance with the civil servants' organizations, in many cases reaching informal joint agreement on amendments before they were formally issued as 'unilateral directives'. But the full, formal right to conclude collective agreements had not yet been achieved, as civil servants were not permitted to take industrial action.

The 1969 Civil Servants Act redressed this situation by establishing the formal right of civil servants to negotiate and conclude collective agreements. The Act stipulated that the central organizations (union federations), with which the state employer concludes main agreements, are individually entitled to conclude agreements covering their respective areas. There were four such major union groupings, and it was a prior requirement that the federations were to be represented by a single, joint negotiating committee. Here again a high degree of centralization was introduced formally into the collective bargaining system, and at a very early stage. Despite the formalization of the right to conclude collective agreements, civil servants were not granted the right to take industrial action. The outcome is that if negotiations on the renewal of the current collective agreement end in deadlock, pay and working conditions for the ensuing period are settled by legislation.

In the past, pay and working conditions for other public sector employees were regulated by the same 'unilateral governance' applied by the employers to civil servants. Although the first collective agreements were concluded in the 1920s and 1930s, they were not established as normal practice until the 1960s and 1970s. Today virtually all public sector employees, including the civil servants and those with quasi-civil servant status, are covered by collective agreements. There is, however, a small group – mainly at senior executive level – who are employed on the basis of individual contracts (Due and Madsen, 1988, 1991, 1996; Finansministeriet, 1996a; Pedersen, 1993).

In principle, agreement-covered public sector employees have the same form of collective bargaining system as that governing the private sector. Pay and working conditions are fixed via collective agreements, and if a bargaining round ends in deadlock the employees can call a strike, and the employers can impose a lockout, as long as due notice is given. The Public Conciliator can also take steps to resolve the dispute, by providing conciliation/arbitration services and by submitting a draft agreement for adoption by the parties.

In both the state and the county/municipal sectors, senior employees are usually granted the status of civil servant. This status is otherwise the norm only in areas which were originally regarded as core areas of the state sector: the police, railways, postal services, primary and lower secondary schools, the 'established' Church. In the 1990s, however, the state as employer has tried to change the traditional form of employment. The number of public sector employees with civil servant status will decline as a result of the transfer in 1992 of most teachers to the municipal segment, so that all new staff are now working under the terms of collective agreements. The transfer of some state services to the enterprise structure means that newly recruited employees will be agreement-covered, not civil servants (Due and Madsen, 1996).

Collective bargaining structure

In formal terms separate bargaining rounds are conducted in the state and municipal/county sub-sectors. In the state sector, the Minister of Finance acts as the employer, in his/her capacity as minister for salaries and pensions. On the other side of the table the workers are represented by the Danish Central Federation of State Employees, a coalition of four trade union federations, or central organizations, which are, in turn, coalitions of trade unions with members in the state sector. On the employer side, the local and regional government sub-sector covers both municipalities and counties, so that the employer coalitions cover four independent groupings: one representing municipal employers (KL), one for the counties (ARF), the municipality of Copenhagen and the municipality of Frederiksberg. These two municipalities have a special dual status as both local and regional authorities. The workers are represented by the KTO, a coalition, covering many independent organizations whose members work in the municipal and county

Table 7.4 The structure of public sector collective bargaining

Employers	Employees/trade unions
The state sector	
Ministry of Finance	*CFU* Danish Central Federation of State Employees (cartel with 225,000 members) *StK* Association of Danish State Employee Organizations: 41 unions, 136,000 members *CO II* State Public Servants' Trade Union: 13 unions, 35,000 members *TOK* Association of Danish Trade Unions for Public Servants and Agreement-covered Employees: 21 unions, 21,500 members *AC* Danish Confederation of Professional Associations: 21 unions, 33,000 members in the state sector
The local and regional government sector	
Employers' negotiating team *KL* National Association of Local Authorities, 273 municipalities *ARF* Federation of County Councils, 14 counties The municipalities of Copenhagen and Frederiksberg	*KTO* Association of Local Government Employees' Organizations (638,500 members) Fourteen LO affiliated unions with 399,000 members, (*DKK* Danish Confederation of Municipal Employees) Twenty-six FTF affiliated unions with 198,000 members, (*FTF-K* Confederation of Salaried Employees – Municipal) Sixteen AC-affiliated unions with 36,000 members Four unions with 5,500 members from LH (Organization of Managerial and Executive Staff in Denmark) or without any main organization affiliation.

sectors. Although the bargaining is conducted by KTO, collective agreements are concluded by the organizations.

As Table 7.4 shows, the various groupings in both sub-sectors maintain links with the three major trade union organizations: LO, FTF and AC. But of these three only AC, which is both a confederation and a bargaining cartel, plays a direct role in the collective bargaining system. Neither LO nor FTF has direct bargaining competence, so that the negotiators on the employees' side are the individual unions, federations or bargaining cartels.

Bargaining in the two sub-sectors is co-ordinated, especially on the employers' side, and the main rule is that the state segment should be the first to complete the process, by reaching agreement on a framework and on the main components of a settlement, not only for the state sector but also for the municipal sector, which can subsequently adapt the agreement, within the agreed framework, to match its special requirements. One of the most significant features of public sector collective bargaining is its scope. The negotiations cover all grades in the hierarchy, from the highest to the lowest paid. CFU and KTO are thus coalitions, covering groups with a wide range of different and often diverging interests.

This means that some core issues are negotiated internally in CFU and KTO, where, behind closed doors, there is a struggle to determine the allocation of pay awards and other potential gains which can later shape the final outcome of the negotiations with the employer side.

The collective bargaining system has thus assumed some coalition characteristics which largely determine its mode of functioning. This means that bargaining is intended not only to resolve a clash of interests between two opposing parties, but also to resolve conflicts of interest on each side of the negotiation table. Thus we refer to the 'compromise equilibrium', using the term as a designation for the end goal of bargaining in coalitions: namely, to ensure the conclusion of a collective agreement incorporating a balancing of all the various and often conflicting interests at stake within the broader framework of the system (Due and Madsen, 1988, 1996; Due *et al.*, 1996).

The role of coalitions in Denmark's public sector collective bargaining system is based on a common principle, observed by all the parties involved in the negotiations: no organization must be capable of achieving a better result by pursuing a separate course outside the coalition structure. This is a prior requirement if centralized bargaining and the negotiating coalitions are to survive. The negotiations are conducted in relatively narrowly based constellations. In the state sub-sector the line-up consists of CFU's negotiating team (the chairpersons of the four central organizations) on one side and the Minister of Finance on the other. The meetings are attended by civil servants (assisting the minister) and CFU (non-elected) executives. These professional advisers play an important role in drafting the material to be discussed. In practice, agreement has already been reached – prior to the meeting – on a considerable part of the agenda, via negotiations conducted between the professionals, within the guidelines and limits defined by the elected union representatives and by the politicians. During the bargaining process there are shifts in the positions adopted by the parties, often the result of informal contact at 'professional' and political levels. For the decisive phase – focusing on unresolved issues, such as the framework of the overall pay award, the only negotiators present are CFU's chairperson and the Minister of Finance.

Similar negotiating procedures have been developed in the regional/municipal collective bargaining system, although here the picture is necessarily more complex, as the employers' side is also a coalition. The workers are represented by KTO's eight-member negotiating committee, consisting of four representatives from the LO organizations (in DKK), three from FTF organizations (in FTF-K) and one from an AC member organization. The employers' side comprises two representatives from KL, one from ARF, and one from Copenhagen and from Frederiksberg. Informal contacts between the professionals, and between the elected representatives, play an important role throughout negotiations. The final steps towards a settlement are taken at meetings with KTO's chair and chief executive officer on one side, and the chair of the municipal employers' delegation and KL's salaries director on the other.

Although the outcome of the bargaining conducted at central level determines the general pay levels and working conditions, the subsequent bargaining at federation or trade union level – within the centrally agreed framework – determines more specific improvements. In the state sector, the Civil Servants Act and the related main agreement are applied to reach a joint decision on the outcome of the negotiations (i.e. the draft settlement), initially for the single bargaining cartels and then for CFU as a whole. KTO has clung to the principle that the single unions/federations can determine whether they will adopt the draft settlement. This has caused greater turbulence in the regional/municipal sub-sector than in the state sub-sector during the final phase of collective bargaining.

The trade unions/federations in the regional/municipal sub-sector, in practice, have little opportunity to influence the outcome, as the KTO negotiations are based on the musketeer principle: 'one for all and all for one'. This derives from a realization that the KTO bargaining is conducted at central level and simultaneously, so that all groups are obliged to accept or reject the same draft settlement. If individual trade unions or federations could reject the settlement negotiated on their behalf by KTO, and subsequently achieve a better deal as a result of another sequence of negotiations, via conciliation or industrial action, it would weaken the will of the more timid unions to adopt a settlement at the appropriate stage of the next bargaining round. Employers are not the only party to frown upon splinter factions or 'dissidents'. The unions/federations which have tried to plough their own furrow have reaped a bitter harvest – a result of the above mentioned coalition characteristics.

The only group of workers to achieve success by pursuing a separate course is the large and influential nurses' organization DSR, which took industrial action during the 1995 bargaining round. The subsequent political intervention conferred greater benefits than those achieved in the draft settlement already reached on the nurses' behalf by KTO. The reasons for the success of the DSR arose from a shortage of nurses and the sympathetic attitude of the public. But DSR had to pay a price by conceding potential gains on other points. Indeed, some observers have doubted whether DSR achieved any net gains at all. At the same time, both KTO and the regional/municipal employers became convinced that a repetition of this sectional action would endanger the integrity of the municipal bargaining system; the musketeer principle may be a prerequisite for the survival of the existing centralized system.

Although the public sector collective bargaining system is still highly centralized, there has been a growing tendency during the past decade to refer a greater number of issues to direct negotiation, and subsequent agreement, between the parties in the separate ministries, counties and municipalities, or even at institution level. This course is taken in the case of negotiations on some issues related to personnel policy, which is becoming a regular item on the collective bargaining agenda. But delegation is also practised in the case of pay, where matters such as the reclassification of jobs can – to a small extent – be agreed at local level, and where the local or decentralized pay 'pools' are distributed on the basis of agreement between the parties.

There appears to be a hierarchy in the overall system of labour relations: the public sector has played second fiddle to the private sector, and the regional/

municipal sub-sector has been overshadowed by the state sub-sector. But the growth of the public sector, concentrated largely in the regional/municipal sub-sector and thus leading to a huge increase in the number of agreement-covered employees, has reduced the potential significance of the hierarchy. It still exists, however, and for the past ten years has influenced the content and priorities of the collective bargaining agenda – although with some important exceptions.

During the 1989 collective bargaining round, the municipal negotiators revealed a high level of self-reliance by reaching a settlement before the state parties did. Moreover, the terms of the settlement were ones which the Minister of Finance could not have accepted *vis-à-vis* CFU. The municipal parties introduced full pay during parental leave, and commenced work on a pension scheme for the relatively large group of public sector employees who hitherto had no pension scheme (apart from the universal old age pension). As the process of collective bargaining in the different sectors of the Danish labour market normally takes place simultaneously (every other year), the parties able to conclude the first agreement will often set the trend for the agreements in the other sectors – this also happened in 1989.

The results from the regional/municipal sector were transferred to – and adopted by – the state sub-sector, and set the agenda for the subsequent negotiations in the private sector. The outcome was that pension schemes were introduced in the private sector – with industry taking the lead – in 1991; paid parental leave was adopted in the industrial sector in 1995, with effect from the spring of 1997, when the other segments of the private sector agreed to follow suit. The state sub-sector had come into prominence in 1991 by concluding its negotiations before a settlement had been reached in the dominant area of the private sector labour market.

The 1997 bargaining round was the last one in which funding had to be allocated to the new pension scheme, which is now fully funded. But the 1997 bargaining round marks the commencement of a determined effort to reform the public sector pay system. Its implementation will be the main goal for the next decade. This raises some structural questions. The delegation of a number of decisions on pay and working conditions to local level has extended the scope of negotiations in the counties and municipalities, and this local activity is expected to increase, following the full introduction of the new pay system adopted during the 1997 collective bargaining round. The question is whether the parties at the local level will prove capable of performing this function without the formation of bargaining alliances corresponding to the cartels formed by the trade union federations and KTO at central level. If not, new local structures may emerge.

Industrial disputes

As indicated earlier, relations between the parties in Denmark's public sector are characterized by a large measure of consensus. One of the results is that industrial disputes are resolved without high levels of confrontation. This is not to suggest that serious disputes have never arisen – indeed, there have been both 'official' (or 'legal') strikes and lock-outs, in connection with the renewal of collective

Table 7.5 Working days lost in the county and municipal sub-sectors, 1980–96

Year	Counties	Municipalities	Total
1980	11,068	6,154	17,222
1981	107,020	180	107,200
1982	1,709	1,250	2,959
1983	2,792	4,448	7,240
1984	13,234	816	14,050
1985	115,770	47,212	162,982
1986	7,942	2,587	10,529
1987	6,341	9,668	16,009
1988	4,211	4,593	8,803
1989	961	108	1,069
1990	1,777	6,837	8,614
1991	1,332	3,308	4,640
1992	1,436	5,106	6,542
1993	945	1,472	2,417
1994	2,585	674	3,259
1995	36,807	7,841	44,648
1996	434	1,294	1,728

Source: Danmarks Statistik, separate processing run, October 1997.

agreements, and unofficial (or 'illegal') protest strikes, in response to political intervention or to steps which might have an adverse impact on working conditions. The 1970s and 1980s were marked by a certain radicalization of public sector trade unions. Work stoppages – as a protest against cuts in public sector spending – were not uncommon. For a number of years this sort of industrial action was often taken by staff at day care centres, and on some occasions civil servants also took part in these strikes, despite the ban on work stoppages.

The number and scope of work stoppages in the public sector as a whole are not treated as specific items in any official statistics. The annual report published by Danmarks Statistik covers the counties/regions and the municipalities but not the state sub-sector. Besides, the published reports (e.g. Danmarks Statistik, 1997a: 10) do not specify the number of work stoppages in the counties and municipalities. For this chapter, separate processing of the data was commissioned, to trace the trend in the number of working days lost in stoppages during the period 1980–96, limiting the search to stoppages amounting to losses of more than 100 working days.

The figures for 1981 convey a misleading impression of the level of work stoppages in the municipal sub-sector, as the most extensive industrial action, taken by social workers, is entered under 'Counties', although the actual stoppages occurred mainly in the municipal sub-sector. More generally, the data in Table 7.5 confirm the impression of a low level of industrial disputes in the county/regional sub-sector throughout the entire period, with the exception of 1981, 1985 and 1995. The high figure for 1981 is accounted for by an official strike of social workers, and a lock-out and a work stoppage by doctors in breach of the terms of

Table 7.6 Work stoppages in the state sub-sector

Year	No. of stoppages	No. of workers involved	No. of working days lost
1993	18	1,462	1,525
1994	56	2,307	1,742
1995	36	4,073	3,120
1996	22	1,354	1,085

Sources: Agency for Financial Management and Administrative Affairs, statistics on work stoppages by state employees, 1996, October 1997. Danmarks Statistik, separate processing run, October 1997.

their collective agreement. The 1985 figure reflects a dispute, called in response to government intervention, especially widespread in the public sector. The relatively high figure for 1995 arose from the dispute between nurses and their employers. Since 1993 the Agency for Financial Management and Administrative Affairs (under the Ministry of Finance) has published statistics on all work stoppages in the state sub-sector. Table 7.6 confirms the above assessment of a low level of industrial disputes in this sub-sector.

The level of industrial disputes is far higher in the private sector than in the public sector. If the size of the work force in the selected areas is compared (200,000 state employees; 400,000 county/municipal employees; roughly 600,000 workers in the DA part of the private sector), only 0.5–1.0 per cent of public sector employees were involved in work stoppages in 1996, while in the private sector the figure is 5–10 per cent (Agency for Financial Management and Administrative Affairs; statistics for work stoppages in the state sub-sector in 1996).

Workers' participation

Various forms of workers' participation in decision making at local level are widespread in the public sector. As in the private sector, most of the measures introduced to promote worker participation are based on collective agreements between the labour market parties, not legislation. One of the important pillars of the system of participation is the works council, referred to in Denmark's public sector as a *co-operation committee*, in accordance with agreements concluded between public sector employers (the Minister of Finance and KL) and the trade union groupings (CFU and KTO). This structure covers both workplace and higher levels: a county can have works councils at single institutions; for the administrative bodies to which the institutions belong; and an overarching works council for the county as a whole.

In the works councils, employee representatives may exert an influence on strategic decisions – in so far as they have the right to be consulted before such decisions are reached. Some critics of the works council system argue that consultation does not facilitate much influence, that it is only a safety valve. Another reason put forward for regarding the works council as a 'talking shop' is that it is not empowered to conclude agreements with the same validity as those concluded within the framework of collective bargaining. Such agreements are concluded between the employers at local level and the shop stewards. It can be argued that works councils cover most of the issues subject to management prerogative, issues on which the workers are entitled to negotiate but not to conclude agreements. None the less, employee representatives on the works councils are usually the shop stewards, and now that more and more personnel policy issues are being covered by collective agreements there is some overlap between collective agreement issues and what are formally classified as 'negotiating issues'. It may seem odd that the works council structure cannot be applied to solve problems related to these issues by concluding continuous local agreements.

In the worker participation structure, health and safety organizations deal with issues related to the working environment and, unlike works councils, are based on legislation. In many public sector areas, the working environment has not been given a very high priority, compared with the works council or the status and function of the shop steward. The comparative neglect of the working environment, and the problem of the relations between the works council and the shops steward system, have led to the implementation of pilot projects in the public sector. In 1991, in the county/municipal sub-sector and, commencing in 1995, in the state sub-sector, a project on 'Extended Joint Influence for Employees', and another on 'Job Development and the Development of Human Resources', were initiated. Also in the county/municipal sub-sector, a new framework agreement was concluded on worker participation, and both there and in the state sub-sector, in connection with the settlement on a pay reform in 1997, it was agreed to improve working conditions for shop stewards. Recent developments in worker participation seem to indicate an ultimate merging of the existing structures, suggesting that the works council and health and safety systems may be reinforced, by linking them with the representative system applied to the collective agreements.

Public sector consensus and informal relations

The strategies of Danish public service unions and the values of their members have been based on reformist goals. They have sought to influence pay and working conditions, but have been reluctant to challenge the 'management prerogative' of their employers. Since 1929, a period during which most governments have been led by the Social Democrats, it has not proved difficult to maintain close co-operation between the government and the politicians/civil servants and the organizations representing public sector workers. The Danish model, in which the labour market parties regulate industrial relations via collective agreements, and where both parties are guaranteed influence on legislation, in particular on the fairly rare items of labour market legislation, is also applied in the public sector labour market. But in this latter case the *dual role* of the employer is strikingly obvious. In the private sector the influence exercised in relation to the political authorities has been granted to the main organizations of workers and employers – in particular to LO and DA. But in the public sector, the chief negotiator on the employer side sitting down to negotiate with the workers' representatives can turn out to be the same minister who is responsible for drafting the legislation on which the labour market parties wish to exert an influence. This applies, for example, to overall economic policy, for which the Minister of Finance is responsible.

More or less consensual relations are sustained by an elaborate network of informal contacts. This can be illustrated by an analysis of public sector bargaining rounds from the early 1980s to the mid-1990s (Due and Madsen, 1988, 1996). It can be argued that negotiations between organizations with conflicting interests in complex social systems generally presuppose the use of informal relations if results are to be achieved. Informal relations in a collective bargaining system can be defined as contacts established and maintained with the aim of, first, testing the reaction to specific proposals or attitudes and, second, attempting to promote a settlement without entering into any commitment and with the guarantee of full confidentiality. The necessity of informal relations is supported by a number of structural features of the collective bargaining system in the public sector.

The first feature is that the system has to accommodate potentially conflicting interests, while at the same time maintaining a pragmatic and compromise-oriented approach to collective bargaining. The inviolable basic principle of negotiations is that the parties enter the process with the desire to reach a settlement. The negotiators attempt to establish consensual, not adversarial, relations (Walton and McKersie, 1965). The range of negotiating tactics encompasses both adversarial and consensual methods and adds complexity and controversy to the attempts made to achieve compromise settlements. This process may be facilitated by a second feature of the system, namely the high degree of centralization of bargaining, which can isolate the negotiator from the groups or organizations represented.

The third feature is the representative political system, from which the negotiators receive their authorization to negotiate – the system which must finally approve any draft settlement reached by the negotiators. This creates a situation in which the negotiators are compelled to strike a balance between demands, mobilization and settlement. For example, ordinary members must be mobilized to generate support for the demands and to ensure the basis for the implementation of the resulting measures. But the mobilization must not engender a mood of unjustified optimism, leading members to expect an unrealistic settlement. The negotiators – as a sort of occupational imperative – must complete the process by adding their signatures to the expected award. And the span of the possible approaches to the bargaining – ranging from the desirable to the possible – makes the negotiators aware of the need for informal relations.

The fourth feature, which partly derives from the others, is the coalition character of the collective bargaining system. As suggested earlier, the formation of coalitions, between which most of the negotiations are conducted, can be attributed to the insistence of public sector employers on a negotiating structure in which simultaneous overall negotiations can be conducted for all public sector

employees. This means that the system has to accommodate not only the conflicting interests of the two main parties, but also profound internal conflicts on both
sides of the table. This adds complexity and difficulty to the process of reaching
the compromise equilibrium which will ensure a settlement that balances the
different and conflicting interests between the two sides and between the parties
sitting on the same side of the table. The need for informal relations is increased
by the tension between the compromises which can be reached in coalitions and
the expectations expressed by the groups and organizations represented by
the negotiators. The need is also sharpened by the obligation to comply with the
principle that no single coalition party should achieve any special advantage.

In any discussion of Denmark's public sector labour market this coalition character is probably the single most important reason for such extensive informal
relations. The informal coalition game provides the key to an understanding of
virtually any collective bargaining sequence in the public sector. It has even been
argued that no representative who imagines that the major decisions are taken in
the plenary assembly is equipped to assume the negotiator role. But among the
negotiators informal relations are also regarded with some scepticism, because
the contact which offers one negotiator some sympathy or support for an argument is perceived by another negotiator as a threat, as a risk of being cheated of
a potential gain. Obviously, informal relations pose a problem *vis-à-vis* the group
or groups which elected or appointed the negotiator. The groups may fear that
their interests are being diluted or even sacrificed in the club atmosphere of the
negotiating process. There is thus a potential problem of democracy. In relation
to both the bargaining culture and the organizational cultures, discussion of
informal relations is taboo.

Conciliation and the settlement of disputes

In the law governing Danish industrial relations, a distinction is drawn between
conflicts of interest (disputes arising from the renewal or conclusion of collective
agreements) and agreement-related conflicts[6] (disputes related to breaches or interpretation of the current collective agreement). In the case of agreement-covered
employees there are provisions enshrined in the 'main agreements' and collective
agreements, stipulating a general 'peace obligation' during the period covered
by the agreement. Only in connection with the conclusion of new agreements
or negotiations on the renewal of existing agreements is it possible to resort to
industrial action. Industrial action requires the adoption of a resolution in the
competent assemblies by a qualified majority, and notice in accordance with the
current provisions. In the private sector the usual rule is notice of fourteen days,
and the notice must be lodged twice, with a week's interval. In the public sector,
one month's notice must be given on one occasion.

Before industrial action takes place, the issues in dispute are usually considered
by the Public Conciliator's Institution, where the Public Conciliator is empowered
to convene meetings with the parties, to demand concessions and to submit a
draft settlement for adoption or rejection by the parties. In practice, the conciliator

will submit a draft settlement only if both parties consent. Negotiations on general demands are held simultaneously for civil servants and agreement-covered employees. As civil servants are not covered by the Public Conciliator's Institution, in practice it is not until the negotiations have reached seeming deadlock that the institution becomes involved, with regard to the agreement-covered employees. As the voting on draft settlements is via the central organizations in the state sub-sector, the vote-counting procedure amounts to aggregation or concatenation, which has hitherto meant that the services of the Public Conciliator's Institution have not been required. In this sub-sector, the choice is between either an aggregate settlement or political intervention covering all state employees. Almost half the state employees have no right to strike, and as pay and working conditions for this group are determined by an Act of the *Folketing* if the parties fail to reach agreement, it is difficult to imagine a situation in which the other half – the agreement-covered employees – are allowed to take industrial action and thus possibly achieve a more favourable settlement than their colleagues with civil servant status.

In the municipal sub-sector the same rule applies; civil servants have not been given the right to resort to industrial action in the event of a conflict of interests when renewing a collective agreement. This situation is subject to 'dual governance' – civil law and collective agreement. The civil servants have a right – governed by civil law – to conclude collective agreements on pay and terms of employment. But the conditions of the collective agreement are determined unilaterally by the employers – via legislation or statutory regulations – and the right to conclude collective agreements is nullified the moment the parties declare that they have reached deadlock (Pedersen, 1993: 59). Pay and working conditions for the regional/municipal civil servants are subsequently fixed by the Municipal Pay Board, a body appointed under the terms of the Municipal Governance Act, passed as an extension of the 1969 Civil Servants Act and of the municipal reforms adopted in 1970. All the members of the Pay Board represent employers.

Despite these constraints, the Public Conciliator's Institution has played a major role in the regional/municipal area – the role it has not had an opportunity to play in the state sub-sector. This apparent paradox is explained by the fact that the municipal area has a far higher number of agreement-covered employees, while the voting on the negotiated result is conducted in the individual trade unions. The fragmented voting procedure has meant that in most of the collective bargaining rounds individual trade unions have rejected the negotiated settlement and thus created a situation fraught with the risk of industrial strife. In these cases the usual procedure has been to involve the Public Conciliator's Institution, so that the disputes have subsequently been settled by acceptance of the latter's draft settlement, even when the conciliator has made only minor adjustments to the settlement rejected earlier. The two main examples of this procedure were in 1981 (social workers) and 1995 (nurses).

In the event of agreement-related conflicts (disputes pertaining to the interpretation or breaches of the collective agreements), the general 'peace obligation' also applies to the agreement-covered employees. They have as little opportunity as their civil servant colleagues of using the strike weapon during the duration of an agreement. In principle, agreement-covered employees in the public sector are subject to the same terms as employees in the private sector. This means that interpretation-related disputes are to be settled by arbitration, either in accordance with the parties' own rules as stipulated in the collective agreement, or in accordance with the ordinary rules of arbitration, which the Industrial Court Act states shall apply in all cases in which the parties have not themselves adopted adequate rules for treating industrial disputes. But *breaches* of the collective agreements, such as work stoppages during the agreement period, must be treated in the Industrial Court.

In the public sector, however, some trade unions have special arbitration clauses in their main agreements. This means that disputes can be settled by the parties' own arbitration courts. This arrangement ensures that the resolution of disputes is not removed from their own domain to a higher level – to the federations, which conduct the cases (on behalf of the member unions) and nominate the judges on the union side in the Industrial Court. Since 1931 similar conflicts relating to civil servants have been dealt with by a Court of Arbitration.

During the 1970s and 1980s work stoppages in protest against cuts in public sector spending were not uncommon. A three-hour work stoppage in connection with the bargaining on collective agreements in 1979 marked a turning point. On this occasion hundreds of thousands of public sector employees protested against parliamentary intervention – and among the strikers were many civil servants. Unlike their agreement-covered colleagues, the civil servants could not be collectively charged with this breach of the peace obligation. A separate civil service case would have had to be brought against every individual civil servant, and this presented insuperable difficulties in terms of the time and resources required. Thus one of the most important outcomes of this strike was the reform of the Arbitration Court, establishing a state civil service court and a municipal civil service court, so that civil servants who resorted to 'illegal' strike action could be collectively charged and sentenced to pay a collective fine. The new, more effective system of sanctions was introduced via legislation in 1981. The state civil service court was empowered to treat disputes – and impose fines – arising from either breaches of or the interpretation of the currently valid agreements. In the municipal area, only breaches of the agreement were to be treated by the civil service court, whereas the Arbitration Court was retained to deal with cases related to interpretation. The setting up of the civil service court was perceived as an indirect recognition of the right of civil servants to resort to strike action. The decision to establish a system of collective sanctions can in itself be seen as *de facto* acceptance of disputes as a phenomenon that could no longer be ignored. The distinctive character of the civil service system was thus partly eroded.

Conclusion

Public sector employment relations in Denmark have been shaped by the legislative constraints imposed on collective agreements by the 1969 Civil Servant Act.

This maintained civil servant status as the hub of labour market relations and decreed that, if trade unions were to influence pay and working conditions, a centralized and highly co-ordinated collective bargaining system covering the entire public sector was necessary. The Act stipulated that the right to conclude collective agreements was to be granted to central trade union federations with which the state employers concluded a main agreement.

In practice, four trade union federations met the statutory requirements, and the main agreement stated that they were to negotiate *as a single entity* by forming a joint negotiating committee. The provisions of the Act and of the main agreement thus established a bargaining system in which the actors were to be the four trade union federations representing the state civil servants and their joint negotiating committee. It was assumed that a corresponding collective bargaining system would be established for the regional/municipal sub-sector, and a joint negotiating cartel was formed to represent more than sixty trade unions in 1975. The goal of centralization had thus been achieved, as in both sub-sectors employees were represented by single entities.

The agreements for agreement-covered public sector employees are not negotiated until the general negotiations of the two civil servant groupings have been completed. The post-1969 structure of organizations and collective agreements marked a reversal of trends in the public sector during the 1960s. The 1969 legislation was a conservative reform, and since then the development of the collective bargaining system has been a process of continuous adaptation to meet the exigencies of the new context, in which the agreement-covered employees are the numerically dominant group and in which working conditions have changed, as a consequence of the general process of decentralization and adaptation since the 1980s. The process is reflected in the changes taking place in the rigid pay system, negotiated almost exclusively at central level, which governed pay in the public sector until 1997. The system was based on the principles adopted when passing the Civil Servants Act in 1919, a system which also governed the agreement-covered public sector employees, even though their working conditions are in some respects fundamentally different from those of the traditional civil servant group.

From 1987, public sector employers had little success in trying to introduce a more flexible and more decentralized pay system, in experiments with various forms of local 'pay pools'. The pools were too small to have any real impact, and many public sector employees regarded them as little more than fringe benefits for 'toadies', despite the fact that they were supposed to be awarded only following agreement between the parties. The new pay reforms were launched as a three-year pilot scheme in the state sub-sector, commencing in January 1998. In the regional/municipal sub-sector a large percentage of employees have been covered from April 1998: 50 per cent of county employees, and 60 per cent of municipal employees. Under the new system, the basic pay fixed at central level will be supplemented by locally agreed allowances for job functions, qualifications and performance, and the local supplementary allowances will constitute a sizeable percentage of total pay – between 15 per cent and 20 per cent.

The pay reforms of 1997 may be regarded as an important turning point in Denmark's public sector collective bargaining system. It represents a shift from a pay system based on employment with civil servant status to a system based on employment under the terms of a collective agreement. It is important to note that the system is intended to cover not only the agreement-covered employees but also large groups with civil servant status, in so far as that form of employment is retained in the future.

The nature of the change in the state sub-sector can be described as a movement from an *étatiste* system subject to hierarchical governance by a directorate-general (for which a minister was ultimately responsible) to a division-based system, which is being 'firmatized' (i.e. given many of the features of a business entity) and being managed partially in line with 'market principles' (although still with a minister assuming the ultimate responsibility). It is mainly the provision of public services that is being transferred to business-type structures, by moving functions from state to semi-state or private production units. So far these changes have had only a limited impact on the collective bargaining system, although the long-term consequences may be a gradual erosion of the system in the state sub-sector. For example, Copenhagen Airports A/S has joined an association of private employers (DI). The restructuring of the postal services serves as an example of gradual development from public to private sector employment.

The question is how large a part of state public services in the longer term will remain in the domain of the state collective bargaining system, and thus be included in the negotiations between CFU and the Ministry of Finance. It seems certain that the remaining state part of the 'welfare' area, covering institutions of higher education and research, will remain part of the state domain, and these functions, along with others relating to the exercise of public authority, will ensure the continued existence of a sizeable area of state employment, to the extent of perhaps 175,000 employees. Even though the state area will be somewhat reduced in size, it will probably remain the hub of the negotiations in the public sector as a whole. The position of the state sub-sector appears impregnable, if only because of the central importance of the Ministry of Finance, and the role of the minister in shaping overall socio-economic policy and in co-ordinating economic policy and political initiatives to develop the public sector and influence pay policy. The reallocation of 60,000 primary and lower secondary school teachers to the municipal segment in 1992 led many observers to predict a significant loss of influence for the state sector, but the departure of the teachers has not shifted the balance of power. The dominance of the state collective bargaining system does not, it would appear, depend on the size of the sub-sector, although the declining number of employees may influence its legitimacy.

The status of the state sub-sector in the overall system in no way challenges the central position of the regional/municipal area in the provision of essential welfare functions. It is thus at regional and local level that the demands for modernization will be expressed with greatest urgency, and those demands will probably include a call for further reform of the collective bargaining system. The new pay system, facilitated by the 1997 agreement, potentially can be integrated with the personnel policy and goals of the individual public institution, and with the steps taken to adapt to the changing qualitative and quantitative requirements govern- ing the development of public services. The pay system corresponds closely to the flexible pay systems – based on negotiations at local level – found in the private sector. This may lead to a form of convergence which reflects developments in a public sector in which governance is based to a growing extent on various market- type mechanisms.

It remains to be seen whether the parties at local level are capable of introduc- ing the new pay system. In many places management has not yet achieved the requisite competence to develop a personnel policy combined with pay policy. And the trade union organizations – which have a key role in the new collective bargaining system via the function and status of the shop stewards – may also experience difficulties. In the regional/municipal sub-sector the new pay system came into force for large groups of staff from April 1998. As the system has been introduced at central level in the negotiations on special demands with the indi- vidual trade unions, the prediction is that at local level it will also be introduced in fragmented form.

In AC, however, a co-ordinated policy has been adopted, to avoid a situation in which one group of graduates is played off against the others. Similar co- ordination is also being considered with regard to the main staff groups in the FTF and LO unions. But the question is whether a locally based pay system can be efficiently implemented if local KTO structures are not created; that is, coali- tions corresponding to the central structures. The latter were developed because they were seen as a prior requirement if single groups of employees were not to be played off against the others. Also, the coalitions were accepted by the employers as a prerequisite of the development of a framework for negotiations with more than sixty trade unions. Now that a considerable part of the right to engage in collective bargaining has been delegated to local level, it must be assumed that the shift will generate the same pressure to develop coalitions at the local level. The recurring crises experienced by KTO show that it is difficult to maintain a coalition-based structure, and it is likely to prove even more difficult at local level, because the creation of regional and municipal coalitions by individual trade unions can be perceived as a threat to their right to conclude agreements for their own members. If the immanent conservatism of organizations has been an obstacle to the development of KTO at central level, it will act as an even more powerful curb on moves to establish local co-operation – that is, the structure required for successful implementation of a new locally based pay system.

Notes

1 Institutions subsidized by central and/or local government: (1) employees in state- and/ or municipality-subsidized private and autonomous institutions, where at least half the institution's income comes from the public purse, and (2) employees in institutions and enterprises with other forms of links with the state and municipalities, e.g. the established (Lutheran Evangelical) Church, municipal organizations, Danmarks Radio

or supply enterprises, in which the state and/or municipalities own at least half the
share capital or constitute the majority of those with a financial interest in the entity.

2 *Translator's note.* The Danish term is more earthy, more graphic. But its use here might
offend some sensitive readers. No prizes for guessing the English equivalent.

3 Pedersen's analysis is restricted to the state segment of the public sector, but it seems
evident that some of the same trends in development can be found in the county/
municipal sector.

4 The competence of KL and ARF outside the employer area has, however, been
questioned. In the other areas, the two groupings have not been delegated formal competence, and are thus prevented from concluding binding agreements in those areas. For
example, KL's and ARF's agreements with the Minister of Finance on the regional/
local economies are consultative, not binding, because – it is argued – as 'private organizations' KL and ARF are not empowered to bind democratically elected organs such as
the single municipal and county councils. In practice, however, there is a high degree of
compliance with such consultative agreements.

5 *Translator's note.* The English designations used for trade unions, employer organizations
and other Danish institutions are, virtually without exception, the official English designations used by these entities.

6 It should be noted that the Danish term is *retskonflikter*, literally 'law or court conflicts/
disputes', but we prefer to refer to these as *agreement-related conflicts*, because they are
(1) related to the collective agreements and (2) settled by an arbitration court or the
Industrial Court ('the parties' *own* court'). The disputes thus remain within the purview
of the labour market parties and are not referred to the ordinary civil courts.

References

Betænkning 1150 (1988) *90'ernes aftaler og overenskomster.* Betænkning skrevet af 'Udvalget
om større fleksibilitet i det offentlige aftale- og overenskomstsystem,' Copenhagen: Statens
Informationstjeneste.

Danmarks Statistik (1996) *Statistisk årbog 1996,* Copenhagen: Danmarks Statistik.

Danmarks Statistik (1997a) *Statyistiske Efterretninger,* Arbejdsmarked 10, Copenhagen:
Danmarks Statistik.

Danmarks Statistik (1997b) *Statistiske Efterretninger,* Arbejdsmarked 23, Copenhagen:
Danmarks Statistik.

Due, J. and Madsen, J. S. (1988) *Når der slås søm i: overenskomstforhandlinger og organisationskultur,*
Copenhagen: Jurist- & Økonomforbundets forlag.

Due, J., and Madsen, J. S. (1991) 'Centraliseret decentralisering. Overenskomstforhandlingerne
på det offentlige område i 1970'erne og 1980'erne', in N. F. Christiansen (ed.) *Årbog
for Arbejderbevægelsens Historie – 1990* xx, Copenhagen: Selskabet til Forskning i
Arbejderbevægelsens Historie, pp. 135–65.

Due, J. and Madsen, J. S. (1996) *Forligsmagerne: de kollektive forhandlingers sociologi,* Copenhagen: Jurist- & Økonomforbundets forlag.

Due, J., Madsen, J. S., Andersen, S. K., Navrbjerg, S. E., Lubanski, N. and Vistisen, H.
(1996) 'Industrial relations in Denmark's public sector: structure; approaches to restructuring', paper presented at ARAN workshop, 'The Restructuring of Employment Relations in Public Services in Western Europe', Rome, 25–8 January.

Finansministeriet (1993) *Nyt syn på den offentlige sektor,* Copenhagen: Finansministeriet.

Finansministeriet (1995) *Budgetredegørelse 95,* Copenhagen: Finansministeriet.

Finansministeriet (1996a) *Budgetredegørelse 96: velfærdssamfundets veje*, Copenhagen: Finansministeriet.

Finansministeriet (1996b) 'Employment in the Danish State', paper presented at the European Conference on Developing the Public Sector through Social Dialogue, Copenhagen, 21–2 March.

Finansministeriet (1996c) *Lønpolitik 96*, Copenhagen: Finansministeriet.

Finansministeriet/Indenrigsministeriet (1995) *Erfaringer med udbud og udlicitering*, Copenhagen: Finansministeriet/Indenrigsministeriet.

Folkeskolen (1997) *Særnummer om overenkomstforhandlingerne 1997* 21, Copenhagen: Danmarks Lærerforening.

KL (1997) *KL's organisation*, Copenhagen: Kommunernes Landsforening's homepage.

Lægreid, P. and Pedersen, O. K. (1994) *Forvaltningspolitik i Norden*, Conpenhagen: Jurist- & Økonomomforbundets forlag.

Ligestillingsrådet (1995) *Ligestillingsrådets Årsberetning 1995: kvinder og mænd*, Copenhagen: Danmarks Statistik.

Naschold, F. (1996) *New Frontiers in Public Sector Management*, Berlin and New York: de Gruyter.

Pedersen, D. (1993) *Offentlig løn*, Copenhagen: Samfundslitteratur.

Pedersen, D. (1996) 'Personaleorganisationer og forvaltningspolitik i Danmark' in P. Lægreid, and Pedersen, O. K. (eds): *Integration og decentralisering*, Copenhagen: Jurist- & Økonomforbundets forlag.

Sygeplejersken (1997) *Ekstra-forliget i hovedtræk, Marts 1997*, Copenhagen: Dansk Sygeplejeråd.

Walton, R. E. and Mackersie, R. B. (1965) *A Behavioural Theory of Labor Negotiations: An Analysis of a Social Interaction System*, New York: McGraw-Hill.

Index